It's *your* country. **Learn it. Love it.** Explore it.

NATIONAL GEOGRAPHIC KiDS

UNITED STATES ATLAS

SIXTH EDITION

NATIONAL GEOGRAPHIC
WASHINGTON, D.C.

TABLE OF CONTENTS

Northeast: Maine lighthouse, p. 34

Southeast: Manatee in Florida waters, p. 62

Title page: Mountain lion; Chocorua Lake, New Hampshire; John F. Kennedy Space Center, Florida; Gateway Arch, Missouri; Zuni woman, Arizona; Statue of Liberty, New York Harbor; brown tree snake, Guam; sunflowers, North Dakota.

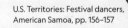

Southwest: Albuquerque balloon festival, New Mexico, p. 120

U.S. Territories: Festival dancers, American Samoa, pp. 156–157

Midwest: Illinois hay field with tractor, pp. 88–89

West: Wyoming ranch, p. 152

GETTING STARTED

How to Use This Atlas

This atlas is much more than just another book of maps about the United States. Of course you will find plenty of maps—country, regional, state, and territory—that have been designed to help you learn about the people and places that make up our country. But there's much more. There are essays filled with history and current facts about each state, and photos that provide an up close view of natural and cultural features. In addition, you will discover state flags and nicknames, state flowers and birds, statistics and fun facts, and even graphs and charts. Follow the captions below and to the right to discover all the special features that are waiting for you in this atlas. Turn to page 160 to find outside websites that will lead you to additional sources of information on topics of interest to you.

STATE FACT BOX

The fact box is full of key information you need at a glance about a state: its flag, statehood, statistics about land and population*, racial and ethnic makeup** and other population characteristics, plus some Geo Whiz facts and the state bird and flower.

*Population figures are estimates from the U.S. Census Bureau: state, city (city proper unless otherwise specified), and metropolitan area, 2018; racial/ethnic groups, 2017; foreign born, 2013–2017; urban population, 2010; population density, 2018.

**Racial percentages total less than 100 percent because very small racial groups are not included. Hispanics are an ethnic group and can be included in any racial group.

COLOR BARS

Each section of the atlas has its own color. Look for the color in the Table of Contents and across the top of the pages in the atlas. The name of the section and the title for each topic or map is in the color bar.

- THE NORTHEAST
- THE SOUTHEAST
- THE MIDWEST
- THE SOUTHWEST
- THE WEST
- U.S. TERRITORIES

44 THE NORTHEAST

THE EMPIRE STATE
NEW YORK

New York

When Englishman Henry Hudson explored New York's Hudson River Valley in 1609, the territory was already inhabited by large tribes of Native Americans, including the powerful Iroquois. In 1624 a Dutch trading company established the New Netherland colony, but after just 40 years the colony was taken over by the English and renamed for England's Duke of York. In 1788 New York became the 11th state. The powerful port city of New York, center of trade and commerce and a gateway to immigrants, is the largest city in the United States. Its metropolitan area, which extends into the surrounding states of Connecticut, New Jersey, and Pennsylvania, has more than 20 million people. Cities such as Buffalo and Rochester are industrial centers, and Ithaca and Syracuse boast major universities. Agriculture is also important, and the state is a leading producer of dairy products, fruits, and vegetables.

THE BASICS

Statehood
July 26, 1788; 11th state
Total area (land and water)
54,555 sq mi (141,297 sq km)
Land area
47,126 sq mi (122,057 sq km)
Population
19,542,209
Capital
Albany
Population 97,279
Largest city
New York City
Population 8,398,748
Racial/ethnic groups
69.6% white; 17.7% African American; 9.1% Asian; 1.0% Native American; 19.2% Hispanic origin (any race)
Foreign born
22.7%
Urban population
87.9%
Population density
414.7 per sq mi
(160.1 per sq km)

GEO WHIZ

The National Baseball Hall of Fame, established in 1939 in Cooperstown, includes a museum that houses more than 40,000 artifacts of the game, including bats, balls, gloves, and uniforms.

The Erie Canal, built in the 1820s between Albany and Buffalo, opened the Midwest to development by linking the Hudson River and the Great Lakes.

LADY LIBERTY. Standing in New York Harbor, the Statue of Liberty is a symbol of freedom and democracy.

EASTERN BLUEBIRD

ROSE

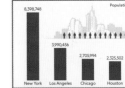

URBAN GIANT

Population of city proper, 2018 data

8,398,748 — New York
3,990,456 — Los Angeles
2,705,994 — Chicago
2,325,502 — Houston
1,660,272 — Phoenix

With more than twice the population of the next largest city, New York—known as the Big Apple—is the country's largest city.

NATURAL WONDER. Each year more than eight million tourists visit Niagara Falls on the U.S.-Canada border. Visitors in rain slickers trek through the mists below Bridal Veil Falls on the American side.

130 THE WEST
131 THE WEST

The West

THE HIGH FRONTIER

The western states, which make up almost half of the country's land area, have diverse landscapes and climates, ranging from the frozen heights of Denali, in Alaska, to the desolation of Death Valley, in California, and the lush, tropical islands of Hawai'i. More than half the region's population lives in California, and the Los Angeles metropolitan area is second in population only to that of New York City. Yet many parts of the region are sparsely populated, and much of the land is set aside as parkland and military bases. The region also faces many natural hazards—earthquakes, landslides, wildfires, and even volcanic eruptions.

WHERE ARE THE PICTURES?

If you want to know where a picture in any of the regional sections in the atlas was taken, check the map in the regional photo essay. Find the label that describes the photograph you are curious about, and follow the line to its location.

CHARTS AND GRAPHS

The photo essay for each state includes a chart or graph that highlights economic, physical, cultural, or some other type of information related to the state.

MAP SYMBOLS

Maps use symbols to represent many physical, political, and economic features. Below is a complete list of the map symbols that appear in map keys in this atlas.

- Aspen .... town of under 25,000 residents
- Frankfort .... town of 25,000 to 99,999
- San Jose .... city of 100,000 to 999,999
- New York .... city of 1,000,000 and over
- ⊛ National capital
- ★ State capital
- ⊙ Territory capital
- ■ Point of interest
- + Mountain peak with elevation above sea level
- ▼ Low point with elevation below sea level
- ——— River
- – – – Intermittent river
- ⊥⊥⊥⊥ Canal
- ——— Interstate or selected other highway
- •–•–• Pipeline
- – – – Trail
- •••••• State or national boundary
- •••••• Continental divide
- Lake and dam
- Intermittent lake
- Dry lake
- Swamp
- Glacier
- National Wild & Scenic River, N.W.&S.R.
- Area below sea level

- ▦ Indian Reservation, I.R. *(All Indian Reservations are not shown due to map scale and the size of the I.R.)*
- ▩ **State Park unit**
  State Park, **S.P.**
  State Historical Park, S.H.P.
  State Historic Site, S.H.S.
- ▩ **National Park Service unit**
  National Battlefield, N.B.
  National Battlefield Park, N.B.P.
  National Battlefield Site, N.B.S.
  National Historic Site, N.H.S.
  National Historic Area, N.H.A.
  National Historical Park, N.H.P.
  National Lakeshore
  National Military Park, N.M.P.
  National Memorial, NAT. MEM.
  National Monument, NAT. MON.
  National Park, N.P.
  National Parkway
  National Preserve
  National Recreation Area, N.R.A.
  National River
  National Riverway
  National Scenic Area
  National Seashore
  National Volcanic Monument
- ▤ National Forest, N.F.
- ☐ National Grassland, N.G.
- ▨ National Wildlife Refuge, N.W.R.
- ☐ National Marine Sanctuary, N.M.S.

METRIC CONVERSIONS

CONVERSIONS TO METRIC MEASUREMENTS

WHEN YOU KNOW	MULTIPLY BY	TO FIND
INCHES (IN)	2.54	CENTIMETERS (CM)
FEET (FT)	0.30	METERS (M)
MILES (MI)	1.61	KILOMETERS (KM)
ACRES	0.40	HECTARES (HA)
SQUARE MILES (SQ MI)	2.59	SQUARE KILOMETERS (SQ KM)
POUNDS (LB)	0.45	KILOGRAMS (KG)
GALLONS (GAL)	3.79	LITERS (L)

CONVERSIONS FROM METRIC MEASUREMENTS

WHEN YOU KNOW	MULTIPLY BY	TO FIND
CENTIMETERS (CM)	0.39	INCHES (IN)
METERS (M)	3.28	FEET (FT)
KILOMETERS (KM)	0.62	MILES (MI)
HECTARES (HA)	2.47	ACRES
SQUARE KILOMETERS (SQ KM)	0.39	SQUARE MILES (SQ MI)
KILOGRAMS (KG)	2.20	POUNDS (LB)
LITERS (L)	0.26	GALLONS (GAL)

YOU ARE HERE
This and other locator maps show you where each region or state within the region is in relation to the rest of the United States. Each region is shown in its regional color; featured states are in yellow.

BAR SCALE
Each map has a bar scale in miles and kilometers to help you find out how far on Earth's surface it is from one place to another on the map.

THE NORTHEAST | 45

THE EMPIRE STATE: **NEW YORK**

MAP KEY
⊛ State capital
● City
■ Point of interest
+ Mountain peak
•••••• State or national boundary
– – – Trail
National Wild & Scenic River
▦ Indian Reservation
▩ State Park unit
▩ National Park Service unit
▤ National Forest
▨ National Wildlife Refuge

0 ———— 50 miles
0 ———— 50 kilometers
Albers Conic Equal-Area Projection

ⓘ **SWEET HARVEST.** The Finger Lakes region, with its unique combination of soils and climate conditions, is well suited to growing wine grapes. With more than 10,000 acres (4,047 ha) of vineyards, it is the center of New York's wine industry, producing varieties for both domestic and export markets.

INDEX AND GRID
A grid system makes it easy to find places listed in the index. For example, the listing for Tarrytown, NY, is followed by **45** G8. The bold type is the page number; G8 tells you the city is near the point where imaginary lines drawn from G and 8 on the grid bars meet.

The Physical United States

The United States is the world's third largest country in area. It stretches from the Atlantic Ocean in the east to the Pacific Ocean and Hawai'i in the west, with Alaska, its largest state, bordering the Arctic Ocean. Physical features range from mountains to fertile plains, tropical forests, and deserts. Shading on the map indicates changes in elevation. Colors suggest vegetation patterns.

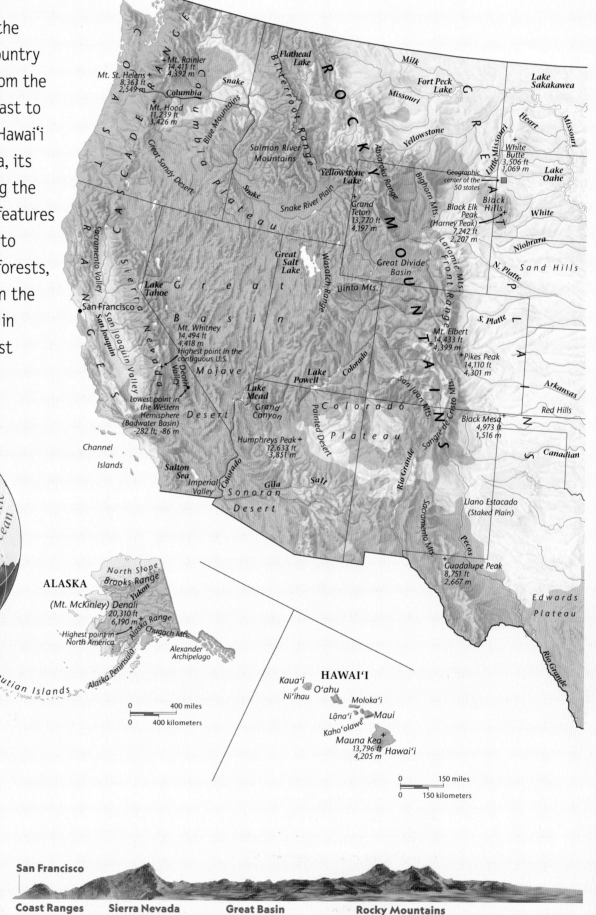

◐ ALASKA AND HAWAI'I.
These two states are not directly connected to the other 48 states. If their correct relative sizes and locations were shown, the map would not fit on this page. The locator globe shows the correct relative size and location of each.

San Francisco

Coast Ranges   Sierra Nevada   Great Basin   Rocky Mountains

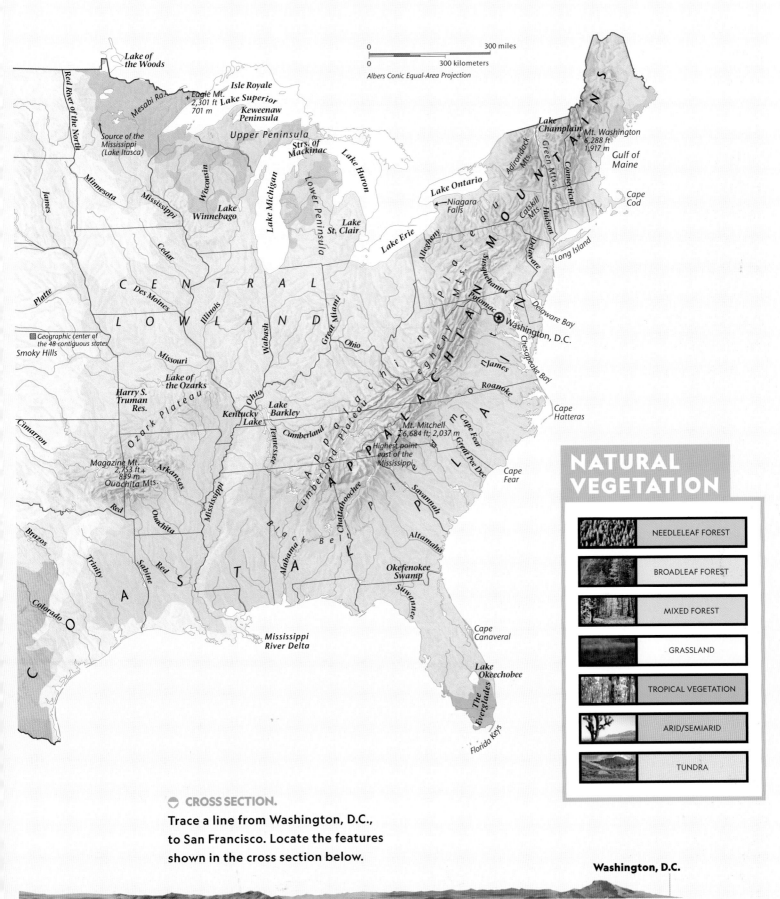

Lake of the Woods

Red River of the North

Mesabi Ra.

+ Eagle Mt. 2,301 ft 701 m

Isle Royale

Lake Superior

Keweenaw Peninsula

Upper Peninsula

Source of the Mississippi (Lake Itasca)

Minnesota

Wisconsin

Mississippi

Lake Winnebago

Lake Michigan

Strs. of Mackinac

Lower Peninsula

Lake Huron

Lake St. Clair

Lake Erie

James

Platte

CENTRAL

Des Moines

Illinois

LOWLAND

Cedar

Wabash

Geographic center of the 48 contiguous states

Smoky Hills

Cimarron

Missouri

Lake of the Ozarks

Harry S. Truman Res.

Ozark Plateau

Kentucky Lake

Lake Barkley

Ohio

Great Miami

Ohio

Tennessee

Cumberland

Magazine Mt. 2,753 ft + 839 m

Ouachita Mts.

Arkansas

Red

Ouachita

Mississippi

Brazos

Trinity

Sabine

Red

Colorado

COAST

Alabama

Black Belt

Chattahoochee

Appalachian Plateau

Cumberland Plateau

Mt. Mitchell 6,684 ft; 2,037 m

Highest point east of the Mississippi

APPALACHIAN

Blue Ridge

Savannah

Altamaha

Okefenokee Swamp

Suwannee

PLAIN

Mississippi River Delta

Cape Canaveral

Lake Okeechobee

The Everglades

Florida Keys

Lake Ontario

Niagara Falls

MOUNTAINS

Lake Champlain

Adirondack Mts.

Green Mts.

Connecticut

Mt. Washington 6,288 ft 1,917 m

Gulf of Maine

Cape Cod

Catskill Mts.

Hudson

Allegheny Plateau

Susquehanna

Delaware

Long Island

Potomac

Washington, D.C.

Delaware Bay

Chesapeake Bay

James

Roanoke

Cape Fear

Great Pee Dee

Cape Hatteras

Cape Fear

0 — 300 miles
0 — 300 kilometers
Albers Conic Equal-Area Projection

NATURAL VEGETATION

	NEEDLELEAF FOREST
	BROADLEAF FOREST
	MIXED FOREST
	GRASSLAND
	TROPICAL VEGETATION
	ARID/SEMIARID
	TUNDRA

⬡ CROSS SECTION.

Trace a line from Washington, D.C., to San Francisco. Locate the features shown in the cross section below.

Washington, D.C.

Great Plains   Ozark Plateau   Appalachian   Atlantic
                                                     Mountains   Coastal Plain

CLIMATE

Climate

A big part of the natural environment of the United States is the climate. With humid areas near the coasts, dry interior regions far from any major water body, and land areas that extend from frigid northern Alaska to tropical Hawai'i and southern Florida, the country experiences great variation in climate. Location is the key to the country's climate patterns. Distance from the Equator, nearness to water, wind patterns, temperature of nearby water bodies, and elevation are things that influence temperature and precipitation. Climate affects the types of vegetation that grow in a particular place and plays a part in soil formation.

CHANGING CLIMATE

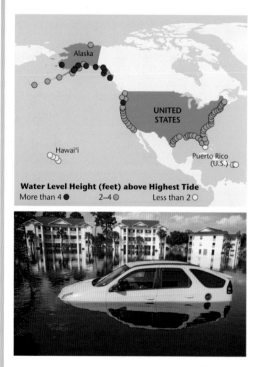

Water Level Height (feet) above Highest Tide
More than 4 ● 2–4 ◉ Less than 2 ○

Scientists generally agree that human activity has played an important role in recent changes in Earth's climate. The years 2014–2018 are the five warmest years ever recorded. Increases in average temperatures are likely to contribute to more severe storms, changes in precipitation patterns, and the spread of desert conditions. Rising temperatures also contribute to higher ocean levels and coastal flooding as glaciers melt and warmer ocean waters expand. Average sea level has risen nearly eight inches (20 cm) since 1900. Almost 40 percent of the U.S. population lives in coastal areas at risk of severe flooding. Above, floodwaters caused by Hurricane Florence in 2018 trap a car in Longs, South Carolina.

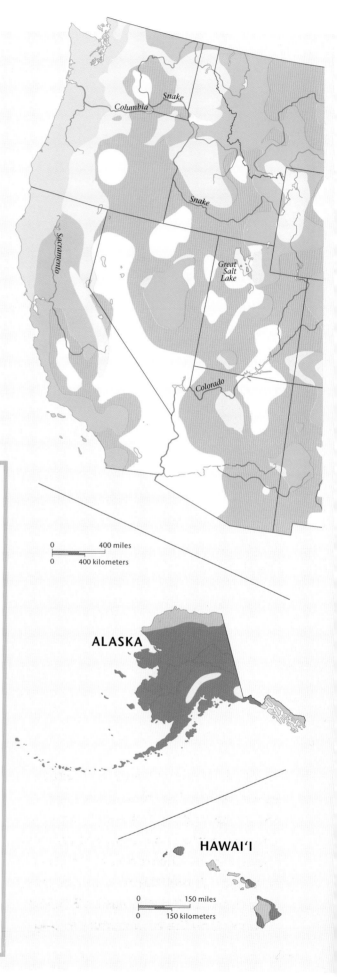

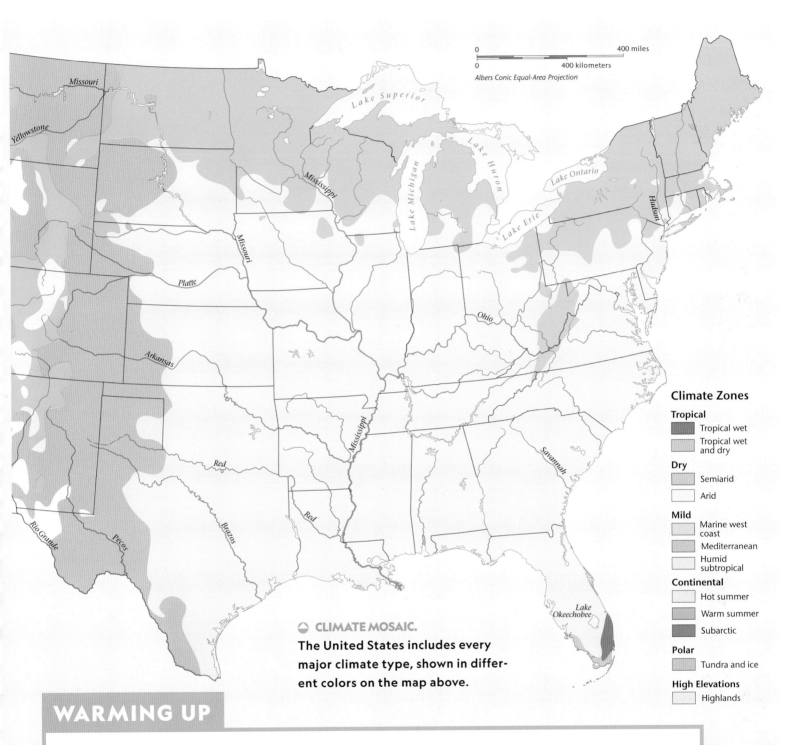

0   400 miles

0   400 kilometers

Albers Conic Equal-Area Projection

Climate Zones

Tropical

- Tropical wet
- Tropical wet and dry

Dry

- Semiarid
- Arid

Mild

- Marine west coast
- Mediterranean
- Humid subtropical

Continental

- Hot summer
- Warm summer
- Subarctic

Polar

- Tundra and ice

High Elevations

- Highlands

CLIMATE MOSAIC.
The United States includes every major climate type, shown in different colors on the map above.

WARMING UP

Evidence indicates that Earth is experiencing a warming trend unlike any ever recorded. In 2017 all of the 48 contiguous states reported above average temperatures; five experienced record-setting averages. Overall the average temperature in these 48 states was 2.6°F (1.4°C) warmer than the 20th-century average.

Average temperature ranks in 2017 (for 48 contiguous states)

- Above average
- Much above average
- Record warmest

Natural Hazards

The natural environment of the United States provides much diversity, but it also poses many dangers, especially when people locate homes and businesses in places at risk of natural disasters. Tornadoes bring destructive winds, and hurricanes bring strong winds, rain, the possibility of dangerous storm surges in coastal areas, and more. The shifting of Earth's crust along fault lines rattles buildings; floodwaters and wildfires threaten lives and property. More than one-third of the U.S. population lives in hazard-prone areas. Compare this map to the population map on pages 16–17.

Mount Baker
Glacier Peak
Mount Rainier
North Cascades, 1872
Mount St. Helens
Columbia River, 1996
Columbia
Mount Hood
Three Sisters
West Coast flooding, 1982–1983, 1996–1997
Newberry Crater
Hebgen Lake, 1959
California-Oregon Coast, 1873
Medicine Lake
Mount Shasta
Snake
Tsunami, 1964
Lassen Peak
Western Wildfires, 1994, 2000, 2012, 2016, 2017, 2018
California flooding, 1995
Central California wildfires, 2018, 2019
San Francisco, 1906
Oakland firestorm, 1991
Long Valley Caldera
Western & Plains drought, 2013
Western drought, 2014, 2015, 2018
Owens Valley, 1872
California drought, 2016
Ridgecrest, 2019
Kern County, 1952
Fort Tejon, 1857
Landers, 1992
Wildfires, 2011
Southern California wildfires, 1993, 2003, 2008, 2009, 2018, 2019
Colorado
Gila
Imperial Valley, 1892

ALASKA

Alaska has about 80 major volcanic centers.
More earthquakes occur in Alaska than in the other 49 states combined.

Alaskan wildfires, 2015
Prince William Sound, 1964
Novarupta, 1912
Tsunami, 1964
Tsunami, 1958
Tsunami, 1946, 1957

0   400 miles
0   400 kilometers

HAWAI'I

Iniki, 1992
Tsunami, 1946
Haleakala
Tsunami, 1868, 1946
Hualalai
Mauna Loa
Kilauea
Kau District, 1868
Loihi

0   150 miles
0   150 kilometers

NATURAL HAZARDS

BLIZZARD. Severe storm with bitter cold temperatures and wind-whipped snow and ice particles that reduce visibility to less than 650 feet (198 m), paralyzing transportation systems

FLOOD. Inundation of buildings or roadways caused by overflow of a river or stream swollen by heavy rainfall or rapid snowmelt; may involve displacement of people

DROUGHT. Long and continuous period of abnormally low precipitation, resulting in water shortages that negatively affect people, animals, and plant life; may result in crop loss

HURRICANE. Tropical storm in the Atlantic, Caribbean, Gulf of Mexico, or eastern Pacific with a minimum sustained wind speed of 74 miles an hour (119 km/h)

ICE STORM. Damaging accumulations of ice associated with freezing rain; may pull down trees or utility lines, causing extensive damage and creating dangerous travel conditions

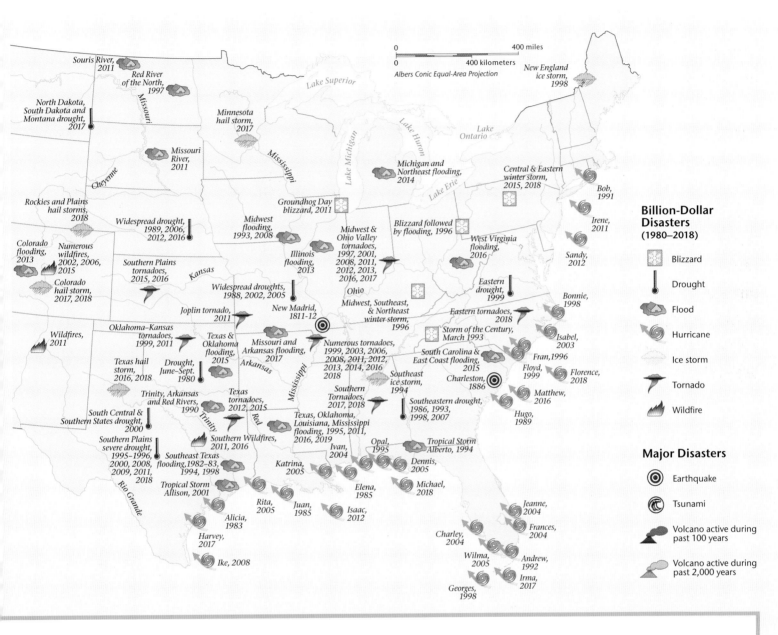

0 _____ 400 miles
0 _____ 400 kilometers
Albers Conic Equal-Area Projection

Souris River, 2011
Red River of the North, 1997
North Dakota, South Dakota and Montana drought, 2017
Minnesota hail storm, 2017
Missouri River, 2011
New England ice storm, 1998
Lake Superior
Lake Huron
Lake Ontario
Lake Erie
Lake Michigan
Michigan and Northeast flooding, 2014
Central & Eastern winter storm, 2015, 2018
Bob, 1991
Irene, 2011
Rockies and Plains hail storms, 2018
Widespread drought, 1989, 2006, 2012, 2016
Midwest flooding, 1993, 2008
Groundhog Day blizzard, 2011
Blizzard followed by flooding, 1996
West Virginia flooding, 2016
Sandy, 2012
Colorado flooding, 2013
Numerous wildfires, 2002, 2006, 2015
Southern Plains tornadoes, 2015, 2016
Illinois flooding, 2013
Midwest & Ohio Valley tornadoes, 1997, 2001, 2008, 2011, 2012, 2013, 2016, 2017
Eastern drought, 1999
Bonnie, 1998
Colorado hail storm, 2017, 2018
Widespread droughts, 1988, 2002, 2005
Ohio
Midwest, Southeast, & Northeast winter storm, 1996
Eastern tornadoes, 2018
Isabel, 2003
Wildfires, 2011
Joplin tornado, 2011
New Madrid, 1811-12
Storm of the Century, March 1993
Fran, 1996
Oklahoma–Kansas tornadoes, 1999, 2011
Texas & Oklahoma flooding, 2015
Missouri and Arkansas flooding, 2017
Numerous tornadoes, 1999, 2003, 2006, 2008, 2011, 2012, 2013, 2014, 2016, 2018
South Carolina & East Coast flooding, 2015
Floyd, 1999
Florence, 2018
Texas hail storm, 2016, 2018
Drought, June–Sept. 1980
Arkansas
Southeast ice storm, 1994
Charleston, 1886
Matthew, 2016
Trinity, Arkansas and Red Rivers, 1990
Texas tornadoes, 2012, 2015
Southern Tornadoes, 2017, 2018
Southeastern drought, 1986, 1993, 1998, 2007
Hugo, 1989
South Central & Southern States drought, 2000
Texas, Oklahoma, Louisiana, Mississippi flooding, 1995, 2011, 2016, 2019
Southern Plains severe drought, 1995-1996, 2000, 2008, 2009, 2011, 2018
Southern Wildfires, 2011, 2016
Southeast Texas flooding, 1982–83, 1994, 1998
Opal, 1995
Ivan, 2004
Tropical Storm Alberto, 1994
Dennis, 2005
Michael, 2018
Tropical Storm Allison, 2001
Katrina, 2005
Elena, 1985
Rita, 2005
Juan, 1985
Isaac, 2012
Alicia, 1983
Harvey, 2017
Ike, 2008
Jeanne, 2004
Frances, 2004
Charley, 2004
Wilma, 2005
Andrew, 1992
Irma, 2017
Georges, 1998

Missouri
Cheyenne
Mississippi
Kansas
Mississippi
Arkansas
Trinity
Red
Rio Grande

Billion-Dollar Disasters
(1980–2018)

- Blizzard
- Drought
- Flood
- Hurricane
- Ice storm
- Tornado
- Wildfire

Major Disasters

- ◎ Earthquake
- ⊚ Tsunami
- Volcano active during past 100 years
- Volcano active during past 2,000 years

TORNADO. Violently rotating column of air that, when it reaches the ground, is the most damaging of all atmospheric phenomena; most common in the central region of the country

WILDFIRE. Free-burning fire in a forest or grassland; may result from lightning strikes or accidental or deliberate human activity in areas where conditions are dry

EARTHQUAKE. Shaking or vibration created by energy released by movement of Earth's crust along tectonic plate boundaries; can cause structural damage and loss of life

TSUNAMI. Series of unusually large ocean waves caused by an underwater earthquake, landslide, or volcanic eruption; very destructive in coastal areas

VOLCANO. Vent or opening in Earth's surface through which lava (molten rock), ash, and gases are released; often associated with tectonic plate boundaries

The Political United States

Like a giant patchwork quilt, the United States is made up of 50 states. Each is uniquely different, but collectively these units create a national fabric that is held together by a Constitution and a federal government. State boundaries, outlined in various colors on the map, set apart internal political units within the country. The national capital—Washington, D.C.—is marked by a star in a double circle. Each state capital is marked by a star in a single circle.

TIME ZONES. Earth is divided into 24 time zones, each about 15 degrees of longitude wide, reflecting the distance Earth turns from west to east each hour. The U.S. is divided into six time zones, indicated by red dotted lines on these maps. When it is noon in Boston, what is the time in Seattle?

POLITICAL MAP

11:00 AM   12:00 PM

0   300 miles
0   300 kilometers
Albers Conic Equal-Area Projection

Lake of the Woods
Isle Royale
Lake Superior
MAINE
Minot
Grand Forks
International Falls
Bangor
NORTH DAKOTA
Duluth
Marquette
Augusta
Bismarck Fargo
MINNESOTA
Superior
MICHIGAN
Burlington
VT.
Portland
Aberdeen
WISCONSIN
Lake Champlain
N.H.
Montpelier
SOUTH DAKOTA
Minneapolis
Green Bay
Concord
Pierre
St. Paul
Lake Michigan
Lake Huron
Syracuse
Albany
MASS.
Boston
Cape Cod
Rapid City
Madison
Grand Rapids
Lansing
Lake Ontario
Rochester
NEW YORK
Hartford
Providence
Sioux Falls
Missouri
Milwaukee
Detroit
Buffalo
CONN.
RHODE ISLAND
NEBRASKA
IOWA
Cedar Rapids
Rockford
Chicago
Gary
Fort Wayne
Toledo Cleveland
Lake Erie
Erie
Newark
Long Island
New York
PENNSYLVANIA
Trenton
Grand Island
Omaha
Des Moines
Davenport
Peoria
OHIO
Columbus
Harrisburg
Pittsburgh
NEW JERSEY
Philadelphia
S. Platte
Platte
Lincoln
ILLINOIS
INDIANA
Dayton
Baltimore
Dover
DELAWARE
Kansas City
Springfield
Indianapolis
Cincinnati
WEST VIRGINIA
Washington, D.C.
Annapolis
MARYLAND
Topeka
Jefferson City
St. Louis
Louisville
Frankfort
Charleston
Richmond
Chesapeake Bay
KANSAS
Dodge City
Arkansas
Wichita
MISSOURI
Springfield
Evansville
Lexington
Roanoke
VIRGINIA
Norfolk
Virginia Beach
Paducah
KENTUCKY
Greensboro
Raleigh
Cape Hatteras
Tulsa
Nashville
Knoxville
NORTH CAROLINA
Charlotte
OKLAHOMA
Fort Smith
Memphis
Chattanooga
Greenville
Amarillo
Oklahoma City
ARKANSAS
Huntsville
Atlanta
Columbia
SOUTH CAROLINA
Lawton
Little Rock
Birmingham
GEORGIA
Charleston
Lubbock
Wichita Falls
Red
Jackson
MISSISSIPPI
ALABAMA
Macon
Savannah
Fort Worth
Shreveport
Montgomery
Columbus
Midland
Abilene
Dallas
Brazos
LOUISIANA
Red
Natchez
Mobile
Tallahassee
Jacksonville
Odessa
Waco
Jackson
Biloxi
FLORIDA
Gainesville
TEXAS
Austin
Beaumont
Lafayette
Baton Rouge
New Orleans
Mobile Bay
Apalachee Bay
Orlando
Cape Canaveral
Houston
San Antonio
Mississippi River Delta
Tampa
St. Petersburg
Lake Okeechobee
Corpus Christi
Laredo
Fort Lauderdale
The Everglades
Miami
Rio Grande
Brownsville
Florida Keys

Red River basin ceded by Great Britain, 1818
Ceded by Great Britain, 1842
Ceded by Great Britain, 1842
Oregon Country ceded by Great Britain, 1846
Louisiana Purchase from France, 1803
United States, 1783
Ceded by Mexico, 1848
Texas annexed by U.S., 1845
Western boundary of original 13 colonies, 1775
Alaska purchased from Russia, 1867
Gadsden Purchase from Mexico, 1853
Area acquired from Spain, 1810-1821
Hawai'i annexed, 1898

◖ **WESTWARD EXPANSION.** The United States had its origins in 13 British colonies along the Atlantic coast. After winning independence in 1783, the young country began adding new territory, as shown on the map at left.

Population

More than 327 million* and growing! The population of the United States topped the 300 million mark in 2006, and it continues to grow by more than two million people each year. Before the arrival of European settlers, the population consisted of Native Americans living in tribal groups scattered across the country. In the 17th century, Europeans began settling along the eastern seaboard. By the early 18th century, the population was increasing and included African slaves brought as unpaid labor for the growing plantation economy. By 1790 when the first U.S. census was taken, the country's population was almost four million people. Today, New York City alone has a population more than double that number. The country's population is unevenly distributed. The greatest densities are in the East and along the West Coast, especially around major cities. The most rapid growth is occurring in the South and the West—an area referred to as the Sunbelt—as well as in suburban areas around cities.

*July 2018 figure

⬠ **COMMUTER RUSH HOUR.** Crowds of people press toward trains in New York City's Grand Central Station. With more than three-quarters of the population living in urban areas, commuter transportation poses a major challenge to cities in the United States.

◗ **WHERE WE LIVE.** In 1790 only 5 percent of Americans lived in towns. Today most people live in urban places (blue) and surrounding suburbs (orange), rather than in rural areas (green).

ALASKA

0   400 miles
0   400 kilometers

HAWAI'I

0   150 miles
0   150 kilometers

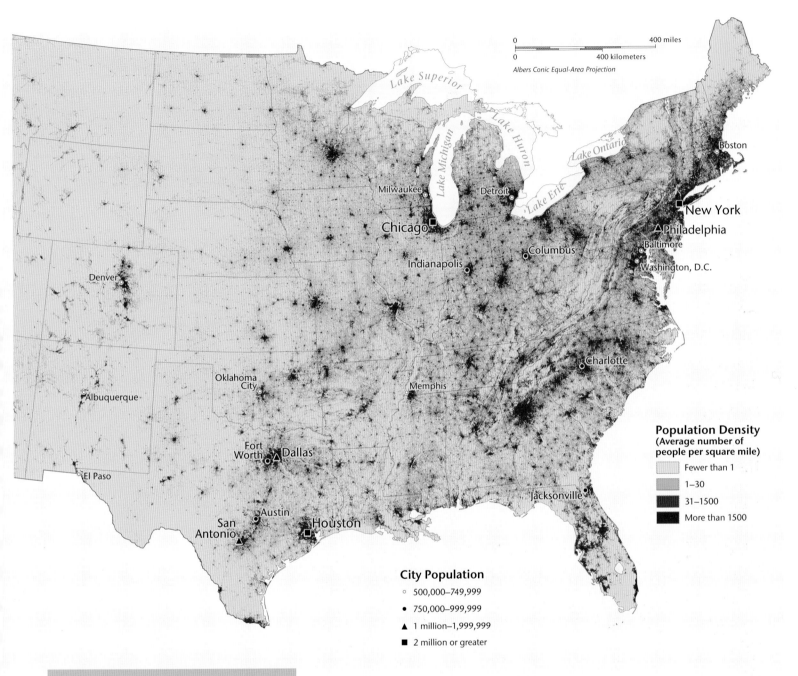

0   400 miles
0   400 kilometers
Albers Conic Equal-Area Projection

Lake Superior
Lake Michigan
Lake Huron
Lake Ontario
Lake Erie

Boston
Milwaukee
Detroit
New York
Chicago
Philadelphia
Columbus
Baltimore
Indianapolis
Washington, D.C.
Denver
Charlotte
Oklahoma City
Memphis
Albuquerque
Fort Worth
Dallas
El Paso
Jacksonville
Austin
San Antonio
Houston

Population Density
(Average number of
people per square mile)

Fewer than 1
1–30
31–1500
More than 1500

City Population

○   500,000–749,999
●   750,000–999,999
▲   1 million–1,999,999
■   2 million or greater

HOW OLD ARE WE?

Population pyramids show distribution of population by sex and age groups. In 1960 the largest group, born after World War II and called Baby Boomers (highlighted in the graphs), were under 15 years of age. By 2040 they will reach the top of the pyramid.

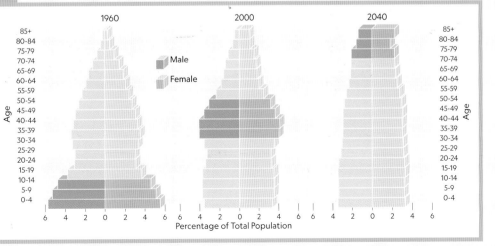

1960   2000   2040

Male
Female

Age: 85+, 80-84, 75-79, 70-74, 65-69, 60-64, 55-59, 50-54, 45-49, 40-44, 35-39, 30-34, 25-29, 20-24, 15-19, 10-14, 5-9, 0-4

Percentage of Total Population

People on the Move

From earliest human history, the land of the United States has been a focus of migration. Ancestors of today's Native Americans arrived thousands of years ago. The first European settlers came in the 16th and 17th centuries, and slave ships brought Africans by way of the West Indies. Today, people are still on the move. Since the mid-1900s, most immigrants have come from Latin America, especially Mexico and Central America; and Asia, particularly China, the Philippines, and India. Although most of the population is still of European descent, certain regions have large minority concentrations (see main map) that influence the local cultural landscape.

ALASKA

0   400 miles
0   400 kilometers

HAWAI'I

0   150 miles
0   150 kilometers

⬤ **BRIDGE OF HOPE.** Many Mexicans enter the U.S. (foreground) daily for work or commerce by bridges across the Rio Grande, such as this one between Nuevo Laredo, Mexico, and Laredo, Texas.

⬤ **IMMIGRANT INFLUENCE.** A dual-language street sign in San Francisco's Chinatown shows how immigrants have contributed to the cultural landscape.

⬤ **SUNBELT SPRAWL.** Spreading suburbs are becoming a common feature of the desert Southwest as people flock to the Sunbelt.

PEOPLE ON THE MOVE

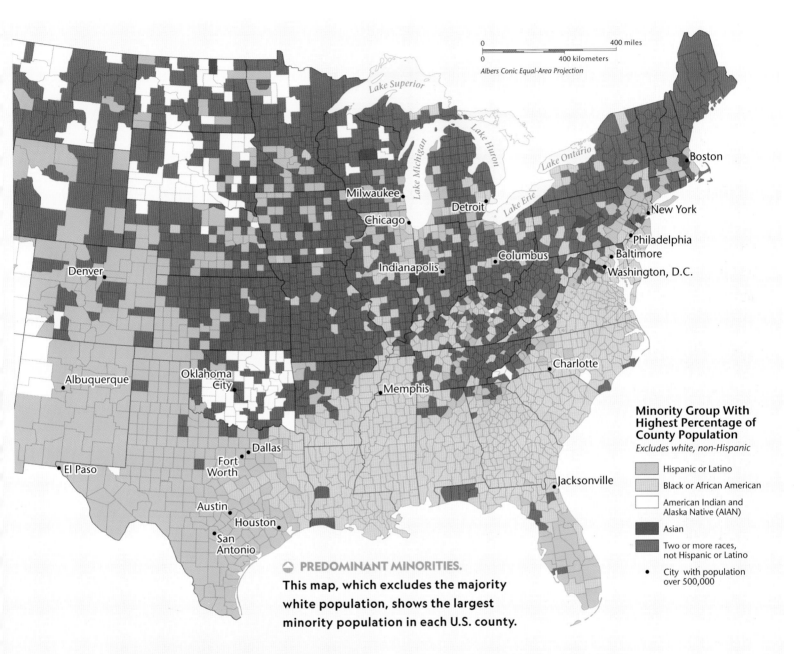

Minority Group With Highest Percentage of County Population
Excludes white, non-Hispanic

- Hispanic or Latino
- Black or African American
- American Indian and Alaska Native (AIAN)
- Asian
- Two or more races, not Hispanic or Latino
- • City with population over 500,000

⊜ PREDOMINANT MINORITIES.
This map, which excludes the majority white population, shows the largest minority population in each U.S. county.

POPULATION SHIFT

In the late 1900s, people began moving from the industrial and agricultural regions of the Northeast and Midwest toward the South and West, attracted by the promise of jobs and generally lower living costs. This trend is reflected in the wide variations in state population changes in the map at right.

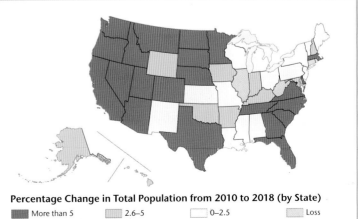

Percentage Change in Total Population from 2010 to 2018 (by State)

- More than 5
- 2.6–5
- 0–2.5
- Loss

Energy

People use energy every day in almost everything they do—from turning on a lamp to using a computer and riding a bus to school or work. Almost 40 percent of all energy is used to create electricity; another 27 percent is consumed by transportation. Energy sources fall into two main categories: nonrenewable and renewable. Nonrenewable energy resources, including fossil fuels (petroleum, natural gas, and coal) and uranium (nuclear power), are in limited supply and are not quickly replenished. Renewable energy sources (wind, water, solar, geothermal, and biomass materials) have an abundant supply that is constantly replenished. Most energy used in the United States comes from nonrenewable sources.

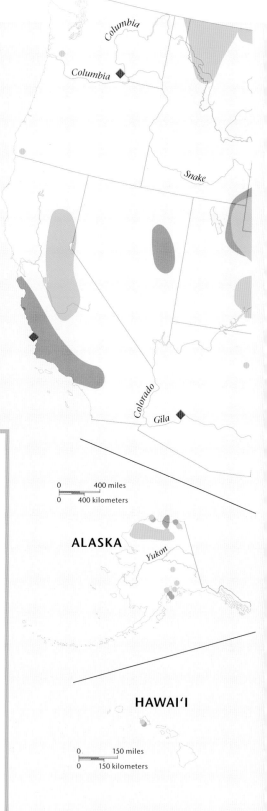

EARTHQUAKES & OIL PRODUCTION

Earthquake activity in the central U.S. increased dramatically after 2009. Geophysicists (scientists who study forces at work within Earth, including earthquakes) concluded that earthquake activity increased as a result of drilling companies pumping toxic wastewater that occurs naturally in oil and gas deposits back into the ground.

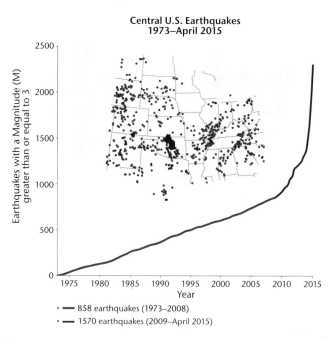

Central U.S. Earthquakes
1973–April 2015

Earthquakes with a Magnitude (M) greater than or equal to 3

Year

• ▬ 858 earthquakes (1973–2008)
• ▬ 1570 earthquakes (2009–April 2015)

From 2009 to early 2016 there were 2,310 earthquakes of magnitude 3 or greater, with most concentrated in central Oklahoma. During this time toxic wastewater pumped back into the ground doubled. In 2015 the state of Oklahoma limited the amount of wastewater that could be pumped back into the ground. Since 2016 the number of earthquakes of magnitude 3 or greater has declined steadily.

ENERGY

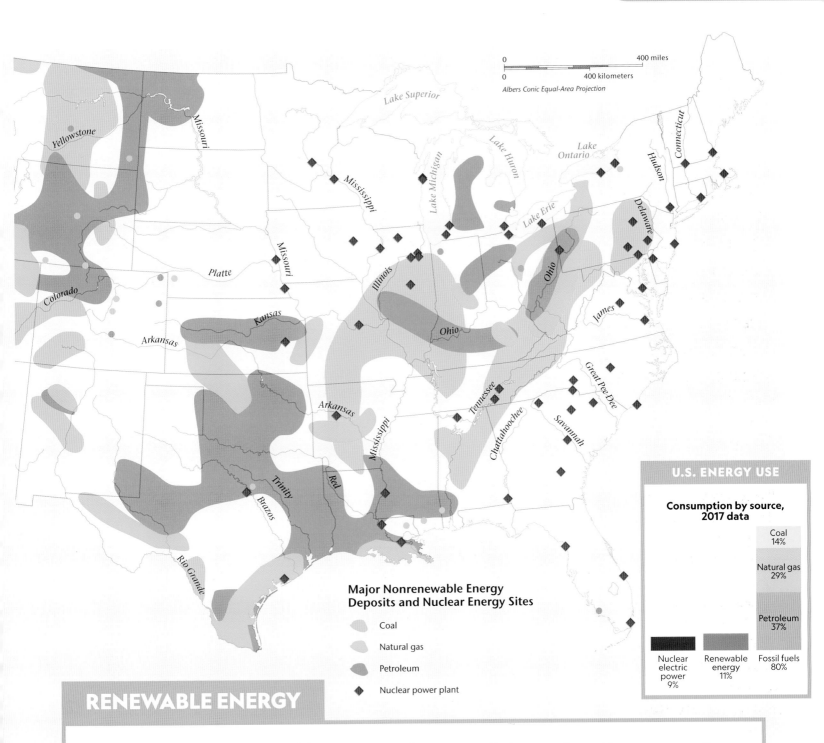

400 miles
400 kilometers

Albers Conic Equal-Area Projection

Major Nonrenewable Energy Deposits and Nuclear Energy Sites

Coal

Natural gas

Petroleum

◆ Nuclear power plant

U.S. ENERGY USE

Consumption by source, 2017 data

Coal 14%	
Natural gas 29%	
Petroleum 37%	

| Nuclear electric power 9% | Renewable energy 11% | Fossil fuels 80% |

RENEWABLE ENERGY

Renewable energy comes from sources that are readily available and naturally replenished. In the United States, 11 percent of all energy consumed comes from renewable sources, including hydroelectric energy from moving water; geothermal energy from heat within Earth's core; solar energy from the sun; wind energy (left) from moving air; and biomass energy from burning organic matter such as wood, plant material, and garbage.

Renewable energy consumption by source, 2017 data*

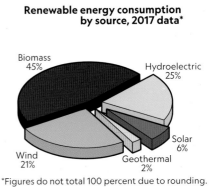

Biomass 45%

Hydroelectric 25%

Solar 6%

Geothermal 2%

Wind 21%

*Figures do not total 100 percent due to rounding.

The National Capital

THE BASICS

Founding
July 16, 1790

Total area (land and water)
68 sq mi (177 sq km)

Land area
61 sq mi (158 sq km)

Population
702,455

Racial/ethnic groups
45.1% white; 47.1% African American; 4.3% Asian; 0.6% Native American; 11.0% Hispanic (any race)

Foreign born
14.0%

Urban population
100.0%

Population density
11,515.7 per sq mi (4,445.9 per sq km)

GEO WHIZ

License plates in the District of Columbia bear the slogan "End Taxation Without Representation," reflecting the fact that residents have no voting representative in either house of the U.S. Congress.

The flag of the District of Columbia, with its three red stars and two red stripes, is based on the shield in George Washington's family coat of arms.

Chosen as a compromise location between Northern and Southern interests and built on land ceded by Maryland and Virginia in the late 1700s, Washington, D.C., is the seat of the U.S. government and symbol of the country's history. The city's design, as laid out by French architect Pierre L'Enfant, is distinguished by a grid pattern cut by diagonal avenues. At its core is the National Mall, a broad park lined by monuments, museums, and stately government buildings.

AMERICAN BEAUTY ROSE

WOOD THRUSH

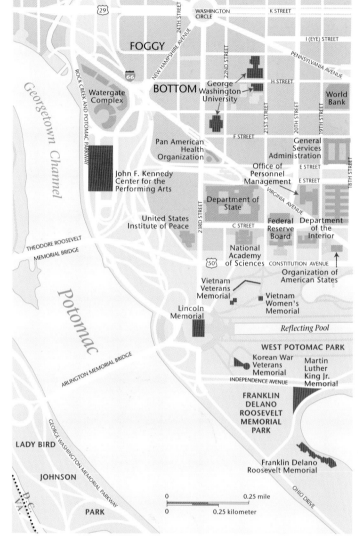

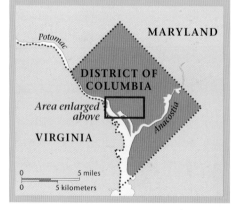

◑ **DISTRICT OF COLUMBIA.** Originally on both sides of the Potomac River, the city returned land to Virginia in 1846.

◑ **GREAT LEADER.** Abraham Lincoln, who was president during the Civil War and a strong opponent of slavery, is remembered in a monument that houses this seated statue at the west end of the National Mall.

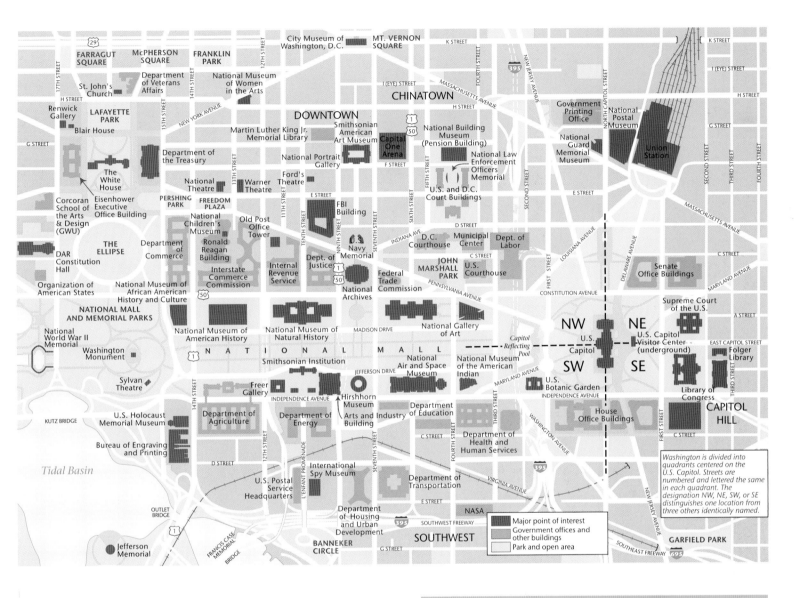

FARRAGUT SQUARE
McPHERSON SQUARE
FRANKLIN PARK
City Museum of Washington, D.C.
MT. VERNON SQUARE
K STREET
K STREET

17TH STREET
14TH STREET
12TH STREET
FOURTH STREET
I (EYE) STREET
I (EYE) STREET

St. John's Church
Department of Veterans Affairs
National Museum of Women in the Arts
CHINATOWN
H STREET
G STREET
G STREET

H STREET
Renwick Gallery
LAFAYETTE PARK
DOWNTOWN
Smithsonian American Art Museum
Capital One Arena
National Building Museum (Pension Building)
Government Printing Office
National Postal Museum
Union Station

Blair House
Martin Luther King Jr. Memorial Library
National Law Enforcement Officers Memorial
National Guard Memorial Museum

G STREET
Department of the Treasury
National Portrait Gallery
F STREET
U.S. and D.C. Court Buildings

The White House
National Theatre
Warner Theatre
Ford's Theatre
FBI Building
D STREET

PERSHING PARK
FREEDOM PLAZA
Old Post Office Tower
Dept. of Justice
D.C. Courthouse
Municipal Center
Dept. of Labor

Corcoran School of the Arts & Design (GWU)
Eisenhower Executive Office Building
National Children's Museum
U.S. Navy Memorial
C STREET

THE ELLIPSE
Department of Commerce
Ronald Reagan Building
Internal Revenue Service
Federal Trade Commission
JOHN MARSHALL PARK
U.S. Courthouse

DAR Constitution Hall
Interstate Commerce Commission
National Archives
PENNSYLVANIA AVENUE
CONSTITUTION AVENUE

Organization of American States
National Museum of African American History and Culture

NATIONAL MALL AND MEMORIAL PARKS
National Museum of American History
National Museum of Natural History
National Gallery of Art
Supreme Court of the U.S.
A STREET

National World War II Memorial
MADISON DRIVE
NW
NE
U.S. Capitol Visitor Center (underground)
EAST CAPITOL STREET

Washington Monument
NATIONAL MALL
Smithsonian Institution
National Air and Space Museum
National Museum of the American Indian
Capitol Reflecting Pool
U.S. Capitol
SW
SE
Folger Library

Sylvan Theatre
JEFFERSON DRIVE
Library of Congress

Freer Gallery
Hirshhorn Museum
U.S. Botanic Garden
INDEPENDENCE AVENUE
CAPITOL HILL

KUTZ BRIDGE
INDEPENDENCE AVENUE
Arts and Industry Building
Department of Education
House Office Buildings

Tidal Basin
U.S. Holocaust Memorial Museum
Department of Agriculture
Department of Energy
Department of Health and Human Services

Bureau of Engraving and Printing
D STREET
International Spy Museum
Department of Transportation

OUTLET BRIDGE
U.S. Postal Service Headquarters
E STREET
NASA

Jefferson Memorial
Department of Housing and Urban Development
SOUTHWEST FREEWAY
SOUTHWEST
GARFIELD PARK

BANNEKER CIRCLE
G STREET

Washington is divided into quadrants centered on the U.S. Capitol. Streets are numbered and lettered the same in each quadrant. The designation NW, NE, SW, or SE distinguishes one location from three others identically named.

Major point of interest
Government offices and other buildings
Park and open area

KEEPER OF HISTORY. The Smithsonian Institution, the world's largest museum, is actually made up of 19 museums. Established in 1846, the Smithsonian is sometimes referred to as our nation's attic because of its large collections.

NATIONAL ICON. The gleaming dome of the U.S. Capitol, home to the House of Representatives and the Senate, is a familiar symbol of Washington's main business—the running of the country's government.

THE REGION

PHYSICAL

Total area (land and water) 196,214 sq mi (508,192 sq km)	**Lowest point** Sea level, shores of the Atlantic Ocean	**Vegetation** Needleleaf, broadleaf, and mixed forest
Highest point Mount Washington, NH 6,288 ft (1,917 m)	**Longest rivers** St. Lawrence, Susquehanna, Connecticut, Hudson	**Climate** Continental to mild, with cool to warm summers, cold winters, and moderate precipitation throughout the year
	Largest lakes Erie, Ontario, Champlain	

POLITICAL

Total population 63,120,968	**Smallest state** Rhode Island: 1,545 sq mi (4,001 sq km)
States (11): Connecticut, Delaware, Maine, Maryland, Massachusetts, New Hampshire, New Jersey, New York, Pennsylvania, Rhode Island, Vermont	**Most populous state** New York: 19,542,209
	Least populous state Vermont: 626,299
Largest state New York: 54,555 sq mi (141,297 sq km)	**Largest city proper** New York, NY: 8,398,748

THE NORTHEAST

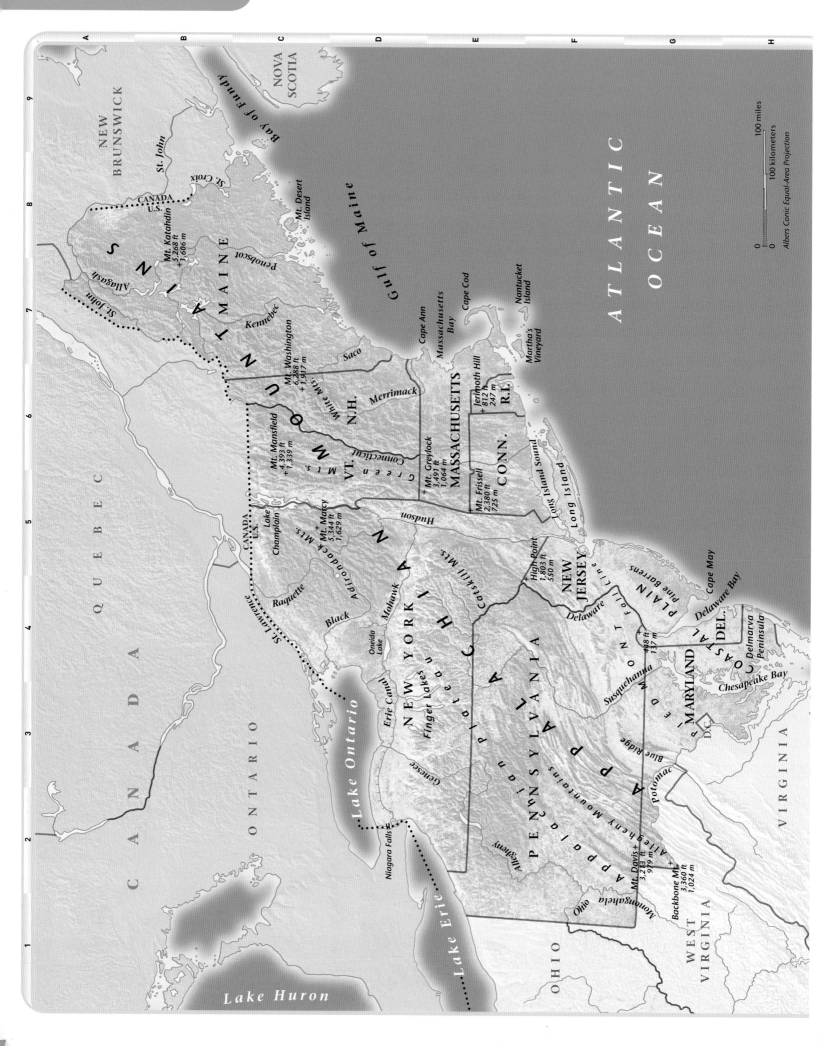

A B C D E F G H

100 miles
100 kilometers
0
0
Albers Conic Equal-Area Projection

NEW
BRUNSWICK

NOVA
SCOTIA

Bay of Fundy

St. John

St. Croix

CANADA
U.S.

MAINE

Mt. Katahdin
5,268 ft
1,606 m

Allagash

St. John

Penobscot

Mt. Desert
Island

Gulf of Maine

Kennebec

Saco

Mt. Washington
6,288 ft
1,917 m

White Mts.

N.H.

Merrimack

Cape Ann

Massachusetts
Bay

Cape Cod

ATLANTIC

OCEAN

Nantucket
Island

Martha's
Vineyard

Mt. Mansfield
4,393 ft
1,339 m

Green Mts.

VT.

Connecticut

Mt. Greylock
3,491 ft
1,064 m

MASSACHUSETTS

Jerimoth Hill
812 ft
247 m

R.I.

Mt. Frissell
2,380 ft
725 m

CONN.

Long Island Sound

Long Island

CANADA
U.S.

Lake
Champlain

Mt. Marcy
5,344 ft
1,629 m

Adirondack Mts.

Hudson

QUEBEC

St. Lawrence

Raquette

Black

Mohawk

Oneida
Lake

Catskill Mts.

NEW YORK

A P P A L A C H I A N

High Point
1,803 ft
550 m

NEW
JERSEY

Delaware

Pine Barrens

COASTAL

Cape May

Delaware Bay

Erie Canal

Finger Lakes

Plateau

fall line

fall line

48 ft
137 m

DEL.

Delmarva
Peninsula

Genesee

Susquehanna

PLAIN

PIEDMONT

MARYLAND

Chesapeake Bay

ONTARIO

CANADA

Lake Ontario

Niagara Falls

Allegheny

PENNSYLVANIA

Appalachian Mountains

Allegheny Mountains

Blue Ridge

Potomac

D.C.

VIRGINIA

Lake Erie

Mt. Davis
3,213 ft
979 m

Monongahela

Ohio

Backbone Mt.
3,360 ft
1,024 m

WEST
VIRGINIA

OHIO

Lake Huron

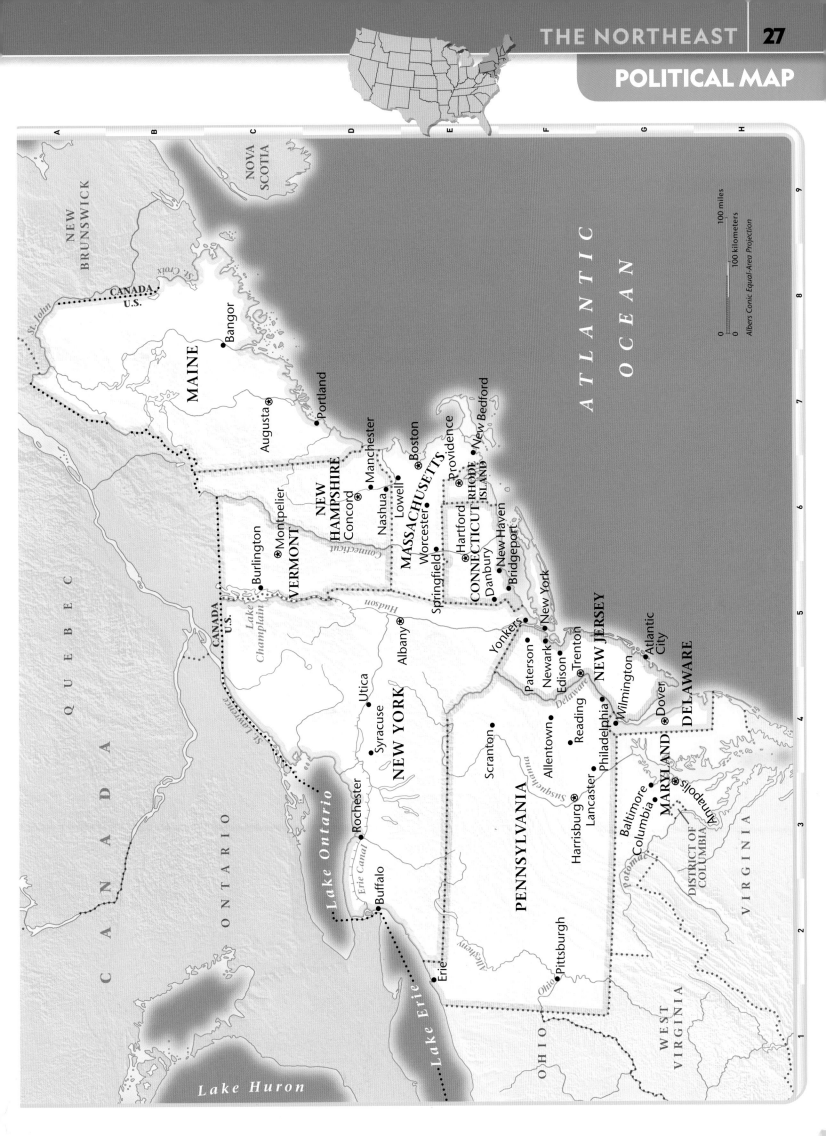

ATLANTIC OCEAN

100 miles
100 kilometers
Albers Conic Equal-Area Projection

NEW BRUNSWICK

NOVA SCOTIA

St. Croix

CANADA
U.S.

St. John

MAINE

Bangor

Portland

Augusta

NEW HAMPSHIRE

VERMONT

Montpelier

Burlington

Concord

Manchester

Nashua

Lowell

MASSACHUSETTS

Worcester

Boston

Springfield

Hartford

Providence

New Bedford

RHODE ISLAND

CONNECTICUT

New Haven

Danbury

Bridgeport

Connecticut

QUEBEC

CANADA

Lake Champlain

CANADA
U.S.

Hudson

Albany

NEW YORK

Utica

Syracuse

Scranton

Yonkers

New York

Paterson

Newark

Edison

Trenton

NEW JERSEY

Atlantic City

DELAWARE

Wilmington

Dover

Allentown

Reading

Delaware

Philadelphia

Lancaster

PENNSYLVANIA

Susquehanna

Harrisburg

Baltimore

Columbia

MARYLAND

Annapolis

DISTRICT OF COLUMBIA

Potomac

VIRGINIA

ONTARIO

Lake Ontario

Rochester

Erie Canal

Buffalo

Erie

Allegheny

Pittsburgh

Ohio

OHIO

WEST VIRGINIA

Lake Erie

Lake Huron

St. Lawrence

The Northeast

BIRTHPLACE OF A NATION

DINNER DELICACY. Lobsters turn bright red when cooked. These tasty crustaceans live in the cold waters of the Atlantic Ocean. Fishermen catch them using baited traps.

Long before the arrival of Europeans, the Northeast was inhabited by various Native American tribes who were mainly hunter-gatherers and farmers. European adventurers, traders, and settlers took over much of their land and began establishing colonies in the 17th century. Immigrants from around the globe soon followed, creating a very diverse population. Today, the Northeast includes the nation's financial center (New York City) and its political capital (Washington, D.C.). Although the region boasts tranquil mountains, lakes, and rivers, its teeming cities have always been the heart of the Northeast.

CHANGING FACES. The Northeast has been a gateway for immigration since colonial times. These young people, performing in traditional clothing in an India Cultural Festival in New Jersey, reflect the rich diversity of the region.

DEFENDER OF FREEDOM. Rising 548 feet (167 m) above Penn Square, Philadelphia's City Hall, with its statue of William Penn, is the country's largest municipal building. Penn was the founder of the Pennsylvania colony and a defender of equal rights for men and women.

◯ **SPARKLING LIGHTS.** The lights of New York City's skyline sparkle in the dark. The tall buildings of Lower Manhattan, reflected in the dark waters of the East River, are home to companies with influence that reaches around the world.

◯ **STILL WATERS.** A father and son enjoy a quiet day of fishing on the smooth-as-glass waters of Chocorua Lake in New Hampshire's White Mountains. Deciduous trees turning red and gold will soon shed their leaves, and the hillsides will turn white with winter's snow, attracting skiers to the valley.

WHERE THE PICTURES ARE

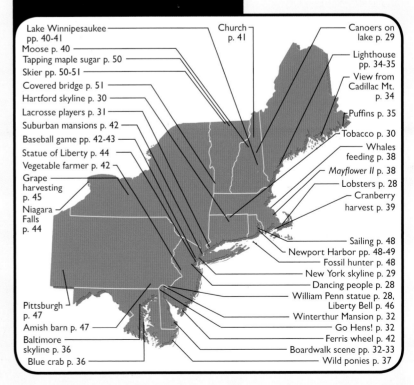

Lake Winnipesaukee pp. 40-41
Moose p. 40
Tapping maple sugar p. 50
Skier pp. 50-51
Covered bridge p. 51
Hartford skyline p. 30
Lacrosse players p. 31
Suburban mansions p. 42
Baseball game pp. 42-43
Statue of Liberty p. 44
Vegetable farmer p. 42
Grape harvesting p. 45
Niagara Falls p. 44

Church p. 41

Canoers on lake p. 29
Lighthouse pp. 34-35
View from Cadillac Mt. p. 34
Puffins p. 35
Tobacco p. 30
Whales feeding p. 38
Mayflower II p. 38
Lobsters p. 28
Cranberry harvest p. 39
Sailing p. 48
Newport Harbor pp. 48-49
Fossil hunter p. 48
New York skyline p. 29
Dancing people p. 28
William Penn statue p. 28, Liberty Bell p. 46
Winterthur Mansion p. 32
Go Hens! p. 32
Ferris wheel p. 42
Boardwalk scene pp. 32-33
Wild ponies p. 37

Pittsburgh p. 47
Amish barn p. 47
Baltimore skyline p. 36
Blue crab p. 36

THE BASICS

Statehood
January 9, 1788; 5th state

Total area (land and water)
5,543 sq mi (14,357 sq km)

Land area
4,842 sq mi (12,542 sq km)

Population
3,572,665

Capital
Hartford
Population 122,587

Largest city
Bridgeport
Population 144,239

Racial/ethnic groups
80.3% white; 11.9% African American; 4.8% Asian; 0.5% Native American; 16.1% Hispanic origin (any race)

Foreign born
14.2%

Urban population
88.0%

Population density
737.8 per sq mi (284.9 per sq km)

GEO WHIZ

The sperm whale, the state animal of Connecticut, has a brain larger than that of any other creature known to have lived on Earth.

The first hamburgers in U.S. history were served by Louis Lassen at his New Haven lunch wagon in 1895.

The nuclear-powered U.S.S. *Virginia*, the first of a class of technologically advanced submarines, was built at Groton, home of the U.S. Naval Submarine Base.

MOUNTAIN LAUREL

ROBIN

Connecticut

As early as 1614, Dutch explorers founded trading posts along the coast of Connecticut, but the first permanent European settlements were established in 1635 by English Puritans from nearby Massachusetts. The laws established by the colony were an important model for the writing of the U.S. Constitution in 1787, earning the state its nickname: the Constitution State. Even in colonial times Connecticut was an important industrial center, producing goods that competed with factories in England. Today, Connecticut industries make jet aircraft engines, helicopters, and nuclear submarines. The state is home to many international corporations. With headquarters of more than 100 insurance companies, Connecticut is often called the "insurance state."

⬤ **LEAFY HARVEST.** Tents protect shade tobacco. Leaves from the plants, which are grown on two farms in the Connecticut River Valley, are used for premium cigar wrappers.

◗ **BRIGHT CITY LIGHTS.** Established as a fort in the early 1600s, Hartford was one of the earliest cities of colonial America. Today, this modern state capital is a center of economic growth and cultural diversity.

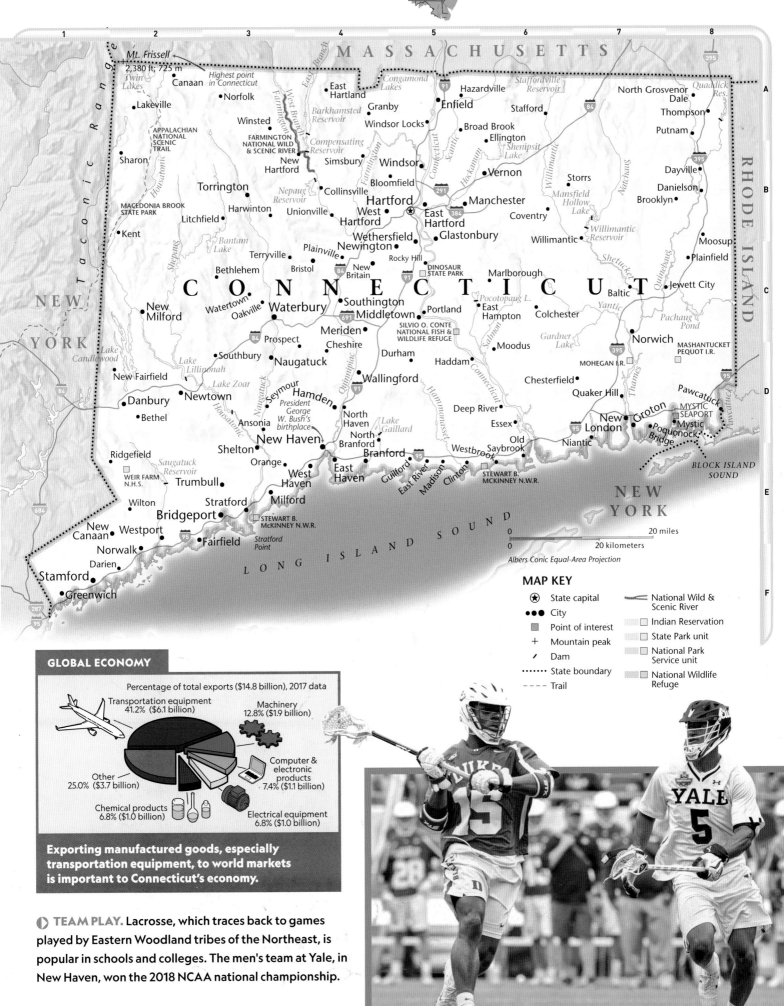

MASSACHUSETTS

Mt. Frissell
2,380 ft; 725 m
Highest point in Connecticut

Twin Lakes
Canaan
Lakeville
Norfolk
East Hartland
Congamond Lakes
Hazardville
Staffordville Reservoir
North Grosvenor Dale
Quaddick Res.

Winsted
Granby
Enfield
Stafford
Thompson

Barkhamsted Reservoir
Windsor Locks
Broad Brook
Putnam

Sharon
APPALACHIAN NATIONAL SCENIC TRAIL
FARMINGTON NATIONAL WILD & SCENIC RIVER
Compensating Reservoir
New Hartford
Simsbury
Windsor
Ellington
Shenipsit Lake
Dayville

Torrington
Nepaug Reservoir
Collinsville
Bloomfield
Vernon
Storrs
Danielson

MACEDONIA BROOK STATE PARK
Harwinton
Unionville
Hartford
Manchester
Mansfield Hollow Lake
Brooklyn

Litchfield
West Hartford
East Hartford
Coventry
Willimantic Reservoir

Kent
Wethersfield
Glastonbury
Willimantic
Moosup

Bantam Lake
Plainville
Newington
Willimantic
Plainfield

Terryville
Bristol
New Britain
Rocky Hill
DINOSAUR STATE PARK
Marlborough
Baltic
Jewett City

Bethlehem
CONNECTICUT
East Hampton
Colchester
Pachaug Pond

New Milford
Watertown
Oakville
Waterbury
Southington
Middletown
Portland
Pocotopaug L.
Norwich
MASHANTUCKET PEQUOT I.R.

Meriden
SILVIO O. CONTE NATIONAL FISH & WILDLIFE REFUGE
Moodus
MOHEGAN I.R.

Prospect
Cheshire
Durham
Gardner Lake

Southbury
Naugatuck
Haddam
Chesterfield
Quaker Hill
Pawcatuck

New Fairfield
Lake Lillinonah
Lake Zoar
Wallingford
MYSTIC SEAPORT

Danbury
Newtown
Seymour
Hamden
President George W. Bush's birthplace
Deep River
Essex
New London
Groton
Mystic

Bethel
Ansonia
North Haven
Lake Gaillard
Old Saybrook
Niantic
Poquonock Bridge

New Haven
North Branford
Westbrook
BLOCK ISLAND SOUND

Ridgefield
Shelton
Branford

WEIR FARM N.H.S.
Saugatuck Reservoir
Orange
East Haven
Guilford
East River
Madison
Clinton
STEWART B. McKINNEY N.W.R.

Trumbull
West Haven
Milford

Wilton
Stratford

Bridgeport
STEWART B. McKINNEY N.W.R.
NEW YORK

New Canaan
Westport
Fairfield
Stratford Point

Norwalk
Darien

Stamford
Greenwich

LONG ISLAND SOUND

NEW YORK

RHODE ISLAND

Taconic Range
Housatonic
NEW YORK
Lake Candlewood
Housatonic
Naugatuck

0   20 miles
0   20 kilometers

Albers Conic Equal-Area Projection

MAP KEY

⊛ State capital	National Wild & Scenic River
●●● City	Indian Reservation
▪ Point of interest	State Park unit
+ Mountain peak	National Park Service unit
∕ Dam	National Wildlife Refuge
⋯⋯ State boundary	
---- Trail	

GLOBAL ECONOMY

Percentage of total exports ($14.8 billion), 2017 data

Transportation equipment
41.2% ($6.1 billion)

Machinery
12.8% ($1.9 billion)

Other
25.0% ($3.7 billion)

Computer & electronic products
7.4% ($1.1 billion)

Chemical products
6.8% ($1.0 billion)

Electrical equipment
6.8% ($1.0 billion)

Exporting manufactured goods, especially transportation equipment, to world markets is important to Connecticut's economy.

◐ **TEAM PLAY.** Lacrosse, which traces back to games played by Eastern Woodland tribes of the Northeast, is popular in schools and colleges. The men's team at Yale, in New Haven, won the 2018 NCAA national championship.

THE BASICS

Statehood
December 7, 1787; 1st state

Total area (land and water)
2,489 sq mi (6,446 sq km)

Land area
1,949 sq mi (5,047 sq km)

Population
967,171

Capital
Dover
Population 38,079

Largest city
Wilmington
Population 70,635

Racial/ethnic groups
69.7% white; 22.8% African American; 4.1% Asian; 0.6% Native American; 9.3% Hispanic origin (any race)

Foreign born
9.1%

Urban population
83.3%

Population density
496.2 per sq mi
(191.6 per sq km)

GEO WHIZ

Each year contestants bring their pumpkins and launching machines to the World Championship Punkin Chunkin in Bridgeville to see who can catapult their big orange squash the farthest.

The Delaware Estuary is one of the most important shorebird migration sites in the Western Hemisphere.

Delaware

Second smallest among the states in area, Delaware has played a big role in the history of the United States. The Delaware River Valley was explored at various times by the Spanish, Portuguese, and Dutch, but the Swedes established the first permanent European settlement in 1638. In 1655 the colony fell under Dutch authority, but in 1682 the land was annexed by William Penn and the Pennsylvania colony. In 1787 Delaware was the first state to ratify the new U.S. Constitution. Delaware's Atlantic coast beaches are popular with tourists. Its fertile farmland, mainly in the south, produces soybeans, corn, dairy products, and poultry. But the state's real economic power is located in the north, around Wilmington, where factories employ thousands of workers to process food products and produce machinery and chemicals. Industry has been a source of wealth, but it also poses a danger to the environment. Protecting the environment is a high priority for Delaware.

PEACH BLOSSOM

BLUE HEN CHICKEN

◉ **TEAM SPIRIT. Enthusiastic** fans and the University of Delaware band support the "Fightin' Blue Hens." Located in Newark, the university traces its roots to 1743.

⬙ **PAST GRANDEUR. Built in 1837** in the fashion of a British country house, Winterthur was expanded from 12 to 196 rooms by the du Ponts, chemical industry tycoons. In 1951 the house was opened to the public as a museum for the family's extensive collection of antiques and Americana.

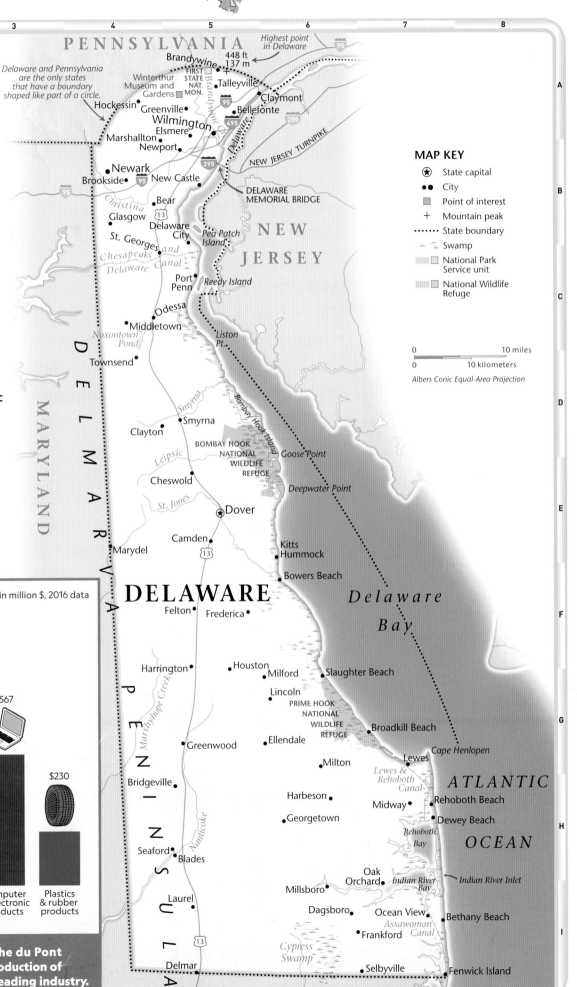

PENNSYLVANIA

Delaware and Pennsylvania are the only states that have a boundary shaped like part of a circle.

Highest point in Delaware
448 ft
137 m

Brandywine

Winterthur Museum and Gardens
FIRST STATE NAT. MON.
Talleyville
Claymont
Hockessin
Greenville
Bellefonte
Wilmington
Elsmere
Marshallton
Newport
Newark
Brookside
New Castle
Bear
Glasgow
Delaware City
St. Georges
Pea Patch Island
Chesapeake and Delaware Canal

NEW JERSEY

NEW JERSEY TURNPIKE

DELAWARE MEMORIAL BRIDGE

Port Penn
Reedy Island
Odessa
Middletown
Noxontown Pond
Liston Pt.
Townsend
Smyrna
Smyrna
Clayton
Bombay Hook Island
Leipsic
BOMBAY HOOK NATIONAL WILDLIFE REFUGE
Goose Point
Cheswold
Deepwater Point
St. Jones
Dover
Camden
Kitts Hummock
Marydel
Bowers Beach
DELAWARE
Felton
Frederica
Delaware Bay
Harrington
Houston
Milford
Slaughter Beach
Lincoln
PRIME HOOK NATIONAL WILDLIFE REFUGE
Greenwood
Ellendale
Broadkill Beach
Bridgeville
Milton
Lewes
Cape Henlopen
Lewes & Rehoboth Canal
ATLANTIC
Harbeson
Midway
Rehoboth Beach
Georgetown
Dewey Beach
Rehoboth Bay
Seaford
Blades
OCEAN
Laurel
Oak Orchard
Indian River Inlet
Millsboro
Indian River Bay
Dagsboro
Ocean View
Bethany Beach
Frankford
Assawoman Canal
Delmar
Cypress Swamp
Selbyville
Fenwick Island

MARYLAND

D E L M A R V A   P E N I N S U L A

Christina
Marshyhope Creek
Nanticoke

MAP KEY
- ⍟ State capital
- •• City
- ▪ Point of interest
- + Mountain peak
- ···· State boundary
- ⁓ Swamp
- ▨ National Park Service unit
- ▨ National Wildlife Refuge

0 ——— 10 miles
0 ——— 10 kilometers
Albers Conic Equal-Area Projection

🌊 **SEASIDE RETREAT.**
Originally established in 1873 as a church campground, Rehoboth Beach is still a popular getaway destination on Delaware's Atlantic coastline. A concrete dolphin overlooks the town's boardwalk, a popular promenade that separates shops and restaurants from the beach. The boardwalk has been destroyed on several occasions by storms.

CHEMICAL GIANT

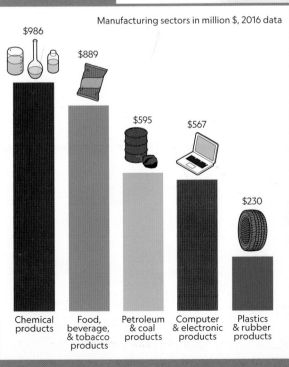

Manufacturing sectors in million $, 2016 data

$986 — Chemical products
$889 — Food, beverage, & tobacco products
$595 — Petroleum & coal products
$567 — Computer & electronic products
$230 — Plastics & rubber products

A gunpowder mill founded by the du Pont family in 1802 gave rise to the production of chemicals that is now the state's leading industry.

THE BASICS

Statehood
March 15, 1820; 23rd state

Total area (land and water)
35,380 sq mi (91,633 sq km)

Land area
30,843 sq mi (79.883 sq km)

Population
1,338,404

Capital
Augusta
Population 18,681

Largest city
Portland
Population 66,417

Racial/ethnic groups
94.7% white; 1.6% African American; 1.2% Asian; 0.7% Native American; 1.6% Hispanic origin (any race)

Foreign born
3.6%

Urban population
38.7%

Population density
43.4 per sq mi (16.8 per sq km)

GEO WHIZ

With world shark populations declining, some conservation-minded deep-sea fishermen in Maine have turned the idea of a shark tournament upside down. They still compete to see who can catch the biggest fish, but they tag and release the sharks.

Glaciers formed during the last ice age carved hundreds of inlets out of Maine's shoreline and created some 2,000 islands.

Maine

Maine's story begins long before the arrival of European settlers in the 1600s. Evidence of ancestors of today's Native Americans dates to at least 3000 B.C., and Leif Erikson and his Viking sailors may have explored Maine's coastline as early as A.D. 1000. English settlements were established along the southern coast in the 1620s, and in 1677 the territory of Maine came under the control of Massachusetts. After the Revolutionary War, the people of Maine pressed for separation from Massachusetts, and in 1820 Maine became a state. Most of Maine's population is concentrated in towns along the coast. Famous for its rugged beauty, the coast is the focus of the tourist industry. Cold offshore waters contribute to a lively fishing industry, and timber from the state's mountainous interior supports wood product and paper businesses. Maine, a leader in environmental awareness, seeks a balance between economic growth and environmental protection.

WHITE PINE CONE
AND TASSEL

CHICKADEE

EASTERN LOOKOUT. Acadia National Park, established in 1929, attracts thousands of tourists each year. The park includes Cadillac Mountain, the highest point along the North Atlantic coast and the site from which the earliest sunrises in the continental United States can be viewed from October 7 through March 6.

BLUEBERRY LEADER

Production in million lb (million kg)

91.1 (41.3)	87.1 (39.5)	104.4 (47.4)	101.1 (45.9)	101.8 (46.2)	67.8 (30.8)
2012	2013	2014	2015	2016	2017

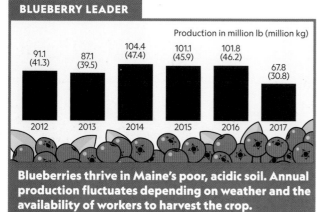

Blueberries thrive in Maine's poor, acidic soil. Annual production fluctuates depending on weather and the availability of workers to harvest the crop.

THE PINE TREE STATE:
MAINE

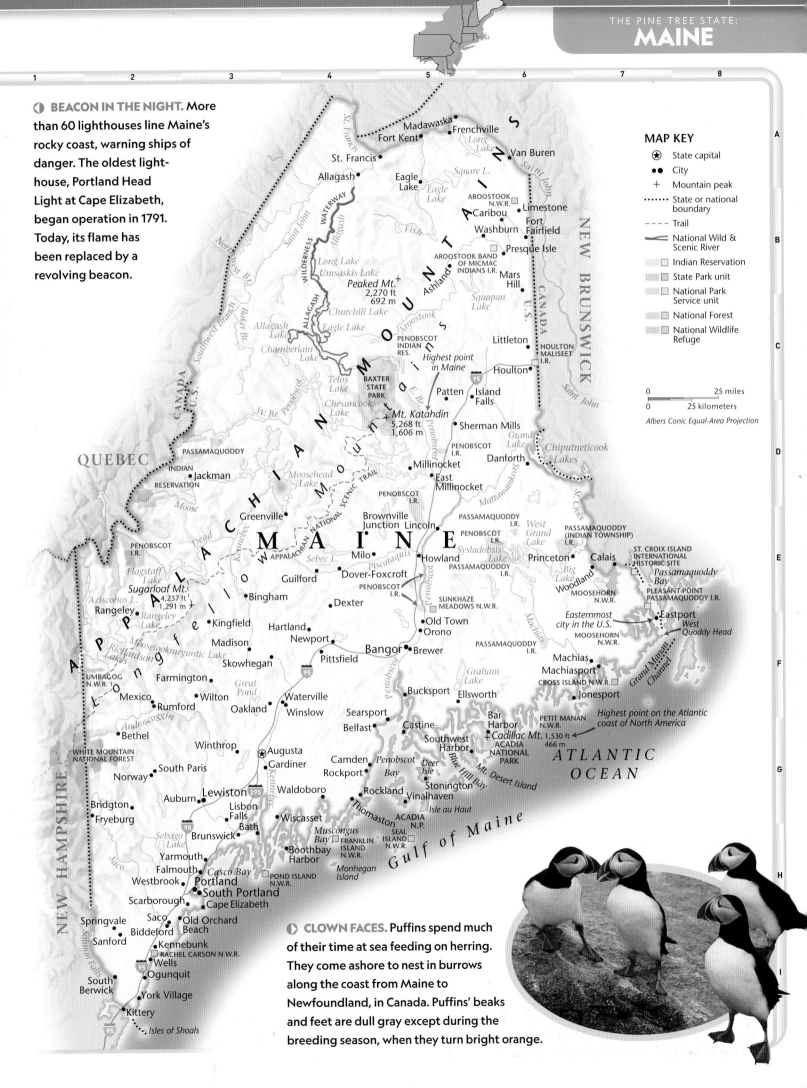

◐ BEACON IN THE NIGHT. More than 60 lighthouses line Maine's rocky coast, warning ships of danger. The oldest lighthouse, Portland Head Light at Cape Elizabeth, began operation in 1791. Today, its flame has been replaced by a revolving beacon.

MAP KEY

⊛ State capital
●● City
+ Mountain peak
••••• State or national boundary
- - - Trail
National Wild & Scenic River
▨ Indian Reservation
▨ State Park unit
▨ National Park Service unit
▨ National Forest
▨ National Wildlife Refuge

0 — 25 miles
0 — 25 kilometers
Albers Conic Equal-Area Projection

Madawaska
Fort Kent
Frenchville
St. Francis
Van Buren
Allagash
Eagle Lake
Square L.
Eagle Lake
AROOSTOOK N.W.R.
Limestone
Caribou
Fort Fairfield
Washburn
Presque Isle
AROOSTOOK BAND OF MICMAC INDIANS I.R.
Ashland
Mars Hill
Peaked Mt. 2,270 ft 692 m
Squapan Lake
Long Lake
Umsaskis Lake
Churchill Lake
Eagle Lake
Allagash Lake
PENOBSCOT INDIAN RES.
Littleton
Chamberlain Lake
Telos Lake
BAXTER STATE PARK
Highest point in Maine
HOULTON MALISEET I.R.
Chesuncook Lake
Mt. Katahdin 5,268 ft 1,606 m
Patten
Island Falls
Houlton
QUEBEC
PASSAMAQUODDY INDIAN RESERVATION
Jackman
Sherman Mills
PENOBSCOT I.R.
Danforth
Grand Lake
Chiputneticook Lakes
Moosehead Lake
Millinocket
East Millinocket
Greenville
Brownville Junction
Lincoln
PENOBSCOT I.R.
PASSAMAQUODDY I.R.
West Grand Lake
PASSAMAQUODDY (INDIAN TOWNSHIP)
ST. CROIX ISLAND INTERNATIONAL HISTORIC SITE
PENOBSCOT I.R.
Flagstaff Lake
Milo
Howland
Sysladobsis Lake
Princeton
Calais
Sugarloaf Mt. 4,237 ft 1,291 m
Guilford
Dover-Foxcroft
PENOBSCOT I.R.
Big Lake
Woodland
Passamaquoddy Bay
Rangeley
Bingham
Dexter
SUNKHAZE MEADOWS N.W.R.
MOOSEHORN N.W.R.
PLEASANT POINT PASSAMAQUODDY I.R.
Kingfield
Hartland
Old Town
Orono
Easternmost city in the U.S.
Eastport
Rangeley Lake
Madison
Newport
PASSAMAQUODDY I.R.
MOOSEHORN N.W.R.
West Quoddy Head
Mooselookmeguntic Lake
Richardson Lakes
Skowhegan
Bangor
Brewer
Pittsfield
Machias
Machiasport
UMBAGOG N.W.R.
Farmington
Graham Lake
CROSS ISLAND N.W.R.
Great Pond
Bucksport
Ellsworth
Jonesport
Mexico
Wilton
Oakland
Waterville
Winslow
Searsport
Rumford
Bethel
Highest point on the Atlantic coast of North America
WHITE MOUNTAIN NATIONAL FOREST
Winthrop
Belfast
Castine
Bar Harbor
PETIT MANAN N.W.R.
Augusta
Gardiner
Southwest Harbor
+ Cadillac Mt. 1,530 ft 466 m
ACADIA NATIONAL PARK
South Paris
Camden
Penobscot Bay
Deer Isle
ATLANTIC OCEAN
Norway
Rockport
Blue Hill Bay
Mt. Desert Island
Auburn
Lewiston
Waldoboro
Rockland
Vinalhaven
Stonington
Bridgton
Fryeburg
Lisbon Falls
Wiscasset
Thomaston
ACADIA N.P.
Isle au Haut
Brunswick
Bath
SEAL ISLAND N.W.R.
Sebago Lake
Muscongus Bay
FRANKLIN ISLAND N.W.R.
Boothbay Harbor
Monhegan Island
Gulf of Maine
Yarmouth
Falmouth
Casco Bay
POND ISLAND N.W.R.
Westbrook
Portland
South Portland
Scarborough
Cape Elizabeth
Springvale
Saco
Old Orchard Beach
Sanford
Biddeford
Kennebunk
RACHEL CARSON N.W.R.
South Berwick
Wells
Ogunquit
York Village
Kittery
Isles of Shoals

NEW BRUNSWICK
CANADA
U.S.
Saint John
St. Croix
Grand Manan Channel
Machias
Penobscot
Kennebec
Androscoggin
Saco
Dead
Moose
Fish
Aroostook
St. Francis
Northwest Br.
Saint John
Southwest Branch
Baker Br.
W. Br. Penobscot
E. Br. Penobscot
Aziscohos L.
NEW HAMPSHIRE
APPALACHIAN MOUNTAINS
ALLAGASH WILDERNESS WATERWAY
APPALACHIAN NATIONAL SCENIC TRAIL
Long Falls
Sebec L.
Piscataquis
Mattawamkeag

◐ CLOWN FACES. Puffins spend much of their time at sea feeding on herring. They come ashore to nest in burrows along the coast from Maine to Newfoundland, in Canada. Puffins' beaks and feet are dull gray except during the breeding season, when they turn bright orange.

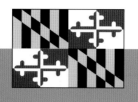

THE BASICS

Statehood
April 28, 1788; 7th state

Total area (land and water)
12,406 sq mi (32,131 sq km)

Land area
9,707 sq mi (25,142 sq km)

Population
6,042,718

Capital
Annapolis
Population 39,174

Largest city
Baltimore
Population 602,495

Racial/ethnic groups
59.0% white; 30.8% African
American; 6.7% Asian; 0.6%
Native American; 10.1%
Hispanic origin (any race)

Foreign born
14.9 %

Urban population
87.2%

Population density
622.5 per sq mi
(240.3 per sq km)

GEO WHIZ

The Naval Support Facility
Thurmont, better known as
Camp David, is the mountain
retreat of American presidents.
It is part of Catoctin Mountain
Park in north-central Maryland.

Residents on Smith Island, in
the lower Chesapeake Bay, face
loss of their land and their
traditional livelihood due to
rising sea levels and dwindling
blue crab harvests.

The name of Baltimore's
professional football
team—the Ravens—was
inspired by the title of a poem
by Edgar Allan Poe, who lived
in Baltimore in the mid-1800s.

Maryland

Native Americans who raised crops and harvested oysters from the nearby waters of Chesapeake Bay lived on the land that would become Maryland long before early European settlers arrived. In 1608 Captain John Smith explored the waters of the bay, and in 1634 English settlers established the colony of Maryland. In 1788 Maryland became the seventh state to ratify the new U.S. Constitution. Chesapeake Bay, the largest estuary in the United States, almost splits Maryland into two parts. East of the bay lies the flat coastal plain, and to the west the land rises through the hills and mountains of the panhandle. Chesapeake Bay, the state's economic and environmental focal point, supports a busy seafood industry. It is also a major transportation artery, linking Baltimore and other Maryland ports to the Atlantic Ocean. Most of the people of Maryland live in an urban corridor between Baltimore and Washington, D.C., where jobs in government, research, and high-tech businesses provide employment.

⬧ **GATEWAY CITY.** Since the early 1700s, Baltimore has been a major seaport and focus of trade, industry, and immigration. Today, the Inner Harbor is not only a modern working port but also the city's vibrant cultural center.

BLACK-EYED SUSAN

NORTHERN (BALTIMORE) ORIOLE

◖ **COLORFUL CRUSTACEAN.** Blue crabs, found in Maryland's Chesapeake Bay waters, have been harvested commercially since the mid-1800s. The tasty meat is a popular menu item—especially in crab cakes—in seafood restaurants throughout the area.

THE OLD LINE STATE:
MARYLAND

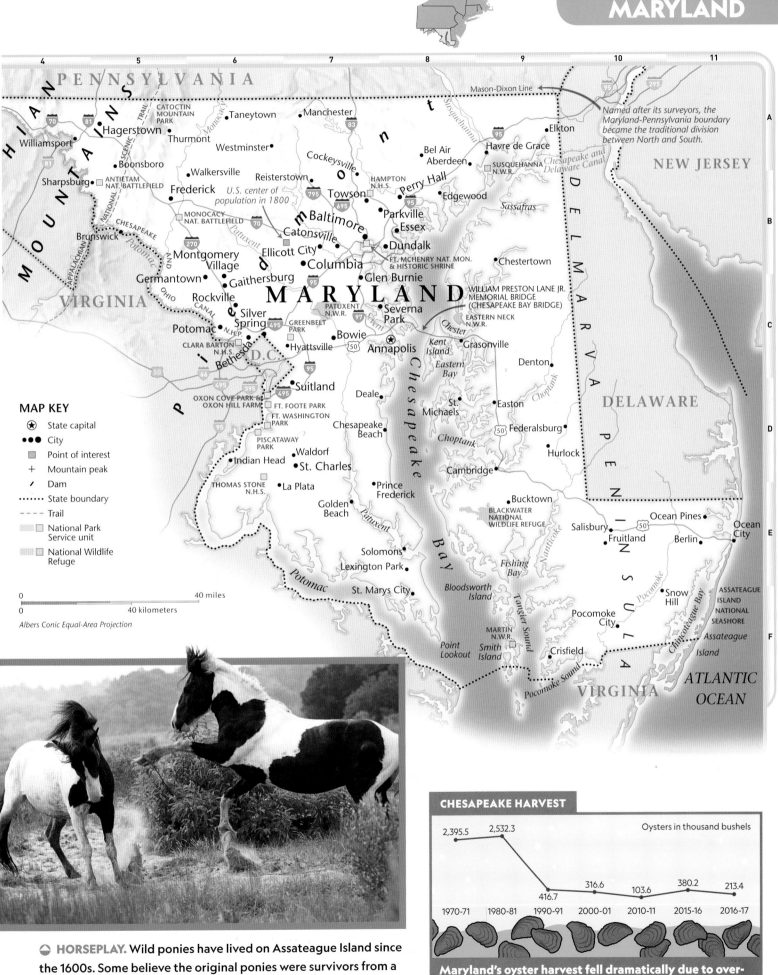

Named after its surveyors, the Maryland-Pennsylvania boundary became the traditional division between North and South.

PENNSYLVANIA

Mason-Dixon Line

NEW JERSEY

Williamsport
Hagerstown
Thurmont
Taneytown
Manchester
CATOCTIN MOUNTAIN PARK
Boonsboro
Westminster
Sharpsburg
ANTIETAM NAT. BATTLEFIELD
Walkersville
Reisterstown
Cockeysville
Elkton
Bel Air
Aberdeen
Havre de Grace
SUSQUEHANNA N.W.R.
Chesapeake and Delaware Canal
Frederick
U.S. center of population in 1800
HAMPTON N.H.S.
Towson
Perry Hall
Edgewood
Sassafras
MONOCACY NAT. BATTLEFIELD
Baltimore
Parkville
Essex
Brunswick
CHESAPEAKE AND OHIO CANAL
Catonsville
Ellicott City
Dundalk
Chestertown
Montgomery Village
Columbia
FT. MCHENRY NAT. MON. & HISTORIC SHRINE
Germantown
Gaithersburg
Glen Burnie
WILLIAM PRESTON LANE JR. MEMORIAL BRIDGE (CHESAPEAKE BAY BRIDGE)
Rockville
MARYLAND
EASTERN NECK N.W.R.
Silver Spring
PATUXENT N.W.R.
Severna Park
Chester
Grasonville
Potomac
GREENBELT PARK
Bowie
Annapolis
Kent Island
Denton
CLARA BARTON N.H.S.
Bethesda
Hyattsville
Eastern Bay
VIRGINIA
D.C.
Suitland
Deale
St. Michaels
Easton
Choptank
DELAWARE
OXON COVE PARK & OXON HILL FARM
FT. FOOTE PARK
FT. WASHINGTON PARK
Chesapeake Beach
Federalsburg
PISCATAWAY PARK
Waldorf
Choptank
Hurlock
Indian Head
St. Charles
Cambridge
THOMAS STONE N.H.S.
La Plata
Prince Frederick
Bucktown
Ocean Pines
Golden Beach
BLACKWATER NATIONAL WILDLIFE REFUGE
Salisbury
Berlin
Ocean City
Solomons
Fruitland
Lexington Park
Fishing Bay
Snow Hill
ASSATEAGUE ISLAND NATIONAL SEASHORE
St. Marys City
Bloodsworth Island
Pocomoke City
Assateague Island
Point Lookout
MARTIN N.W.R.
Smith Island
Crisfield
Tangier Sound
Pocomoke Sound
VIRGINIA
ATLANTIC OCEAN

Chesapeake Bay
Potomac
Patuxent
Monocacy
Susquehanna
Nanticoke
Pocomoke
Chincoteague Bay
DELMARVA PENINSULA
APPALACHIAN MOUNTAINS
NATIONAL SCENIC TRAIL

MAP KEY
- ⍟ State capital
- ●●● City
- ▣ Point of interest
- + Mountain peak
- ⟋ Dam
- ••••• State boundary
- ----- Trail
- ▦ National Park Service unit
- ▦ National Wildlife Refuge

0 _____ 40 miles
0 _____ 40 kilometers

Albers Conic Equal-Area Projection

HORSEPLAY. Wild ponies have lived on Assateague Island since the 1600s. Some believe the original ponies were survivors from a Spanish galleon that sank offshore. Today, more than 300 ponies live on this Atlantic barrier island shared by Maryland and Virginia.

CHESAPEAKE HARVEST

Oysters in thousand bushels

1970-71	1980-81	1990-91	2000-01	2010-11	2015-16	2016-17
2,395.5	2,532.3	416.7	316.6	103.6	380.2	213.4

Maryland's oyster harvest fell dramatically due to over-harvesting, pollution, and disease. It has since struggled to make a comeback.

THE BASICS

Statehood
February 6, 1788; 6th state

Total area
(land and water)
10,554 sq mi
(27,336 sq km)

Land area
7,800 sq mi
(20,202 sq km)

Population
6,902,149

Capital
Boston
Population 694,583

Largest city
Boston
Population 694,583

Racial/ethnic groups
81.3% white; 8.8% African
American; 6.9% Asian; 0.5%
Native American; 11.9%
Hispanic origin (any race)

Foreign born
16.2%

Urban population
92.0%

Population density
884.9 per sq mi
(341.7 per sq km)

GEO WHIZ

**Massachusetts is the birthplace
of several inventors, including
Eli Whitney, Samuel Morse, and
Benjamin Franklin.**

**The country's first lighthouse
was built on Little Brewster
Island in Boston Harbor in 1716.**

CHICKADEE

MAYFLOWER

◗ **LEVIATHANS OF THE DEEP. In the 1800s**
Massachusetts was a major center for the
whaling industry, with more than 300
registered whaling ships. Today, humpback
whales swim in the protected waters of a
marine sanctuary in Massachusetts Bay.

Massachusetts

The earliest human inhabitants of Massachusetts were ancestors of today's Native Americans who arrived more than 10,000 years ago. The first Europeans to visit Massachusetts may have been Norsemen around A.D. 1000, and later fishermen came from France and Spain. But the first permanent European settlement was established in 1620, when people aboard the sailing ship *Mayflower* landed near Plymouth on the coast of Massachusetts. The Puritans arrived soon after, and by 1630 they had established settlements at Salem and Boston.

By 1640 more than 16,000 people, most seeking religious freedom, had settled in Massachusetts. The early economy of Massachusetts was based on shipping, fishing, and whaling. By the 19th century, industry, taking advantage of abundant water power, had a firm foothold. Factory jobs attracted thousands of immigrants, mainly from Europe. In the late 20th century, Massachusetts experienced a boom in high-tech jobs, drawing on the state's skilled labor force and its more than 100 colleges and universities.

⬓ **REMINDER OF
TIMES PAST. Shrouded
in morning mist, this
replica of the *Mayflower*
docked in Plymouth
Harbor is a reminder of
the state's early history.**

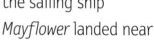

NEW HAMPSHIRE

ATLANTIC OCEAN

One of the ten most populous cities in the U.S. in 1790

MASSACHUSETTS

Massachusetts Bay

STELLWAGEN BANK NATIONAL MARINE SANCTUARY

Turners Falls
Greenfield
Deerfield
Winchendon
Orange
Athol
Gardner
Fitchburg
Leominster
Quabbin Reservoir
N E E R
SILVIO O. CONTE N.W.R.
Amherst
Northampton
South Hadley
Easthampton
Holyoke
Chicopee
Springfield
Agawam
SPRINGFIELD ARMORY N.H.S.
Ludlow
Ware
Spencer
Wachusett Res.
ASSABET N.W.R.
Shrewsbury
Worcester
Lake Quinsigamond
Framingham
Sturbridge
Southbridge
Auburn
Oxford
Webster
Milford
Bellingham
Franklin
North Attleboro
Attleboro
Taunton
Seekonk
Somerset
Fall River
New Bedford
Fairhaven

Amesbury
Haverhill
Methuen
Lawrence
Ipswich
Dracut
Lowell
LOWELL N.H.P.
Chelmsford
Wilmington
Danvers
Peabody
Gloucester
Cape Ann
SALEM MARITIME N.H.S.
Beverly
Salem
Marblehead
Lynn
Malden
Medford
Cambridge
Boston
Brookline
Milton
Quincy
Weymouth
Birthplace of Presidents John Adams and John Quincy Adams
Randolph
Rockland
Whitman
Stoughton
Brockton
Bridgewater
Silver Lake
Middleboro
Assawompset Pond
Great Quittacus Pond
Buzzards Bay
NEW BEDFORD WHALING N.H.P.

LOWELL N.H.P.
SUDBURY, ASSABET & CONCORD NATIONAL WILD & SCENIC RIVER
MINUTE MAN N.H.P.
Concord
Lexington
Woburn
BOSTON N.H.P.
GREAT MEADOWS N.W.R.
Wellesley
Marlborough
President Kennedy's birthplace
President George H.W. Bush's birthplace
Norwood
BOSTON HARBOR ISLANDS N.R.A.
TAUNTON NATIONAL WILD & SCENIC RIVER

Provincetown
CAPE COD NATIONAL SEASHORE
Truro
Plimoth Plantation
Plymouth
MASSASOIT N.W.R.
Wellfleet
Cape Cod Bay
Cape Cod Canal
Orleans
Sandwich
Dennis
Chatham
Barnstable
C A P E C O D
Hyannis
S. Yarmouth
Monomoy Island
MONOMOY N.W.R.
MASHPEE N.W.R.
East Falmouth
Falmouth
Woods Hole
Vineyard Haven
Oak Bluffs
Edgartown
Nantucket Sound
NANTUCKET N.W.R.
Nantucket
Nantucket Island
Chappaquiddick Island
Martha's Vineyard
Gay Head
WAMPANOAG I.R.
Nomans Land
NOMANS LAND ISLAND N.W.R.
Buzzards Bay
Elizabeth Islands
Vineyard Sound
Rhode Island Sound

RHODE ISLAND

TICUT

0   15 miles
0   15 kilometers
Albers Conic Equal-Area Projection

MAP KEY

- ⊛ State capital
- ●●● City
- + Mountain peak
- ⟋ Dam
- ·········· State boundary
- ---- Trail
- ∼∼∼ National Wild & Scenic River
- ▨ Indian Reservation
- ▨ National Park Service unit
- ▨ National Wildlife Refuge
- ▭ National Marine Sanctuary

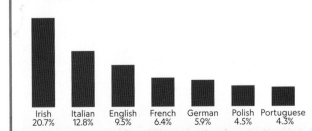

○ **BIG BUSINESS.** Cranberries, grown in fields called bogs, are one of the state's main crops. These tiny berries, one of only a few fruits native to North America, are consumed mainly as juice or as a tasty accompaniment to holiday dishes. Workers harvest floating berries in flooded fields.

EUROPEAN ROOTS

Percentage of European ancestry, 2017 data

Irish	Italian	English	French	German	Polish	Portuguese
20.7%	12.8%	9.5%	6.4%	5.9%	4.5%	4.3%

Most new immigrants to the United States are from Latin America and Asia, but many people in Massachusetts trace their ancestry to Europe.

New Hampshire

THE BASICS

Statehood
June 21, 1788; 9th state

Total area (land and water)
9,349 sq mi (24,214 sq km)

Land area
8,953 sq mi (23,187 sq km)

Population
1,356,458

Capital
Concord
Population 43,412

Largest city
Manchester
Population 112,525

Racial/ethnic groups
93.6% white; 1.6% African American; 2.8% Asian; 0.3% Native American; 3.7% Hispanic origin (any race)

Foreign born
5.9%

Urban population
60.3%

Population density
151.5 per sq mi
(58.5 per sq km)

GEO WHIZ

The Granite State boasts more than 200 different kinds of rocks and minerals, making it a great destination for collectors.

The first potato grown in the United States was planted in 1719 in Londonderry.

The territory that would become the state of New Hampshire, the ninth state to approve the U.S. Constitution in 1788, began as a fishing colony established along the short 18-mile (29-km)-long coastline in 1623. New Hampshire was named a royal colony in 1679, but as the Revolutionary War approached, it was the first colony to declare its independence from English rule. In the early 19th century, life in New Hampshire followed two very different paths. Near the coast, villages and towns grew up around sawmills, shipyards, and warehouses. But in the forested, mountainous interior, people lived on small, isolated farms, and towns provided only basic services. Today, modern industries such as computer and electronic component manufacturing and other high-tech companies, together with biotech and medical research, have brought prosperity to the state. In addition, the state's natural beauty attracts tourists year-round to hike on forest trails, swim in pristine lakes, and ski on snow-covered mountain slopes.

LUMBERING GIANT.
Averaging six feet (2 m) tall at the shoulders, moose are the largest of North America's deer. Moose are found throughout New Hampshire.

PURPLE FINCH
PURPLE LILAC

SUMMER FUN. Children play in the cool waters of Lake Winnipesaukee, a popular New Hampshire vacation spot. The lake's name is derived from an Abenaki word meaning "Smile of the Great Spirit."

ROARING WINDS

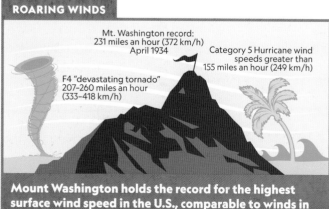

Mt. Washington record:
231 miles an hour (372 km/h)
April 1934

Category 5 Hurricane wind speeds greater than 155 miles an hour (249 km/h)

F4 "devastating tornado"
207–260 miles an hour
(333–418 km/h)

Mount Washington holds the record for the highest surface wind speed in the U.S., comparable to winds in Category 5 hurricanes and F4 tornadoes.

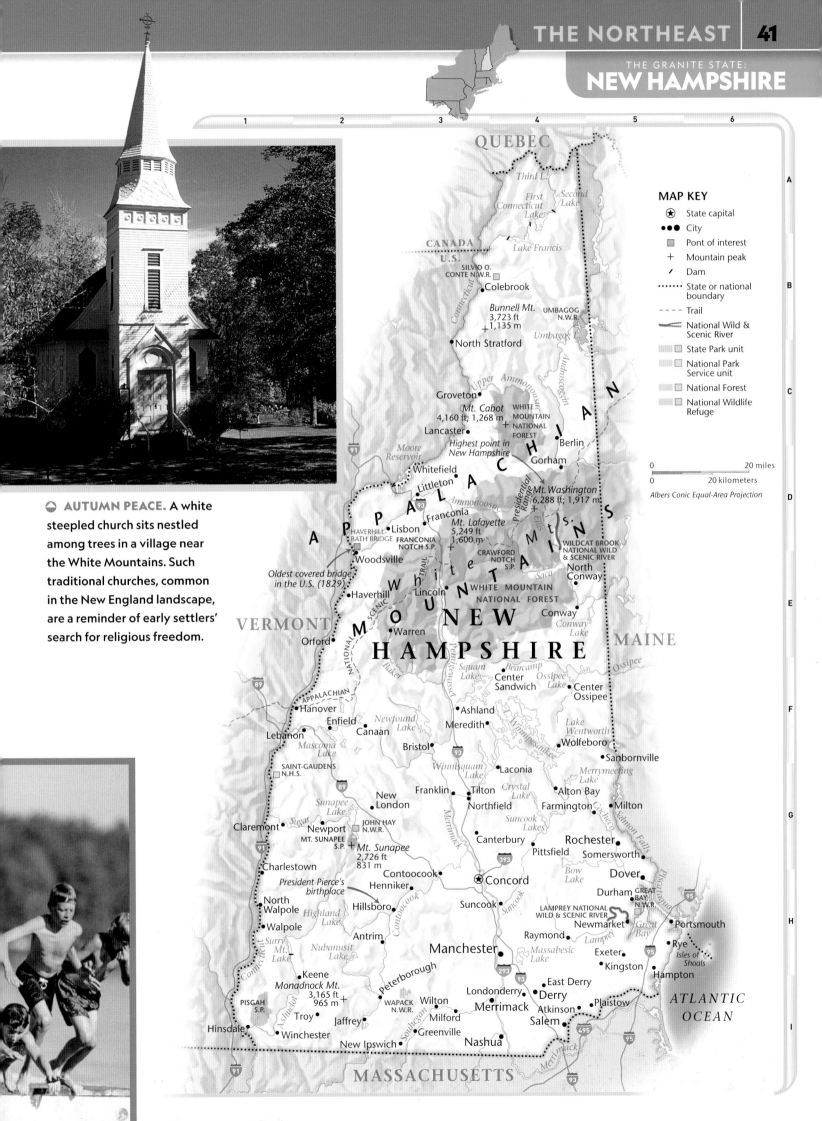

🔔 **AUTUMN PEACE.** A white steepled church sits nestled among trees in a village near the White Mountains. Such traditional churches, common in the New England landscape, are a reminder of early settlers' search for religious freedom.

MAP KEY

⊛ State capital
●●● City
▪ Pont of interest
+ Mountain peak
／ Dam
⋯ State or national boundary
--- Trail
〰 National Wild & Scenic River
▦ State Park unit
▦ National Park Service unit
▦ National Forest
▦ National Wildlife Refuge

0 _____ 20 miles
0 _____ 20 kilometers
Albers Conic Equal-Area Projection

QUEBEC

Third L.

First Connecticut Lakes

Second Lake

Lake Francis

CANADA
U.S.

SILVIO O. CONTE N.W.R.

● Colebrook

Bunnell Mt. 3,723 ft + 1,135 m

UMBAGOG N.W.R.

Umbagog L.

● North Stratford

Upper Ammonoosuc

WHITE MOUNTAIN NATIONAL FOREST

● Groveton

Mt. Cabot 4,160 ft; 1,268 m

● Berlin

● Lancaster

● Gorham

Moore Reservoir

Highest point in New Hampshire

● Whitefield

● Littleton

Ammonoosuc

Presidential Range

Mt. Washington 6,288 ft; 1,917 m

● Franconia

HAVERHILL ● Lisbon
BATH BRIDGE

Mt. Lafayette 5,249 ft 1,600 m

FRANCONIA NOTCH S.P.

CRAWFORD NOTCH S.P.

WILDCAT BROOK NATIONAL WILD & SCENIC RIVER

● Woodsville

Saco

● North Conway

Oldest covered bridge in the U.S. (1829)

● Haverhill

● Lincoln

WHITE MOUNTAIN NATIONAL FOREST

VERMONT

● Orford

● Warren

● Conway

Conway Lake

MAINE

NEW HAMPSHIRE

Baker

Pemigewasset

Squam Lakes

Bearcamp

Ossipee Lake

Ossipee

● Center Sandwich

● Center Ossipee

● Ashland

● Meredith

Lake Wentworth

● Hanover

● Enfield

Newfound Lake

Winnipesaukee

● Wolfeboro

● Canaan

● Sanbornville

● Lebanon

Mascoma Lake

● Bristol

Winnisquam Lake

Merrymeeting Lake

SAINT-GAUDENS N.H.S.

● Laconia

● Franklin

● Tilton

Crystal Lake

● Alton Bay

● Milton

● New London

● Northfield

● Farmington

Cocheco

● Claremont

Sugar

● Newport

JOHN HAY N.W.R.

Merrimack

Suncook Lakes

● Canterbury

● Rochester

Salmon Falls

MT. SUNAPEE S.P.

Mt. Sunapee 2,726 ft 831 m

● Pittsfield

● Somersworth

● Charlestown

President Pierce's birthplace

● Contoocook

● Concord ⊛

Bow Lake

● Dover

● North Walpole

● Henniker

● Suncook

● Durham

GREAT BAY N.W.R.

● Walpole

Highland Lake

● Hillsboro

Contoocook

Suncook

LAMPREY NATIONAL WILD & SCENIC RIVER

● Newmarket

Great Bay

● Portsmouth

● Antrim

● Raymond

Massabesic Lake

Lamprey

Piscataqua

Surry Mt. Lake

Nubanusit Lake

● Manchester

● Exeter

● Rye

Isles of Shoals

● Keene

Monadnock Mt. 3,165 ft + 965 m

● Peterborough

● East Derry

● Kingston

● Hampton

PISGAH S.P.

WAPACK N.W.R.

● Wilton

● Londonderry

● Derry

● Plaistow

ATLANTIC OCEAN

● Troy

● Jaffrey

● Milford

● Merrimack

● Atkinson

● Greenville

● Salem

● Hinsdale

● Winchester

● New Ipswich

● Nashua

Merrimack

MASSACHUSETTS

THE GARDEN STATE:
NEW JERSEY

New Jersey

Long before Europeans settled in New Jersey, the region was home to hunting and farming communities of Delaware Indians. The Dutch set up a trading post in northern New Jersey in 1618, calling it New Netherland, but yielded the land in 1664 to the English, who named it New Jersey after the English Channel Isle of Jersey. New Jersey saw more than 90 battles during the Revolutionary War. It became the third U.S. state in 1787 and the first to sign the Bill of Rights. In the 19th century, southern New Jersey remained largely agricultural, while the northern part of the state rapidly industrialized. Today, highways and railroads link the state to urban centers along the Atlantic seaboard. New Jersey farms grow fruits and vegetables for nearby urban markets. Industries as well as services and trade are thriving. Beaches along the Atlantic coast attract thousands of tourists each year.

⬤ **HOLD ON!** New Jersey's Atlantic coast is lined with sandy beaches that attract vacationers from near and far. Amusement parks, such as this one in Wildwood, add to the fun.

THE BASICS

Statehood
December 18, 1787; 3rd state

Total area (land and water)
8,723 sq mi (22,591 sq km)

Land area
7,354 sq mi (19,047 sq km)

Population
8,908,520

Capital
Trenton
Population 83,974

Largest city
Newark
Population 282,090

Racial/ethnic groups
72.1% white; 15.0% African American; 10.1% Asian; 0.6% Native American; 20.4% Hispanic origin (any race)

Foreign born
22.1%

Urban population
94.7%

Population density
1,211.4 per sq mi
(467.7 per sq km)

GEO WHIZ

Site of a one-time trash heap, the Meadowlands, a swampy lowland along the Hackensack River, is now home to a major sports complex.

In 1930 New Jerseyite Charles Darrow developed the game Monopoly. He named Boardwalk and other streets in the game after those in Atlantic City.

AMERICAN GOLDFINCH

VIOLET

⬤ **SUBURBAN SPRAWL.** With almost 95 percent of the state's population living in urban areas, housing developments with close-set, look-alike houses are a common characteristic of the suburban landscape. Residents commute to city jobs.

CROWDED

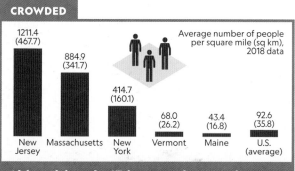

Average number of people per square mile (sq km), 2018 data

New Jersey	Massachusetts	New York	Vermont	Maine	U.S. (average)
1211.4 (467.7)	884.9 (341.7)	414.7 (160.1)	68.0 (26.2)	43.4 (16.8)	92.6 (35.8)

Although it ranks 47th among the states in area, New Jersey has the highest population density—people per square mile—in the country.

THE GARDEN STATE:
NEW JERSEY

SHINE BRIGHT. Designated a National Historic Landmark, the Sandy Hook Lighthouse has been in service since 1764, making it the oldest operating lighthouse in the United States.

HEADED TO MARKET. New Jersey is a leading producer of fresh fruits and vegetables. These vegetables are headed for urban markets in the Northeast.

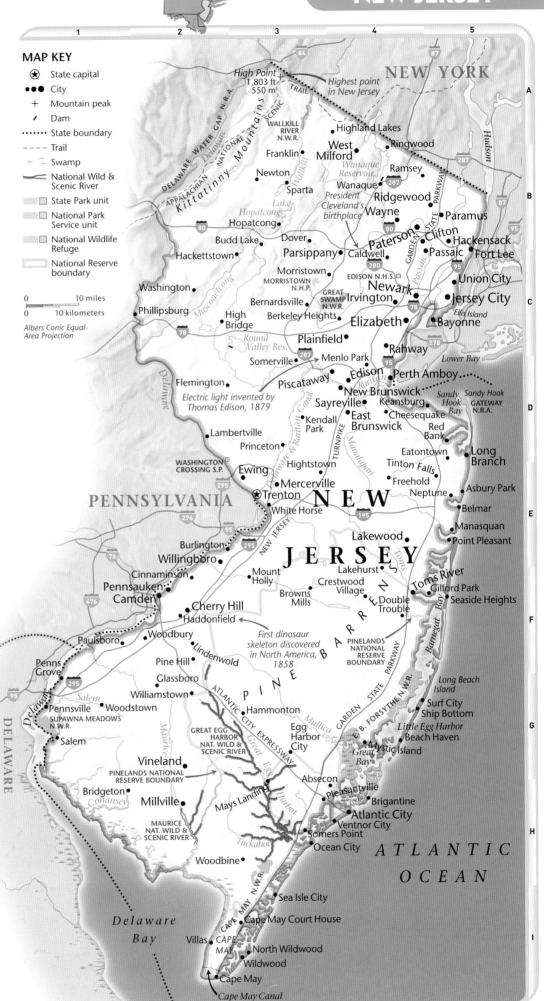

MAP KEY

- ★ State capital
- ●●● City
- ＋ Mountain peak
- ⟍ Dam
- ⋯⋯ State boundary
- --- Trail
- Swamp
- National Wild & Scenic River
- State Park unit
- National Park Service unit
- National Wildlife Refuge
- National Reserve boundary

0   10 miles
0   10 kilometers

Albers Conic Equal-Area Projection

NEW YORK

High Point 1,803 ft 550 m — Highest point in New Jersey

Highland Lakes
Ringwood
West Milford
Franklin
Ramsey
Newton
Wanaque
Sparta
Ridgewood
Paramus
President Cleveland's birthplace
Wayne
Clifton
Hopatcong
Dover
Paterson
Passaic
Hackensack
Budd Lake
Parsippany
Caldwell
Fort Lee
Hackettstown
Morristown
Union City
Washington
Irvington
Newark
Bernardsville
Jersey City
Phillipsburg
Berkeley Heights
Elizabeth
Ellis Island
High Bridge
Plainfield
Bayonne
Somerville
Menlo Park
Rahway
Lower Bay
Flemington
Edison
Perth Amboy
Piscataway
New Brunswick
Sandy Hook Bay
Sandy Hook GATEWAY N.R.A.
Sayreville
Keansburg
Kendall Park
East Brunswick
Cheesequake
Lambertville
Red Bank
Princeton
Eatontown
Long Branch
Hightstown
Tinton Falls
Ewing
Freehold
Asbury Park
Mercerville
Neptune
Trenton
Belmar
White Horse
Manasquan
Point Pleasant
Lakewood
Burlington
Lakehurst
Toms River
Willingboro
Crestwood Village
Gilford Park
Cinnaminson
Mount Holly
Seaside Heights
Pennsauken
Browns Mills
Double Trouble
Camden
Cherry Hill
Haddonfield
Woodbury
Long Beach Island
Paulsboro
Lindenwold
Pine Hill
Surf City
Penns Grove
Ship Bottom
Glassboro
Little Egg Harbor
Williamstown
Beach Haven
Hammonton
Mystic Island
Pennsville
Woodstown
Egg Harbor City
Salem
Great Bay
Vineland
Absecon
Pleasantville
Brigantine
Bridgeton
Mays Landing
Atlantic City
Millville
Ventnor City
Somers Point
Ocean City
Woodbine
Sea Isle City
Cape May Court House
Villas
North Wildwood
Wildwood
Cape May

PENNSYLVANIA
NEW JERSEY
DELAWARE
PINE BARRENS
ATLANTIC OCEAN
Delaware Bay

Electric light invented by Thomas Edison, 1879

First dinosaur skeleton discovered in North America, 1858

WASHINGTON CROSSING S.P.
WALLKILL RIVER N.W.R.
DELAWARE WATER GAP N.R.A.
APPALACHIAN NATIONAL SCENIC TRAIL
Kittatinny Mountains
Lake Hopatcong
Wanaque Reservoir
GREAT SWAMP N.W.R.
MORRISTOWN N.H.P.
EDISON N.H.S.
Round Valley Res.
PINELANDS NATIONAL RESERVE BOUNDARY
SUPAWNA MEADOWS N.W.R.
GREAT EGG HARBOR NAT. WILD & SCENIC RIVER
MAURICE NAT. WILD & SCENIC RIVER
E.B. FORSYTHE N.W.R.
CAPE MAY N.W.R.
Cape May Canal

GARDEN STATE PARKWAY
ATLANTIC CITY EXPRESSWAY

New York

When Englishman Henry Hudson explored New York's Hudson River Valley in 1609, the territory was already inhabited by large tribes of Native Americans, including the powerful Iroquois. In 1624 a Dutch trading company established the New Netherland colony, but after just 40 years the colony was taken over by the English and renamed for England's Duke of York. In 1788 New York became the 11th state. The powerful port city of New York, center of trade and commerce and a gateway to immigrants, is the largest city in the United States. Its metropolitan area, which extends into the surrounding states of Connecticut, New Jersey, and Pennsylvania, has more than 20 million people. Cities such as Buffalo and Rochester are industrial centers, and Ithaca and Syracuse boast major universities. Agriculture is also important, and the state is a leading producer of dairy products, fruits, and vegetables.

THE BASICS

Statehood
July 26, 1788; 11th state

Total area (land and water)
54,555 sq mi (141,297 sq km)

Land area
47,126 sq mi (122,057 sq km)

Population
19,542,209

Capital
Albany
Population 97,279

Largest city
New York City
Population 8,398,748

Racial/ethnic groups
69.6% white; 17.7% African American; 9.1% Asian; 1.0% Native American; 19.2% Hispanic origin (any race)

Foreign born
22.7%

Urban population
87.9%

Population density
414.7 per sq mi (160.1 per sq km)

GEO WHIZ

The National Baseball Hall of Fame, established in 1939 in Cooperstown, includes a museum that houses more than 40,000 artifacts of the game, including bats, balls, gloves, and uniforms.

The Erie Canal, built in the 1820s between Albany and Buffalo, opened the Midwest to development by linking the Hudson River and the Great Lakes.

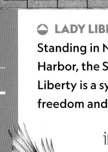

LADY LIBERTY. Standing in New York Harbor, the Statue of Liberty is a symbol of freedom and democracy.

EASTERN BLUEBIRD

ROSE

Map labels: LAKE · Niagara River · Lockport · Erie Canal · Medina · IROQUOIS N.W.R. · TUSCARORA I.R. · Niagara Falls · NIAGARA FALLS · Tonawanda · TONAWANDA I.R. · Amherst · Batavia · ONTARIO · THEODORE ROOSEVELT INAUGURAL N.H.S. · Buffalo · Cheektowaga · W. Seneca · Geneseo · LAKE ERIE · Hamburg · Lake Erie Beach · CATTARAUGUS INDIAN RESERVATION · CANADA U.S. · Dunkirk · Cattaraugus Cr. · Fredonia · Westfield · OIL SPRINGS I.R. · Chautauqua Lake · ALLEGANY INDIAN RES. · Salamanca · Wellsville · Jamestown · ALLEGANY STATE PARK · Olean · Allegheny · Genesee

URBAN GIANT

Population of city proper, 2018 data

City	Population
New York	8,398,748
Los Angeles	3,990,456
Chicago	2,705,994
Houston	2,325,502
Phoenix	1,660,272

With more than twice the population of the next largest city, New York—known as the Big Apple—is the country's largest city.

NATURAL WONDER. Each year more than eight million tourists visit Niagara Falls on the U.S.-Canada border. Visitors in rain slickers trek through the mists below Bridal Veil Falls on the American side.

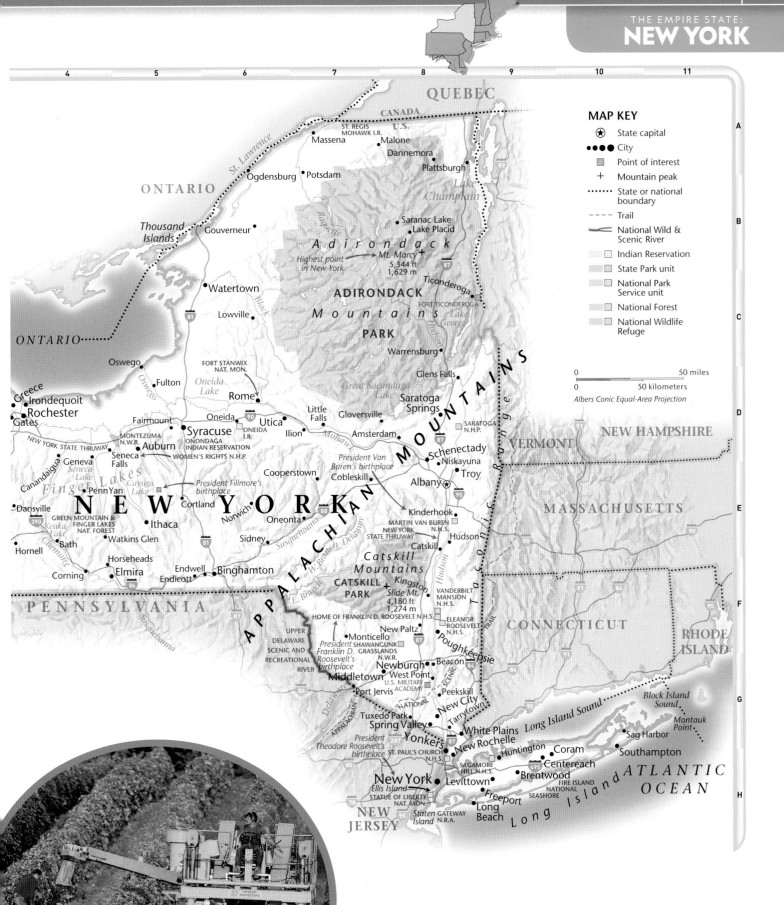

MAP KEY

⭐ State capital
●●● City
▪ Point of interest
+ Mountain peak
····· State or national boundary
--- Trail
〰 National Wild & Scenic River
▫ Indian Reservation
▫ State Park unit
▫ National Park Service unit
▫ National Forest
▫ National Wildlife Refuge

0 _____ 50 miles
0 _____ 50 kilometers
Albers Conic Equal-Area Projection

QUEBEC

CANADA
U.S.

ST. REGIS
MOHAWK I.R.
Massena
Malone
Dannemora
Ogdensburg Potsdam
Plattsburgh

St. Lawrence

ONTARIO

Lake Champlain

Thousand Islands
Gouverneur

Saranac Lake
Lake Placid

A d i r o n d a c k
Highest point in New York
Mt. Marcy +
5,344 ft
1,629 m

Ticonderoga
FORT TICONDEROGA

Watertown

ADIRONDACK
M o u n t a i n s
PARK

Lowville

ONTARIO

Black

Lake George

Hudson

Warrensburg

Oswego

Fulton

FORT STANWIX
NAT. MON.
Oneida Lake
Rome

Greece
Irondequoit
Rochester
Gates

Oswego

Fairmount
Oneida
Syracuse
Utica
Ilion

ONEIDA
I.R.

MONTEZUMA
N.W.R.
ONONDAGA
INDIAN RESERVATION
Auburn
WOMEN'S RIGHTS N.H.P.

Geneva
Seneca Falls

Canandaigua
Seneca Lake

PennYan
Cayuga Lake

Dansville

390
Keuka Lake

F i n g e r   L a k e s

N E W   Y O R K

Cortland

GREEN MOUNTAIN &
FINGER LAKES
NAT. FOREST
Ithaca

Watkins Glen

Hornell
Bath

Chemung

Horseheads
Elmira

Corning
Endicott

Endwell
Binghamton

86

Little Falls
Gloversville

SARATOGA
Saratoga Springs
N.H.P.

Amsterdam
Mohawk

Schenectady
Niskayuna
Troy

President Van
Buren's birthplace

Cooperstown
Cobleskill

Albany ⭐
90

Norwich
Oneonta

Sidney

Susquehanna

88

81

Kinderhook

MARTIN VAN BUREN
N.H.S.
NEW YORK
STATE THRUWAY

Hudson

Catskill

C a t s k i l l
M o u n t a i n s

CATSKILL
PARK
Slide Mt. +
4,180 ft
1,274 m

HOME OF FRANKLIN D. ROOSEVELT N.H.S.

Kingston

VANDERBILT
MANSION
N.H.S.

ELEANOR
ROOSEVELT
N.H.S.

Hudson

T a c o n i c   R a n g e s

VERMONT

NEW HAMPSHIRE

91

MASSACHUSETTS

90

CONNECTICUT

RHODE ISLAND

93

84

W. Branch Delaware
E. Branch

UPPER
DELAWARE
SCENIC AND
RECREATIONAL
RIVER

Monticello

President
Franklin D.
Roosevelt's
birthplace

New Paltz

SHAWANGUNK
GRASSLANDS
N.W.R.

Newburgh
West Point
U.S. MILITARY
ACADEMY

Middletown

Port Jervis

Delaware

APPALACHIAN

A P P A L A C H I A N   M O U N T A I N S

Poughkeepsie

Beacon

Peekskill

New City
Tarrytown

84

84

95

Block Island Sound

Montauk Point

Long Island Sound

Sag Harbor
Southampton

NATIONAL

Tuxedo Park
Spring Valley

Yonkers

President
Theodore Roosevelt's
birthplace
ST. PAUL'S CHURCH
N.H.S.

White Plains
New Rochelle

Huntington
Coram

SAGAMORE
HILL N.H.S.

Centereach
Brentwood

FIRE ISLAND

New York

Ellis Island
STATUE OF LIBERTY
NAT. MON.

Levittown

Freeport
Long Beach

FIRE ISLAND
NATIONAL
SEASHORE

A T L A N T I C
O C E A N

L o n g   I s l a n d

NEW JERSEY

95

Staten Island

GATEWAY
N.R.A.

PENNSYLVANIA

Susquehanna

81

SWEET HARVEST. The Finger Lakes region, with its unique combination of soils and climate conditions, is well suited to growing wine grapes. With more than 10,000 acres (4,047 ha) of vineyards, it is the center of New York's wine industry, producing varieties for both domestic and export markets.

THE BASICS

Statehood
December 12, 1787; 2nd state

Total area (land and water)
46,054 sq mi (119,280 sq km)

Land area
44,743 sq mi (115,883 sq km)

Population
12,807,060

Capital
Harrisburg
Population 49,229

Largest city
Philadelphia
Population 1,584,138

Racial/ethnic groups
82.1% white; 11.9% African American; 3.6% Asian; 0.4% Native American; 7.3% Hispanic origin (any race)

Foreign born
6.6%

Urban population
78.7%

Population density
286.2 per sq mi
(110.5 per sq km)

GEO WHIZ

The Martin Guitar Company in Nazareth has been handcrafting guitars for musicians all over the world since 1833.

For more than a century, streets in Philadelphia have been transformed on New Year's Day for the annual Mummers Parade.

Pennsylvania

Pennsylvania, the 12th of England's 13 American colonies, was established in 1682 by Quaker William Penn and 360 settlers seeking religious freedom and fair government. The colony enjoyed abundant natural resources—dense woodlands, fertile soils, industrial minerals, and water power—that soon attracted Germans, Scotch-Irish, and other immigrants. Pennsylvania played a central role in the move for independence from Britain, and Philadelphia served as the new country's capital from 1790 to 1800. In the 19th century, Philadelphia, in the east, and Pittsburgh, in the west, became booming centers of industrial growth. Philadelphia produced ships, locomotives, and textiles, while the iron and steel industry fueled Pittsburgh's growth. Jobs in industry as well as agriculture attracted immigrants from around the world. Today, Pennsylvania's economy has shifted toward information technology, health care, financial services, and tourism, but coal and steel production continue to play a role in the state's economy.

◉ **LET FREEDOM RING.** The Liberty Bell, cast in 1753 by Pennsylvania craftsmen, hangs in Philadelphia. Because of a crack, it is no longer rung.

MOUNTAIN LAUREL
RUFFED GROUSE

MAKING COINS

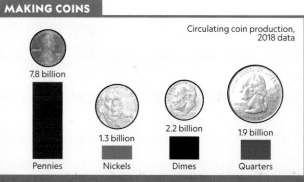

Circulating coin production, 2018 data

7.8 billion	1.3 billion	2.2 billion	1.9 billion
Pennies	Nickels	Dimes	Quarters

The 1792 Coinage Act established the first U.S. mint in Philadelphia. It is still one of the country's main coin-producing facilities.

◗ **RIVER TOWN.** Pittsburgh, one of the largest inland ports in the United States, was established in 1758 where the Monongahela and Allegheny Rivers meet to form the Ohio River. Once a booming steel town, Pittsburgh is now a center of finance, medicine, and education.

Map labels:

LAKE ERIE

OHIO

WEST VIRGINIA

Millcreek • Erie • Corry • Meadville • Titusville • Greenville • Oil City • Sharon • Grove City • New Castle • Butler • Beaver Falls • McCandless • Plum • Pittsburgh • Penn Hills • Aliquippa • McKeesport • Jeannette • Washington • Monessen • Connellsville • Waynesburg • Uniontown

Pymatuning Reservoir
ERIE NATIONAL WILDLIFE REFUGE
OHIO RIVER N.W.R.
FRIENDSHIP HILL N.H.S.
FT. NECESSITY NATIONAL BATTLEFIELD

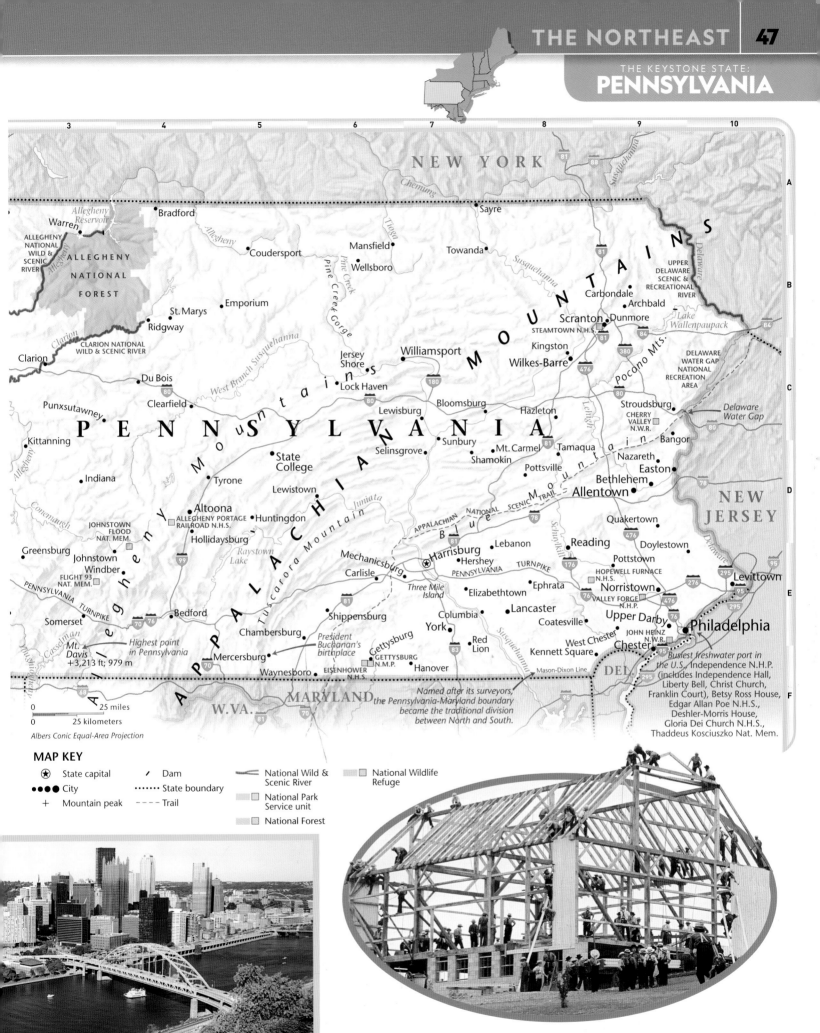

NEW YORK

Warren
Allegheny Reservoir
Bradford
ALLEGHENY NATIONAL WILD & SCENIC RIVER
ALLEGHENY NATIONAL FOREST
Coudersport
Mansfield
Wellsboro
Towanda
Sayre
Chemung
Tioga
Pine Creek
Susquehanna
MOUNTAINS
UPPER DELAWARE SCENIC & RECREATIONAL RIVER
Carbondale
Archbald
Delaware
St. Marys
Emporium
Ridgway
Clarion
CLARION NATIONAL WILD & SCENIC RIVER
Clarion
Du Bois
West Branch Susquehanna
Jersey Shore
Williamsport
Scranton Dunmore
STEAMTOWN N.H.S.
Kingston
Wilkes-Barre
Lake Wallenpaupack
DELAWARE WATER GAP NATIONAL RECREATION AREA
Punxsutawney
Clearfield
Lock Haven
Lewisburg
Bloomsburg
Hazleton
Stroudsburg
CHERRY VALLEY N.W.R.
Delaware Water Gap
Kittanning
PENNSYLVANIA
Sunbury
Mt. Carmel
Tamaqua
Bangor
State College
Selinsgrove
Shamokin
Nazareth
Allegheny
Indiana
Tyrone
Lewistown
Pottsville
Easton
Bethlehem
Allentown
NEW JERSEY
Conemaugh
JOHNSTOWN FLOOD NAT. MEM.
Altoona
ALLEGHENY PORTAGE RAILROAD N.H.S.
Huntingdon
Hollidaysburg
Juniata
APPALACHIAN
NATIONAL
SCENIC TRAIL
Blue
Mountain
Quakertown
Reading
Doylestown
Greensburg
Johnstown
Windber
FLIGHT 93 NAT. MEM.
Raystown Lake
Mechanicsburg
Harrisburg
Hershey
Lebanon
PENNSYLVANIA TURNPIKE
Pottstown
HOPEWELL FURNACE N.H.S.
Levittown
PENNSYLVANIA TURNPIKE
Somerset
Bedford
Carlisle
Three Mile Island
Elizabethtown
Ephrata
Norristown
VALLEY FORGE N.H.P.
Casselman
Mt. Davis +3,213 ft; 979 m
Highest point in Pennsylvania
Shippensburg
Columbia
Lancaster
Coatesville
Upper Darby
Philadelphia
Youghiogheny
Chambersburg
President Buchanan's birthplace
York
Red Lion
West Chester
Kennett Square
Chester
JOHN HEINZ N.W.R.
Mercersburg
Gettysburg
GETTYSBURG N.M.P.
Hanover
Susquehanna
Mason-Dixon Line
Waynesboro
EISENHOWER N.H.S.
DEL.
W.VA.
MARYLAND
Named after its surveyors, the Pennsylvania-Maryland boundary became the traditional division between North and South.

Busiest freshwater port in the U.S. Independence N.H.P. (includes Independence Hall, Liberty Bell, Christ Church, Franklin Court), Betsy Ross House, Edgar Allan Poe N.H.S., Deshler-Morris House, Gloria Dei Church N.H.S., Thaddeus Kosciuszko Nat. Mem.

0   25 miles
0   25 kilometers
Albers Conic Equal-Area Projection

MAP KEY

⊛ State capital
●●●● City
+ Mountain peak
⟋ Dam
⋯⋯ State boundary
---- Trail
⌇ National Wild & Scenic River
▢ National Park Service unit
▢ National Forest
▢ National Wildlife Refuge

🔘 **TEAMWORK.** Amish people in Lancaster County work together to erect a barn. The Amish, who came to Pennsylvania in the early 1700s from Switzerland and Germany, live in traditional farming communities and shun modern technology.

THE BASICS

Statehood
May 29, 1790; 13th state

**Total area
(land and water)**
1,545 sq mi
(4,001 sq km)

Land area
1,034 sq mi
(2,678 sq km)

Population
1,057,315

Capital
Providence
Population 179,335

Largest city
Providence
Population 179,335

Racial/ethnic groups
84.1% white; 8.2% African
American; 3.7% Asian; 1.0%
Native American; 15.5%
Hispanic origin (any race)

Foreign born
13.7%

Urban population
90.7%

Population density
1,022.5 per sq mi
(394.8 per sq km)

GEO WHIZ

Providence is home to the
world's largest artificial
bug—a 58-foot (17.6-m)-long
termite, weighing almost two
tons (1.8 t), that is the mascot
of a local pest control company.

Wild coyotes are living
and thriving on islands in
Narragansett Bay.
Researchers have outfit-
ted some of the animals
with GPS tracking collars
so that their numbers
and whereabouts can
be studied online—even
by schoolkids.

VIOLET

RHODE ISLAND RED

Rhode Island

In 1524 Italian navigator Giovanni da Verrazzano was the first European explorer to visit Rhode Island, but place-names such as Quonochontaug and Narragansett tell of an earlier Native American population. In 1636 Roger Williams, seeking greater religious freedom, left Massachusetts and established the first European settlement in what was to become the colony of Rhode Island. In the years following the Revolutionary War, Rhode Island pressed for fairness in trade, taxes, and representation in Congress as well as greater freedom of worship before becoming the 13th state. By the 19th century Rhode Island had become an important center of trade and textile factories, attracting many immigrants from Europe. In addition to its commercial activities, Rhode Island's coastline became a popular vacation retreat for the wealthy. Today, Rhode Island, like many other states, has seen its economy shift toward high-tech jobs and service industries. It is also promoting its scenic coastline and bays as well as its rich history to attract tourists.

⬤ **CLUES TO THE PAST.**
Fossils embedded in
rocks left behind 10,000
years ago by retreating
glaciers tell of Block
Island's past.

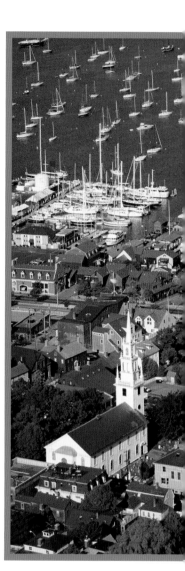

◗ **SETTING SAIL.** Newport Harbor invites sailors of all ages. From 1930 to 1983 the prestigious America's Cup yacht race took place in the waters off Newport. Today, the town provides moorings for boats of all types.

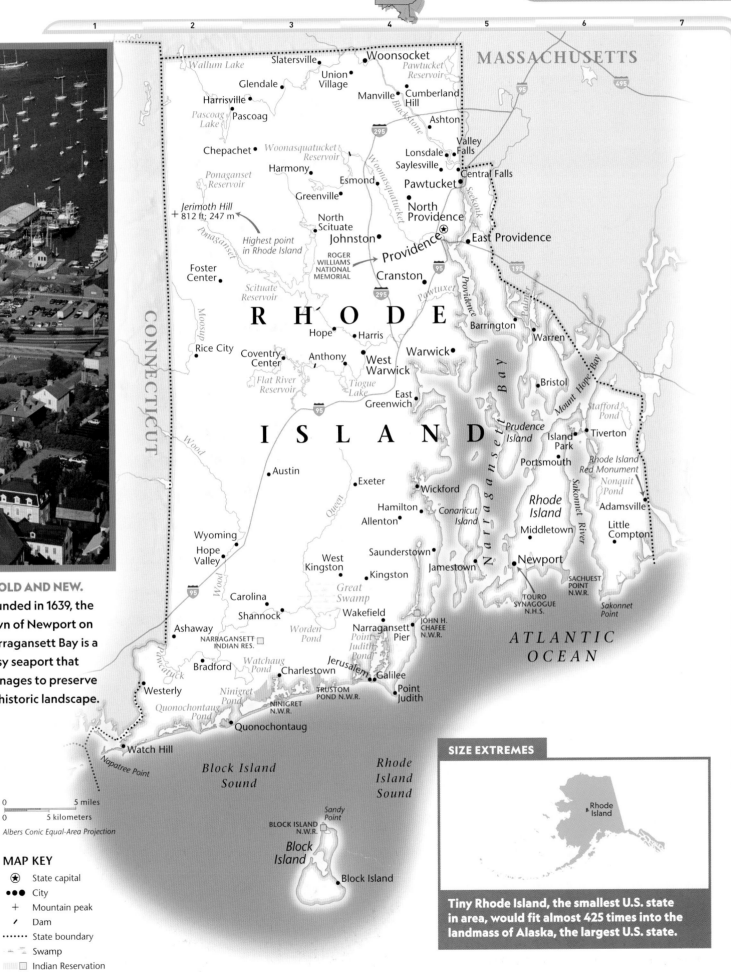

MASSACHUSETTS

Wallum Lake • Slatersville • Woonsocket
Pawtucket Reservoir

Glendale • Union Village
Harrisville • Manville • Cumberland Hill
Pascoag Lake • Pascoag • Ashton
Chepachet • Woonasquatucket Reservoir • Valley Falls
Lonsdale • Saylesville
Harmony • Esmond • Central Falls
Ponaganset Reservoir • Greenville • Pawtucket
Jerimoth Hill • North • North Providence
+ 812 ft; 247 m • Scituate • East Providence
Highest point in Rhode Island • Johnston • Providence ★
ROGER WILLIAMS NATIONAL MEMORIAL • Cranston
Foster Center • Scituate Reservoir
Hope • Harris • Barrington
Rice City • Warwick • Warren
Coventry Center • Anthony • West Warwick
Flat River Reservoir • Bristol
Tiogue Lake • East Greenwich
Prudence Island • Stafford Pond
Austin • Island Park • Tiverton
Exeter • Portsmouth • Rhode Island Red Monument
Wickford • Conanicut Island • Nonquit Pond
Hamilton • Rhode Island • Adamsville
Allenton • Middletown • Little Compton
Wyoming • Saunderstown • Newport
Hope Valley • West Kingston • Jamestown
Kingston • SACHUEST POINT N.W.R.
Carolina • Great Swamp • TOURO SYNAGOGUE N.H.S. • Sakonnet Point
Shannock • Wakefield
Ashaway • Narragansett Pier • JOHN H. CHAFEE N.W.R.
NARRAGANSETT INDIAN RES. • Worden Pond
Bradford • Watchaug Pond • Jerusalem • Galilee
Westerly • Charlestown • Point Judith
Ninigret Pond • TRUSTOM POND N.W.R.
Quonochontaug Pond • NINIGRET N.W.R.
Watch Hill • Quonochontaug
Napatree Point

CONNECTICUT

Moosup • Wood • Ponaganset • Pawcatuck • Queen • Wood

Narragansett Bay • *Mount Hope Bay* • *Sakonnet River* • Providence • Pawtuxet • Palmer • Seekonk • Blackstone • Woonasquatucket

ATLANTIC OCEAN

Block Island Sound • *Rhode Island Sound*

Sandy Point
BLOCK ISLAND N.W.R.
Block Island
Block Island

🜚 **OLD AND NEW.**
Founded in 1639, the town of Newport on Narragansett Bay is a busy seaport that manages to preserve its historic landscape.

0 ———— 5 miles
0 ———— 5 kilometers
Albers Conic Equal-Area Projection

MAP KEY

★ State capital
●●● City
+ Mountain peak
↗ Dam
••••• State boundary
〰 Swamp
▦ Indian Reservation
▦ National Wildlife Refuge

SIZE EXTREMES

Rhode Island

Tiny Rhode Island, the smallest U.S. state in area, would fit almost 425 times into the landmass of Alaska, the largest U.S. state.

Vermont

When French explorer Jacques Cartier arrived in Vermont in 1535, Native Americans living in woodland villages had been there for hundreds of years. Settled first by the French in 1666 and then by the English in 1724, the territory of Vermont became an area of tensions between these colonial powers. The French finally withdrew, but conflict continued between New York and New Hampshire, both of which wanted to take over Vermont. The people of Vermont declared their independence in 1777, and Vermont became the 14th U.S. state in 1791. Vermont's name, which means "green mountain," comes from the extensive forests that cover much of the state and provide the basis for furniture and pulp industries. Vermont also boasts the largest deep-hole granite quarry in the world and the largest underground marble quarry. Both produce valuable building materials. Tourism and recreation are also important. Lakes, rivers, and mountain trails are popular summer attractions, and snow-covered mountains lure skiers throughout the winter.

THE BASICS

Statehood
March 4, 1791; 14th state

Total area (land and water)
9,616 sq mi (24,906 sq km)

Land area
9,217 sq mi (23,871 sq km)

Population
626,299

Capital
Montpelier
Population 7,436

Largest city
Burlington
Population 42,417

Racial/ethnic groups
94.5% white; 1.4% African American; 1.8% Asian; 0.4% Native American; 1.9% Hispanic origin (any race)

Foreign born
4.5%

Urban population
38.9%

Population density
68.0 per sq mi
(26.2 per sq km)

GEO WHIZ

Burlington is the home of Ben & Jerry's ice cream. The company gives its leftovers to local farmers, who feed it to their hogs.

From 1777 until it became a state in 1791, Vermont was an independent country.

Vermont is the only state in New England that does not border the Atlantic Ocean.

◯ **LIQUID GOLD. In spring, sap from maple trees is collected in buckets by drilling a hole in the tree trunk—called "tapping." The sap is boiled to remove water, then filtered, and finally bottled.**

RED CLOVER
HERMIT THRUSH

◑ **WINTER FUN. One of the snowiest places in the Northeast, Jay Peak averages 355 inches (900 cm) of snow each year. With 76 trails, the mountain, near Vermont's border with Canada, attracts beginner and expert skiers from near and far.**

SWEET DELIGHT

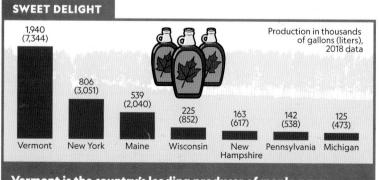

Production in thousands of gallons (liters), 2018 data

State	Production
Vermont	1,940 (7,344)
New York	806 (3,051)
Maine	539 (2,040)
Wisconsin	225 (852)
New Hampshire	163 (617)
Pennsylvania	142 (538)
Michigan	125 (473)

Vermont is the country's leading producer of maple syrup. The syrup is all natural. There are no added ingredients or preservatives, just boiled sap collected from maple trees.

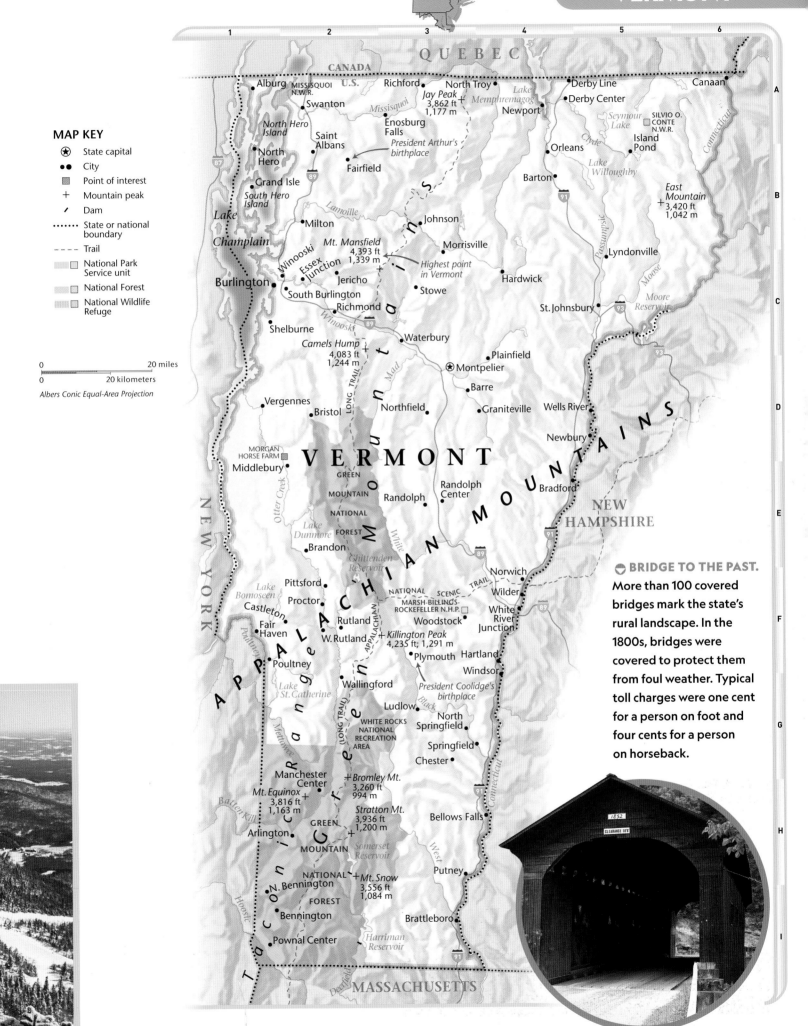

MAP KEY

- ⍟ State capital
- •• City
- ▢ Point of interest
- + Mountain peak
- ⟋ Dam
- ⋯⋯ State or national boundary
- --- Trail
- ▨ National Park Service unit
- ▨ National Forest
- ▨ National Wildlife Refuge

0   20 miles
0   20 kilometers

Albers Conic Equal-Area Projection

QUEBEC

CANADA
U.S.

Alburg
MISSISQUOI N.W.R.
Swanton
Richford
North Troy
Jay Peak
3,862 ft
1,177 m
Lake Memphremagog
Derby Line
Derby Center
Canaan

Missisquoi
Enosburg Falls
Newport
Seymour Lake
SILVIO O. CONTE N.W.R.
Island Pond

North Hero Island
Saint Albans
President Arthur's birthplace
Fairfield
Orleans
Clyde
Lake Willoughby

North Hero
Barton
East Mountain
+ 3,420 ft
1,042 m

Grand Isle
South Hero Island
Lamoille
Johnson
91

Lake Champlain
Milton
Morrisville
Lyndonville

Mt. Mansfield
4,393 ft
1,339 m
Highest point in Vermont
Hardwick
Moose

Winooski
Essex Junction
Jericho
Stowe
St. Johnsbury
93
Moore Reservoir

Burlington
South Burlington
Richmond
Winooski
Waterbury
89
93

Shelburne
Camels Hump
4,083 ft
1,244 m
Plainfield
⍟ Montpelier
Barre

Vergennes
Bristol
Northfield
Graniteville
Wells River
Newbury

MORGAN HORSE FARM
Middleburg

VERMONT

Otter Creek
GREEN
MOUNTAIN
NATIONAL
Randolph
Randolph Center
Bradford

Lake Dunmore
FOREST
White
APPALACHIAN MOUNTAINS
NEW HAMPSHIRE

Brandon
Chittenden Reservoir
91

Pittsford
TRAIL
Norwich
Wilder

Lake Bomoseen
Proctor
NATIONAL MARSH-BILLINGS-ROCKEFELLER N.H.P.
SCENIC
White River Junction
89

Castleton
Rutland
APPALACHIAN
Woodstock

Fair Haven
W. Rutland
Killington Peak
4,235 ft; 1,291 m
Plymouth
Hartland

Poultney
APPALACHIAN
President Coolidge's birthplace
Windsor

Lake St. Catherine
Wallingford
Black

MORE than 100 covered

NEW YORK

Poultney

(LONG TRAIL)
Ludlow
North Springfield

Mettawee
WHITE ROCKS NATIONAL RECREATION AREA
Springfield
Chester

Manchester Center
+ Bromley Mt.
3,260 ft
994 m

Mt. Equinox +
3,816 ft
1,163 m
Batten Kill
Stratton Mt.
3,936 ft
1,200 m
Bellows Falls

Arlington
GREEN
MOUNTAIN
Somerset Reservoir
West

NATIONAL
+ Mt. Snow
3,556 ft
1,084 m
Putney

N. Bennington
FOREST
Brattleboro

Bennington
Hoosic
Harriman Reservoir

Pownal Center

Deerfield
MASSACHUSETTS

Connecticut

◉ BRIDGE TO THE PAST.

More than 100 covered bridges mark the state's rural landscape. In the 1800s, bridges were covered to protect them from foul weather. Typical toll charges were one cent for a person on foot and four cents for a person on horseback.

PHYSICAL

Land area
566,988 sq mi
(1,468,492 sq km)

Highest point
Mount Mitchell, NC
6,684 ft (2,037 m)

Lowest point
New Orleans, LA
8 ft (2.4 m) below sea level

Longest rivers
Mississippi, Arkansas, Red, Ohio

Largest lakes
Okeechobee, Pontchartrain,
Kentucky (reservoir)

Vegetation
Needleleaf, broadleaf, and
mixed forest

Climate
Continental to mild, ranging from cool summers
in the north to humid,
subtropical conditions in
the south

POLITICAL

Total population
84,396,680

States (12):
Alabama, Arkansas, Florida, Georgia,
Kentucky, Louisiana, Mississippi, North
Carolina, South Carolina, Tennessee,
Virginia, West Virginia

Largest state
Florida: 65,758 sq mi (170,312 sq km)

Smallest state
West Virginia: 24,230 sq mi
(62,756 sq km)

Most populous state
Florida: 21,299,325

Least populous state
West Virginia: 1,805,832

Largest city proper
Jacksonville, FL: 903,889

THE SOUTHEAST

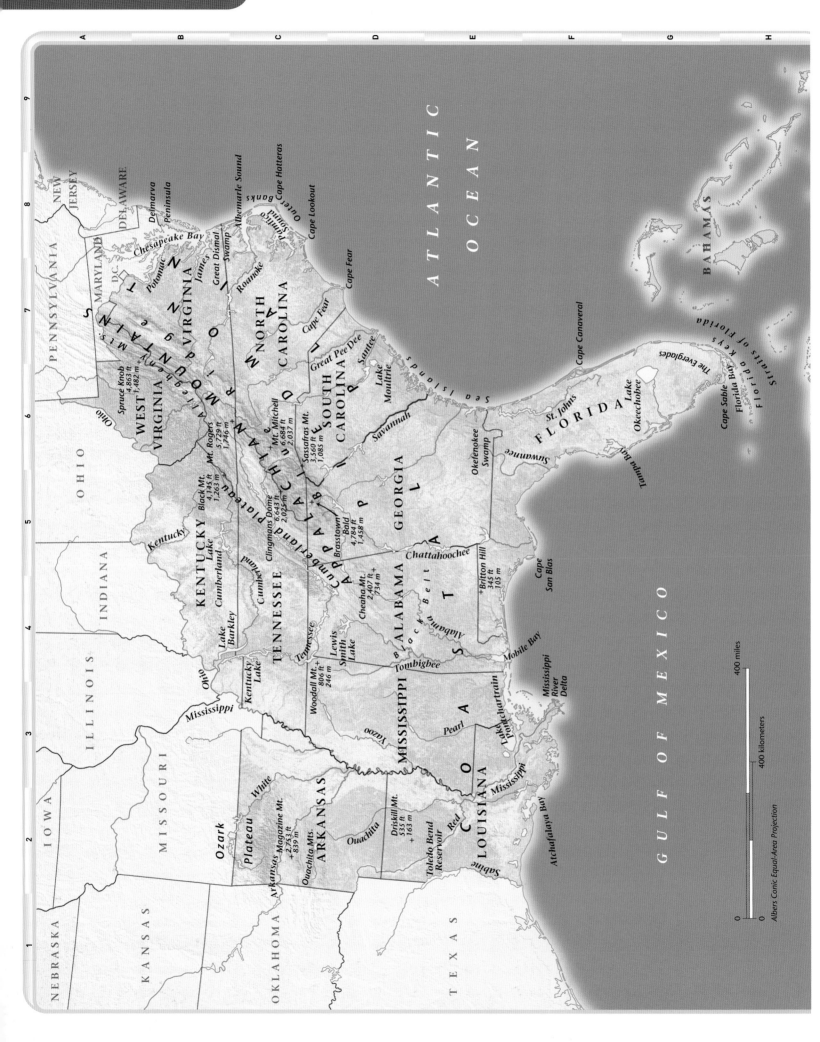

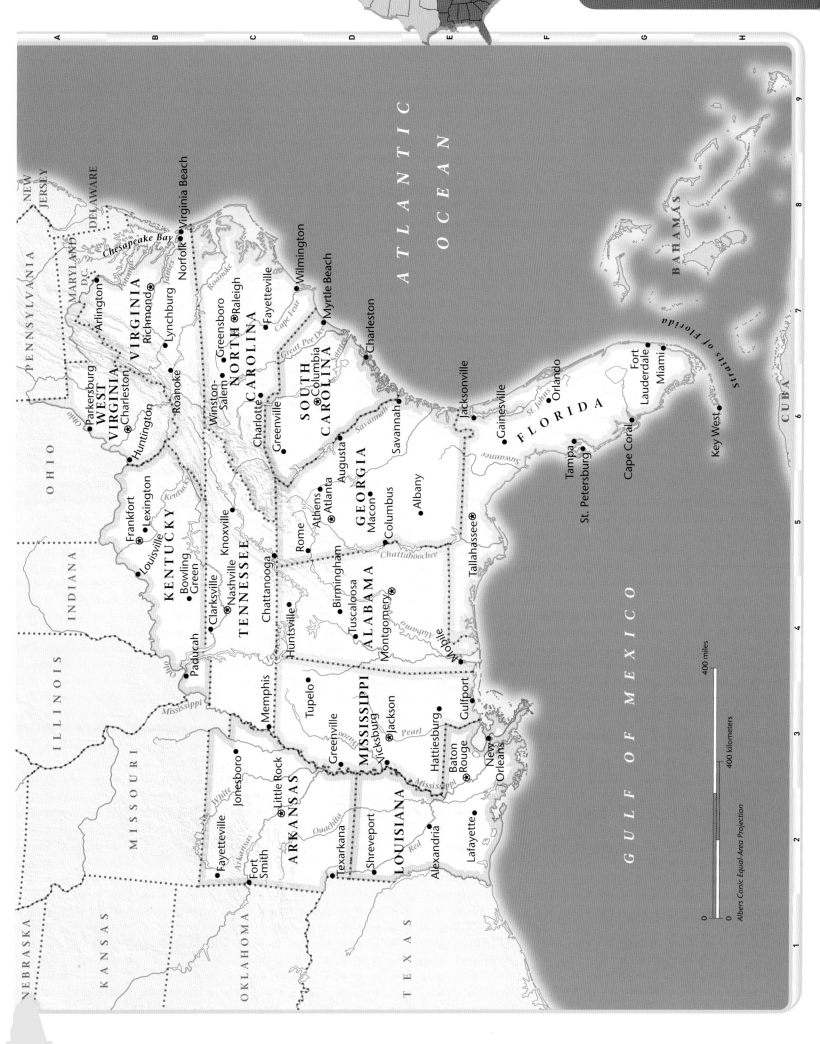

The Southeast

TRADITION MEETS TECHNOLOGY

◐ **OPEN WIDE.** An American alligator in Florida's Big Cypress Swamp shows off its sharp teeth.

From deeply weathered mountains in West Virginia to warm, humid wetlands in south Florida and the Mississippi River's sprawling delta in southern Louisiana, the Southeast is marked by great physical diversity. The region's historical roots are in agriculture—especially cotton and tobacco. The Civil War brought economic and political upheaval in the mid-19th century, but today the Southeast, which is part of the Sunbelt, has three of the country's top 20 metropolitan areas. High-tech industries are redefining the way people in the Southeast earn a living as well as the way the region is connected to the global economy.

◐ **ENCHANTED KINGDOM.** Fireworks light up the night sky above Cinderella Castle at Walt Disney World near Orlando, Florida. The park attracts millions of tourists from around the world each year.

◒ **SOCIAL CONSCIENCE.** Members of the Big Nine Social Aid and Pleasure Club of New Orleans's Lower Ninth Ward march in a parade through a neighborhood devastated by Hurricane Katrina. Such clubs date to the late 19th century and bring support to needy communities.

WHERE THE PICTURES ARE

Banjo playing p. 67
River rafting p. 81
Coal miner p. 80
Horse race p. 66
Cyclists on outcrop pp. 56-57
Black bear family p. 76
Harpers Ferry p. 80
Watts Bar Dam p. 77
Pentagon p. 79
Cherokee woman p. 73
Grand Ole Opry p. 77
Luray Caverns p. 78-79
Rocket display p. 58-59
Dice p. 78
Race car p. 57
Rock climber p. 60
Wright Brothers Memorial p. 72
Bird-watchers p. 60
Blackbeard's cannon p. 57
Diamond hunter p. 61
Boys playing basketball p. 72
Paddleboat p. 70
Beach scene p. 74
Blues museum p. 70
Wild turkey p. 75
Catfish p. 71
Historic Charleston pp. 74-75
New Orleans musicians p. 68
Atlanta p. 64
Oil rig p. 58
Peanuts p. 64
Aerial of Sea Islands p. 64
Katrina parade p. 56
Manatee p. 62
Rocket launch p. 63
Cinderella's Castle p. 56,
Shrimp fisherman p. 68
Girl in parade p. 62
Alligator p. 56

◔ **VIEW FROM ABOVE.** Cyclists look out from a rocky ledge across West Virginia's Germany Valley. The area took its name from German immigrants who moved there in the mid-1700s from North Carolina and Pennsylvania and established farming villages.

◑ **CAR STARS.** For more than 50 years, auto racing has been a leading sport in the U.S., especially in the Southeast. The International Motorsports Hall of Fame, located adjacent to the Talladega Superspeedway in Alabama, features racing cars, motorcycles, and vintage cars.

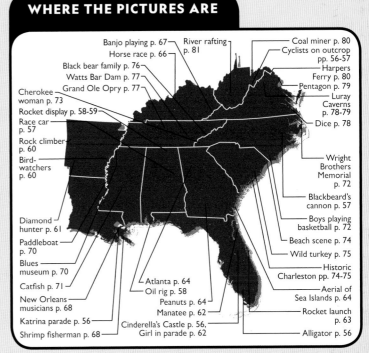

◑ **PIRATE'S DEFENSE.** This cannon was salvaged from the 1718 wreck of the *Queen Anne's Revenge* off North Carolina's coast. The ship probably belonged to the pirate Blackbeard.

THE BASICS

Statehood
December 14, 1819; 22nd state

Total area (land and water)
52,420 sq mi (135,767 sq km)

Land area
50,645 sq mi (131,171 sq km)

Population
4,887,871

Capital
Montgomery
Population 198,218

Largest city
Birmingham
Population 209,880

Racial/ethnic groups
69.2% white; 26.8% African
American; 1.5% Asian; 0.7%
Native American; 4.3%
Hispanic (any race)

Foreign born
3.5%

Urban population
59.0%

Population density
96.5 per sq mi (37.3 per sq km)

GEO WHIZ

Russell Cave, near Bridgeport, was home to prehistoric peoples for more than 10,000 years. Today, visitors can tour the cave and see tools and weapons that were used by these early inhabitants.

In 2004 Hurricane Ivan, one of the worst storms to batter Alabama's Gulf Coast since 1900, struck Orange Beach.

Alabama

In 1702 the French established the first permanent European settlement at Mobile Bay in what is now Alabama, but different groups—British, Native Americans, and U.S. settlers—struggled over control of the land for more than 100 years. In 1819 Alabama became the 22nd state, but in 1861 it joined the Confederacy. During the Civil War, Montgomery was the capital of the secessionist South for a time. After the war Alabama struggled to rebuild its agriculture-based economy. By 1900 the state was producing more than one million bales of cotton annually. In the mid-20th century Alabama was at the center of the civil rights movement, which pressed for equal rights for all people regardless of race or social status. Martin Luther King, Jr., and Rosa Parks were among the key players. Modern industries, including the NASA space program and assembly plants built by automakers from Asia, have given the state's economy a big boost.

⬭ **UNDERWATER RESOURCE.** A massive drill descends from an offshore oil rig to tap petroleum deposits beneath the water of the Gulf of Mexico off Alabama's shore.

**NORTHERN
FLICKER**

CAMELLIA

⬭ **ROCKET POWER.** A giant Saturn V moon rocket dominates a display of rockets in front of the U.S. Space and Rocket Center at NASA's Marshall Space Flight Center in Huntsville. Since it opened in 1970, almost 16 million people have visited the center.

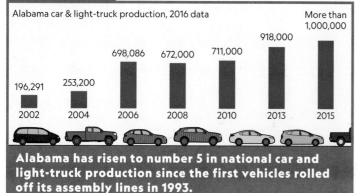

ON THE ROAD

Alabama car & light-truck production, 2016 data

Year	Production
2002	196,291
2004	253,200
2006	698,086
2008	672,000
2010	711,000
2013	918,000
2015	More than 1,000,000

Alabama has risen to number 5 in national car and light-truck production since the first vehicles rolled off its assembly lines in 1993.

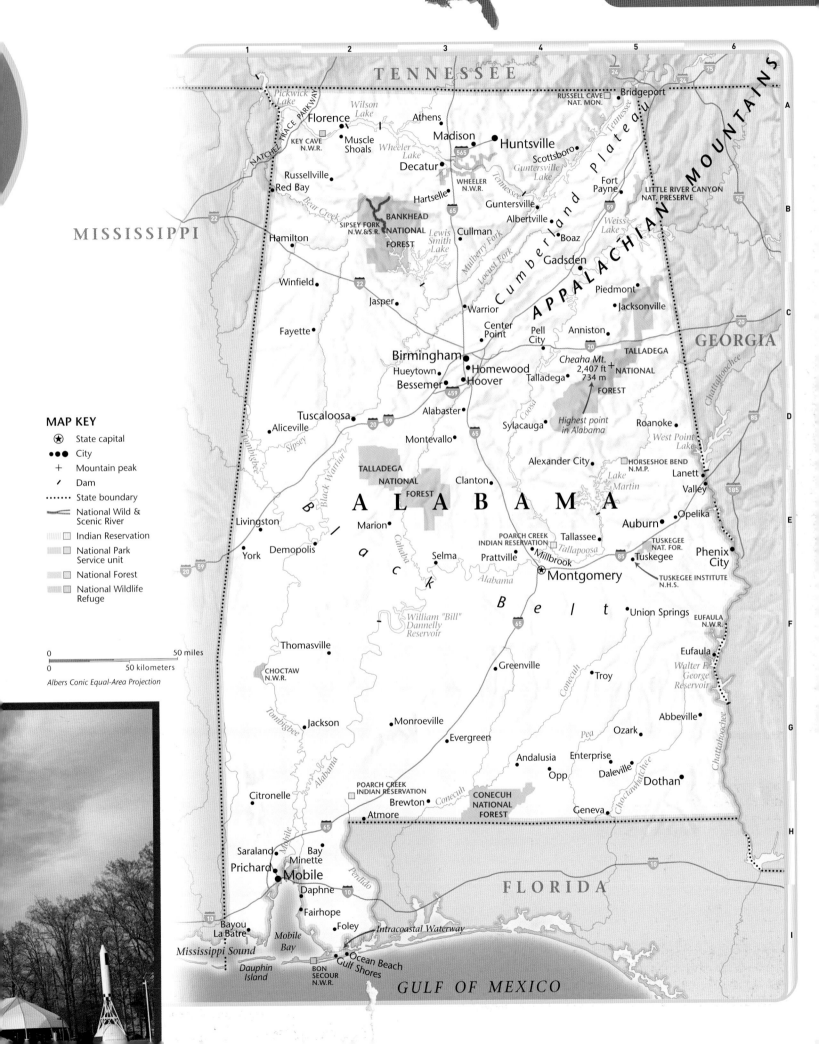

TENNESSEE

MISSISSIPPI

GEORGIA

MAP KEY

⍟ State capital
●●● City
+ Mountain peak
⌐ Dam
••••• State boundary
〜〜 National Wild &
   Scenic River
▦ ▢ Indian Reservation
▨ ▢ National Park
   Service unit
▨ ▢ National Forest
▨ ▢ National Wildlife
   Refuge

0 ———————— 50 miles
0 ———————— 50 kilometers
Albers Conic Equal-Area Projection

A L A B A M A

Pickwick Lake
Wilson Lake
Wheeler Lake
Guntersville Lake
Weiss Lake

Florence
KEY CAVE N.W.R.
Muscle Shoals
Russellville
Red Bay
Hamilton
Winfield
Fayette
Athens
Madison
Huntsville
Decatur
Hartselle
Scottsboro
Fort Payne
Guntersville
Albertville
Boaz
Cullman
Gadsden
Piedmont
Jacksonville
Warrior
Center Point
Pell City
Anniston
Jasper

RUSSELL CAVE NAT. MON.
Bridgeport
LITTLE RIVER CANYON NAT. PRESERVE

BANKHEAD NATIONAL FOREST
SIPSEY FORK N.W.&S.R.

Cumberland Plateau
APPALACHIAN MOUNTAINS

Birmingham
Hueytown
Bessemer
Homewood
Hoover
Talladega
Cheaha Mt. 2,407 ft 734 m
Roanoke
Highest point in Alabama
TALLADEGA NATIONAL FOREST
Tuscaloosa
Aliceville
Alabaster
Montevallo
Sylacauga
TALLADEGA NATIONAL FOREST
Clanton
Alexander City
HORSESHOE BEND N.M.P.
Lanett
Valley
Opelika
Auburn
Livingston
Marion
York
Demopolis
Selma
POARCH CREEK INDIAN RESERVATION
Tallassee
Prattville
Millbrook
Tuskegee
TUSKEGEE NAT. FOR.
Phenix City
Montgomery
TUSKEGEE INSTITUTE N.H.S.

William "Bill" Dannelly Reservoir
Black Belt
Union Springs
EUFAULA N.W.R.
Thomasville
Greenville
Troy
Eufaula
Walter F. George Reservoir
CHOCTAW N.W.R.
Jackson
Monroeville
Evergreen
Andalusia
Opp
Enterprise
Daleville
Ozark
Abbeville
Dothan
Geneva

Citronelle
POARCH CREEK INDIAN RESERVATION
Brewton
Atmore
CONECUH NATIONAL FOREST

Saraland
Bay Minette
Prichard
Mobile
Daphne
Fairhope
Foley
Bayou La Batre
Intracoastal Waterway
Mobile Bay
Ocean Beach
Gulf Shores
BON SECOUR N.W.R.
Dauphin Island
Mississippi Sound

FLORIDA

GULF OF MEXICO

ARKANSAS

THE BASICS

Statehood
June 15, 1836; 25th state

Total area (land and water)
53,179 sq mi (137,732 sq km)

Land area
52,035 sq mi (134,771 sq km)

Population
3,013,825

Capital
Little Rock
Population 197,881

Largest city
Little Rock
Population 197,881

Racial/ethnic groups
79.3% white; 15.7% African American; 1.6% Asian; 1.0% Native American; 7.6% Hispanic (any race)

Foreign born
4.7%

Urban population
56.2%

Population density
57.9 per sq mi (22.4 per sq km)

GEO WHIZ

In 1924 Arkansas's Crater of Diamonds State Park yielded the largest natural diamond ever found in the United States—a 40.23-carat whopper named "Uncle Sam."

Stuttgart has been the site of the annual World's Championship Duck Calling Contest since 1936, when the winner received a hunting coat valued at $6.60. Today, the prize package is worth more than $15,000.

Texarkana is divided by the Arkansas-Texas border. It has two governments, one for each state.

Arkansas

The land that is Arkansas was explored by the Spanish in 1541 and later by the French, but it came under U.S. control with the Louisiana Purchase in 1803. Native Americans were pushed out as settlers arrived, and cotton fields spread across the fertile valleys of the Arkansas and Mississippi Rivers. Arkansas became the 25th state in 1836, but joined the Confederacy in 1861. Following the war Arkansas faced hard times, and many people moved away in search of jobs. Today, agriculture is still an important part of the economy. Rice has replaced cotton as the state's main crop, and poultry and grain production are also important. Natural gas, in the northwestern part of the state, and petroleum, along the southern border with Louisiana, are key mining products in Arkansas. The state is headquarters for Walmart, the world's largest retail chain, and tourism is growing as visitors are attracted to the natural beauty of the Ozark and Ouachita Mountains.

◑ **HOLD ON!** A climber scales the face of Mount Magazine, the highest point in Arkansas, where the Ozark and Ouachita Mountains make up the country's Interior Highlands. Ouachita means "good hunting land" in the language of the Caddo people.

APPLE BLOSSOM MOCKINGBIRD

◑ **BIRD-WATCHERS.** Biologists and volunteers scan the treetops for a rare ivory-billed woodpecker in the White River National Wildlife Refuge. Established in 1935 along the White River near where it joins the Mississippi, the refuge provides a protected habitat for migratory birds.

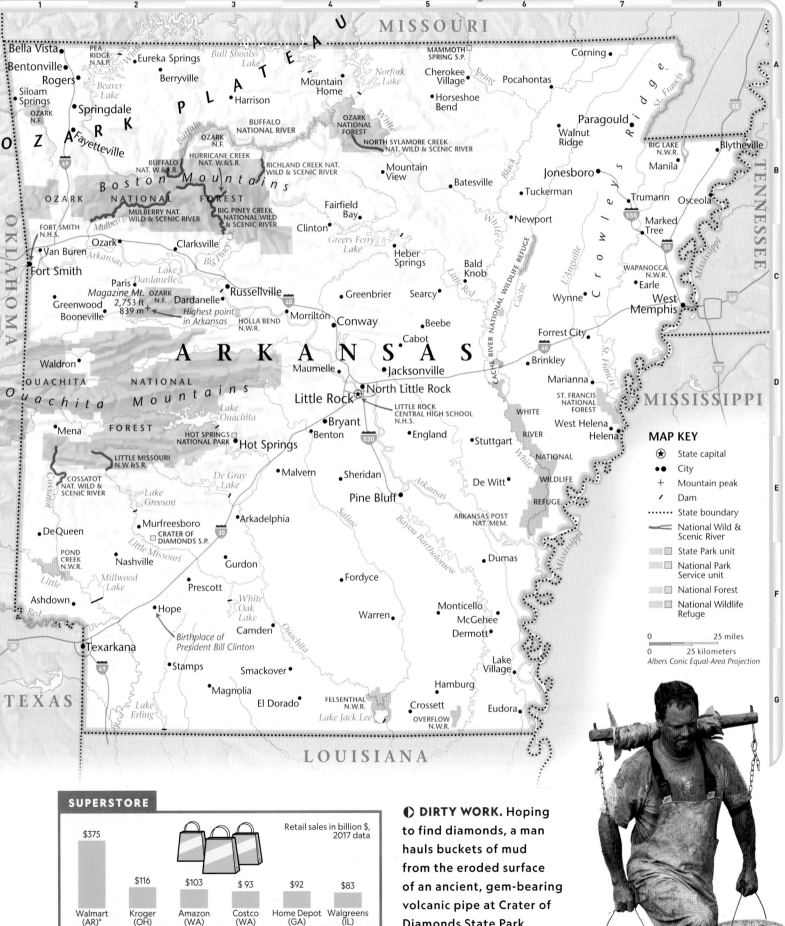

Map labels:

Grid numbers (top): 1 2 3 4 5 6 7 8

Grid letters (right): A B C D E F G

MISSOURI

OZARK PLATEAU

Bella Vista
PEA RIDGE N.M.P.
Bentonville
Rogers
Eureka Springs
Berryville
Bull Shoals Lake
Norfork Lake
MAMMOTH SPRING S.P.
Corning
Siloam Springs
Beaver Lake
Mountain Home
Cherokee Village
Horseshoe Bend
Pocahontas
Spring
Paragould
Springdale
OZARK N.F.
Harrison
BUFFALO NATIONAL RIVER
OZARK NATIONAL FOREST
NORTH SYLAMORE CREEK NAT. WILD & SCENIC RIVER
Walnut Ridge
Crowleys Ridge
St. Francis
BIG LAKE N.W.R.
Blytheville
Fayetteville
Buffalo
OZARK N.F.
HURRICANE CREEK NAT. W.&S.R.
RICHLAND CREEK NAT. WILD & SCENIC RIVER
Mountain View
White
Batesville
Black
Jonesboro
Manila
OZARK
BUFFALO NAT. W.&S.R.
Boston Mountains
Tuckerman
Trumann
Osceola
NATIONAL FOREST
MULBERRY NAT. WILD & SCENIC RIVER
BIG PINEY CREEK NATIONAL WILD & SCENIC RIVER
Fairfield Bay
Newport
Marked Tree
Fort Smith N.H.S.
Mulberry
Ozark
Clarksville
Clinton
Greers Ferry Lake
White
L'Anguille
WAPANOCCA N.W.R.
Earle
Van Buren
Arkansas
Big Piney
Heber Springs
Bald Knob
Cache
Wynne
West Memphis
Fort Smith
Lake Dardanelle
Russellville
Little Red
Paris
Magazine Mt. 2,753 ft 839 m
OZARK N.F.
Dardanelle
Greenbrier
Searcy
Forrest City
Mississippi
Greenwood
Booneville
Highest point in Arkansas
HOLLA BEND N.W.R.
Morrilton
Conway
Beebe
St. Francis
Cabot
Brinkley
ARKANSAS
Maumelle
Jacksonville
Marianna
ST. FRANCIS NATIONAL FOREST
MISSISSIPPI
Waldron
OUACHITA
NATIONAL
Little Rock
North Little Rock
LITTLE ROCK CENTRAL HIGH SCHOOL N.H.S.
WHITE
Mena
Ouachita Mountains
Lake Ouachita
Bryant
Benton
England
West Helena
Helena
FOREST
HOT SPRINGS NATIONAL PARK
Hot Springs
Stuttgart
RIVER
LITTLE MISSOURI N.W.&S.R.
De Gray Lake
Malvern
Sheridan
De Witt
NATIONAL
COSSATOT NAT. WILD & SCENIC RIVER
Lake Greeson
Arkansas
WILDLIFE
Cossatot
Pine Bluff
Saline
REFUGE
DeQueen
Murfreesboro
CRATER OF DIAMONDS S.P.
Arkadelphia
ARKANSAS POST NAT. MEM.
POND CREEK N.W.R.
Little Missouri
Nashville
Gurdon
Fordyce
Bayou Bartholomew
Dumas
Ashdown
Millwood Lake
Prescott
White Oak Lake
Warren
Monticello
Little
Red
Hope
Camden
McGehee
Dermott
TEXAS
Texarkana
Birthplace of President Bill Clinton
Stamps
Smackover
Ouachita
Lake Village
Magnolia
El Dorado
FELSENTHAL N.W.R.
Hamburg
Lake Erling
Lake Jack Lee
OVERFLOW N.W.R.
Crossett
Eudora

LOUISIANA

OKLAHOMA
OZARK N.F.
TENNESSEE

MAP KEY
★ State capital
●● City
+ Mountain peak
⟍ Dam
• • • State boundary
National Wild & Scenic River
State Park unit
National Park Service unit
National Forest
National Wildlife Refuge

0 ____ 25 miles
0 ____ 25 kilometers
Albers Conic Equal-Area Projection

SUPERSTORE

Retail sales in billion $, 2017 data

$375 — Walmart (AR)*
$116 — Kroger (OH)
$103 — Amazon (WA)
$93 — Costco (WA)
$92 — Home Depot (GA)
$83 — Walgreens (IL)

*( ) state where store headquarters is located

Founded in 1962 in Bentonville, retail giant Walmart, with more than 5,300 stores nationwide, leads the country in annual revenue.

◗ **DIRTY WORK.** Hoping to find diamonds, a man hauls buckets of mud from the eroded surface of an ancient, gem-bearing volcanic pipe at Crater of Diamonds State Park.

BASICS

Statehood
March 3, 1845;
27th state

**Total area
(land and water)**
65,758 sq mi
(170,312 sq km)

Land area
53,625 sq mi
(138,887 sq km)

Population
21,299,325

Capital
Tallahassee
Population 193,551

Largest city
Jacksonville
Population 903,889

Racial/ethnic groups
77.4% white; 16.9% African
American; 2.9% Asian; 0.5%
Native American; 25.6%
Hispanic (any race)

Foreign born
20.2%

Urban population
91.2%

Population density
397.2 per sq mi
(153.4 per sq km)

GEO WHIZ

In 1937 Amelia Earhart and
her navigator took off from
Miami with the goal of making
an around-the-world flight,
but they disappeared over the
Pacific Ocean and were never
seen again.

Everglades National Park,
the largest subtropical
wilderness in the United
States, is home to rare and
endangered species such as the
Florida panther and the West
Indian manatee.

Lightning strikes occur more
often in Florida than in any
other U.S. state.

ORANGE BLOSSOM

MOCKINGBIRD

Florida

Florida is home to St. Augustine, the country's oldest permanent European settlement, established by the Spanish in 1565. But various Native American tribes had called Florida home long before then. Florida became a U.S. territory in 1821 and a state in 1845. The state's turbulent early history included the Civil War and three wars with native tribes over control of the land. Railroads opened Florida to migration from northern states as early as the 1890s. Its mild climate and sandy beaches continue to attract people seeking to escape cold winters. Today, the state draws both tourists and retirees. South Florida has a large Hispanic population that has migrated from all over Latin America—especially from nearby Cuba. Florida is working to solve many challenges: competition between city dwellers and farmers for limited water resources; the risk of annual tropical storms; and the need to preserve its natural environment, including the vast Everglades wetland.

CULTURAL PRIDE. A young girl marches in Orlando's Puerto Rican Parade, a celebration of the music, dance, and culture of this U.S. island territory.

GENTLE GIANT. The manatee, which is closely related to the elephant, is Florida's state marine mammal. Averaging 10 feet (3 m) long and 1,000 pounds (454 kg), these endangered animals live on a diet of sea grasses.

ALABAMA

Highest point
in Florida → Britton
Hill
Crestview• 345 ft
105 m
Niceville
Pensacola•
Fort Walton
Beach
FORT GULF ISLANDS
PICKENS NATIONAL SEASHORE

Intracoastal
Waterway

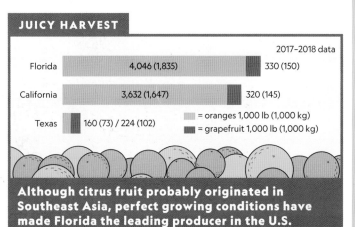

JUICY HARVEST

2017–2018 data

	Oranges	Grapefruit
Florida	4,046 (1,835)	330 (150)
California	3,632 (1,647)	320 (145)
Texas	160 (73)	224 (102)

= oranges 1,000 lb (1,000 kg)
= grapefruit 1,000 lb (1,000 kg)

Although citrus fruit probably originated in
Southeast Asia, perfect growing conditions have
made Florida the leading producer in the U.S.

| 3 | 4 | 5 | 6 | 7 | 8 | 9 | 10 |

G E O R G I A

Marianna

Lake Seminole

OKEFENOKEE
NATIONAL
WILDLIFE
REFUGE

Fernandina Beach

Ochlockonee

Tallahassee ⊛

TIMUCUAN ECOLOGICAL
AND HISTORIC PRESERVE

FORT CAROLINE NAT. MEM.

Apalachicola

OSCEOLA
NAT. FOREST

Jacksonville

Jacksonville Beach

Panama
City

APALACHICOLA
NATIONAL
FOREST

ST. MARKS
N.W.R.

Live
Oak

Lake City

St. Marys

CASTILLO DE SAN
MARCOS NAT. MON.

F L O R I D A

Perry

St. Augustine ← Oldest permanent European
settlement in the U.S.,
established 1565

ST. VINCENT
N.W.R.

FORT MATANZAS
NAT. MON.

Palm Coast

Suwannee

Gainesville

Palatka

St. Johns

Ormond Beach

LOWER
SUWANNEE
NATIONAL
WILDLIFE
REFUGE

Lake George

Ocala

OCALA
NATIONAL
FOREST

LAKE WOODRUFF
N.W.R.

Daytona Beach

New Smyrna Beach

CEDAR KEYS
N.W.R.

The Villages

De Land

CANAVERAL
NATIONAL
SEASHORE

CRYSTAL RIVER N.W.R.

Leesburg

Sanford

Deltona

Titusville

MERRITT ISLAND N.W.R.

Homosassa Springs

Apopka

JOHN F. KENNEDY SPACE CENTER

CHASSAHOWITZKA
N.W.R.

Winter
Garden

Orlando

Cape Canaveral

Spring Hill

WALT DISNEY
WORLD

Merritt Island

Bayonet Point

Kissimmee

Poinciana

Melbourne

Tarpon Springs

TAMPA
I.R.

Lakeland

Haines City

FLORIDA'S TURNPIKE

Palm Bay

Clearwater

Tampa

Winter
Haven

PELICAN ISLAND N.W.R.

St. Petersburg

Tampa Bay

Vero Beach

PINELLAS N.W.R.

Sebring

Kissimmee

Fort Pierce

EGMONT KEY N.W.R.

FORT PIERCE I.R.

DE SOTO NAT. MEM.

Bradenton

Port St. Lucie

Sarasota

Arcadia

Peace

BRIGHTON
SEMINOLE
I.R.

Lake Okeechobee

St. Lucie Canal

HOBE SOUND N.W.R.

Venice

LOXAHATCHEE NAT.
WILD & SCENIC RIVER

Port Charlotte

Punta Gorda

Caloosahatchee

Jupiter

ISLAND BAY N.W.R.

West Palm Beach

Charlotte Harbor

Cape Coral

Fort Myers

Lehigh Acres

Belle
Glade

Delray Beach

J. N. "DING"
DARLING N.W.R.

Immokalee

IMMOKALEE
I.R.

ARTHUR R.
MARSHALL
LOXAHATCHEE
N.W.R.

Boca Raton

Sanibel Island

Bonita
Springs

BIG CYPRESS
SEMINOLE I.R.

Coral Springs

COCONUT CREEK I.R.

Golden Gate

Big Cypress Swamp

BIG
CYPRESS

MICCOSUKEE
INDIAN
RES.

Fort Lauderdale

Naples

NATIONAL
PRESERVE

HOLLYWOOD
I.R.

SEMINOLE I.R.

Hollywood

GULF OF MEXICO

Ten Thousand Islands

Hialeah

Miami

Kendall

Miami Beach

Biscayne Bay

EVERGLADES
NATIONAL

BISCAYNE
N.P.

Largest subtropical wilderness
in the United States

Cape Sable

PARK

Homestead

Key Largo

Florida Bay

ATLANTIC OCEAN

MAP KEY
- ⊛ State capital
- ••• City
- ▪ Point of interest
- + Mountain peak
- ∕ Dam
- ⋯ State boundary
- Swamp
- National Wild & Scenic River
- Indian Reservation
- National Park Service unit
- National Forest
- National Wildlife Refuge
- National Marine Sanctuary

0 ___ 50 miles
0 ___ 50 kilometers
Albers Conic Equal-Area Projection

FLORIDA KEYS NATIONAL MARINE SANCTUARY

FLORIDA KEYS

STRAITS OF FLORIDA

NAT. KEY DEER
REFUGE

Marathon

DRY TORTUGAS
NATIONAL PARK

GREAT WHITE HERON
N.W.R.

KEY WEST
N.W.R.

Key West

Southernmost incorporated place
in the continental United States

⊙ **LIFTOFF!** A NASA rocket rises amid clouds of steam from John F. Kennedy Space Center on Florida's Atlantic coast. The center has been the launch site for many U.S. space exploration projects.

Georgia

When Spanish explorers arrived in the mid-1500s in what would become Georgia, they found the land already occupied by Cherokee, Creek, and other native people. Georgia was the frontier separating Spanish Florida and English South Carolina, but in 1733 James Oglethorpe founded a new colony on the site of present-day Savannah. Georgia became the fourth state in 1788 and built an economy based on agriculture and slave labor. During the Civil War Georgia was part of the Confederacy. The state experienced a long period of poverty following the war. But modern-day Georgia is part of the fast-changing Sunbelt region. Agriculture—especially poultry, cotton, peanuts, and forest products—remains important. Atlanta has emerged as a regional center of banking, telecommunications, and transportation, and Savannah is a major container port near the Atlantic coast, linking the state to the global economy. Historic sites, sports, and beaches draw thousands of tourists to the state every year.

◯ **LIGHT SHOW.** Busy interstate traffic appears as ribbons of light below Atlanta's nighttime skyline. Atlanta is a center of economic growth, with 18 Fortune 500 companies headquartered within its metropolitan area.

◯ **CASH CROP.** Peanuts are a big money-maker in Georgia, where almost half the U.S. crop is grown—about half of which is used to make peanut butter.

BASICS

Statehood
January 2, 1788;
4th state

Total area
(land and water)
59,425 sq mi
(153,910 sq km)

Land area
57,513 sq mi
(148,959 sq km)

Population
10,519,475

Capital
Atlanta
Population 498,044

Largest city
Atlanta
Population 498,044

Racial/ethnic groups
60.8% white; 32.2% African American; 4.2% Asian; 0.5% Native American; 9.6% Hispanic (any race)

Foreign born
10.0%

Urban population
75.1%

Population density
182.9 per sq mi
(70.6 per sq km)

GEO WHIZ

The Okefenokee Swamp, the largest swamp in North America, has meat-eating plants that capture insects and spiders for food.

Founded in 1836 in Macon as the Georgia Female College, Wesleyan College was the first college in the world established to grant degrees to women.

CHEROKEE ROSE
BROWN THRASHER

◯ **PAST MEETS PRESENT.** Georgia's 100-mile (160-km) coastline is laced with barrier islands, wetlands, and winding streams. In the 19th century, plantations grew Sea Island cotton here. Today, tourists are attracted to the area's natural beauty and beaches.

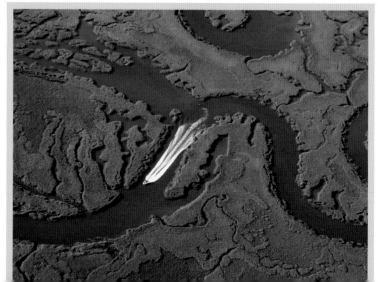

FLYING HIGH

Total passengers in millions, 2017 data

City	Passengers
Atlanta	103.9
Los Angeles	84.6
Chicago O'Hare	79.8
Dallas–Ft. Worth	67.1
Denver	61.4

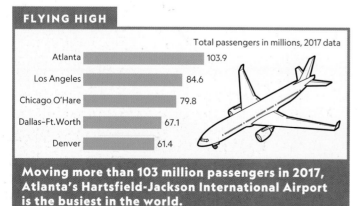

Moving more than 103 million passengers in 2017, Atlanta's Hartsfield-Jackson International Airport is the busiest in the world.

TENNESSEE

NORTH CAROLINA

SOUTH CAROLINA

ALABAMA

G E O R G I A

FLORIDA

ATLANTIC OCEAN

SEA ISLANDS

APPALACHIAN MOUNTAINS

Blue Ridge

MAP KEY

⬢ State capital
●●● City
◾ Point of interest
+ Mountain peak
⌐ Dam
···· State boundary
--- Trail
Swamp
National Wild & Scenic River
State Park unit
National Park Service unit
National Forest
National Wildlife Refuge
National Marine Sanctuary

0   25 miles
0   25 kilometers

Albers Conic Equal-Area Projection

Points of interest and cities

Chickamauga and Chattanooga N.M.P.
LaFayette
Dalton
CHATTAHOOCHEE NATIONAL FOREST
Calhoun
NEW ECHOTA S.H.S.
Rome
Springer Mt. 3,782 ft 1,153 m
Dahlonega
Brasstown Bald + 4,784 ft; 1,458 m
Highest point in Georgia
Rabun Gap
CHATTOOGA NATIONAL WILD & SCENIC RIVER
Toccoa
Hartwell L.
Hartwell
Gainesville
Lake Sidney Lanier
Allatoona Lake
Roswell
KENNESAW MOUNTAIN N.B.P.
CHATTAHOOCHEE RIVER N.R.A.
Marietta
Smyrna
Sandy Springs
Athens
Elberton
Richard B. Russell Lake
MARTIN LUTHER KING, JR. N.H.S.
★ Atlanta
STONE MOUNTAIN
Monroe
Washington
J. Strom Thurmond Reservoir
East Point
OCONEE
Carrollton
Stockbridge
Covington
Lake Oconee
Evans
Martinez
Augusta
Peachtree City
Thomson
NATIONAL
Newnan
Griffin
Eatonton
Lake Sinclair
Waynesboro
FOREST
La Grange
West Point Lake
PIEDMONT N.W.R.
Milledgeville
Sandersville
Thomaston
Macon
OCMULGEE NATIONAL MONUMENT
Millen
Lake Harding
Warner Robins
Perry
Dublin
Swainsboro
Statesboro
Lake Oliver
Columbus
ALABAMA
ANDERSONVILLE N.H.S.
Vidalia
SAVANNAH N.W.R.
JIMMY CARTER N.H.S.
Americus
Eastman
EUFAULA N.W.R.
Plains
President Carter's birthplace
Cordele
Hazlehurst
Savannah
FORT PULASKI NAT. MONUMENT
Tybee Island
WASSAW N.W.R.
Dawson
Fitzgerald
Jesup
Hinesville
Ossabaw Sound
Ossabaw Island
HARRIS NECK N.W.R.
St. Catherines Sound
St. Catherines Island
Walter F. George Reservoir
Albany
Douglas
Sapelo Sound
BLACKBEARD ISLAND N.W.R.
Sapelo Island
Blakely
Tifton
Waycross
WOLF ISLAND N.W.R.
GRAY'S REEF N.M.S.
Camilla
Moultrie
Adel
Satilla
FORT FREDERICA NAT. MONUMENT
Brunswick
St. Simons Island
Jekyll Island
St. Andrew Sound
Bainbridge
Cairo
BANKS LAKE N.W.R.
Valdosta
Kingsland
St. Marys
Cumberland Island
CUMBERLAND ISLAND NATIONAL SEASHORE
Thomasville
Quitman
Okefenokee NATIONAL WILDLIFE REFUGE
Okefenokee Swamp
Lake Seminole

Rivers and waters

Oostanaula
Etowah
Coosa
Coosawattee
Tugaloo
Savannah
Broad
Chattahoochee
Flint
Ocmulgee
Oconee
Ogeechee
Canoochee
Altamaha
Ohoopee
Withlacoochee
Alapaha
Satilla
Ochlockonee
St. Marys
Suwannee

BASICS

Statehood
June 1, 1792; 15th state

Total area (land and water)
40,408 sq mi (104,656 sq km)

Land area
39,486 sq mi (102,269 sq km)

Population
4,468,402

Capital
Frankfort
Population 27,679

Largest city
Louisville/Jefferson County
Population 620,118

Racial/ethnic groups
87.8% white; 8.4% African
American; 1.6% Asian; 0.3%
Native American; 3.7% Hispanic
(any race)

Foreign born
3.6%

Urban population
58.4%

Population density
113.2 per sq mi (43.7 per sq km)

GEO WHIZ

A favorite Kentucky dessert
is Derby Pie, a rich chocolate-
and-walnut pastry that was
first created by George Kern,
manager of the Melrose Inn,
in Prospect, in the 1950s. It
became so popular that the
name was registered with
the U.S. Patent Office and the
Commonwealth of Kentucky.

Pleasant Hill, near Lexington,
was the site of a Shaker
religious community. It is now
a National Historic Site with a
living history museum.

"Happy Birthday to You," one
of the most popular songs in
the English language, was the
creation of two Louisville
sisters in 1893.

GOLDENROD

CARDINAL

Kentucky

The original inhabitants of the area known today as Kentucky were Native Americans, but a treaty with the Cherokee, signed in 1775, opened the territory to settlers—including the legendary Daniel Boone—from the soon-to-be-independent eastern colonies. In 1776 Kentucky became a western county of the state of Virginia. In 1792 it became the 15th state. Eastern Kentucky is a part of Appalachia, a region rich in bituminous (soft) coal but burdened with the environmental problems that often accompany the mining industry. The region is known for crafts and music that can be traced back to Scotch-Irish immigrants who settled there. In central Kentucky, the Bluegrass region produces some of the finest thoroughbred horses in the world, and the Kentucky Derby, held in Louisville, is a part of racing's coveted Triple Crown. In western Kentucky, coal found near the surface is strip-mined, leaving scars on the landscape. Federal laws now require that the land be restored after mining.

⬭ **THEY'RE OFF!** Riders and horses press for the finish line at Churchill Downs, in Louisville. Kentucky is a major breeder of Thoroughbred race horses, and horses are the leading source of farm income in the state.

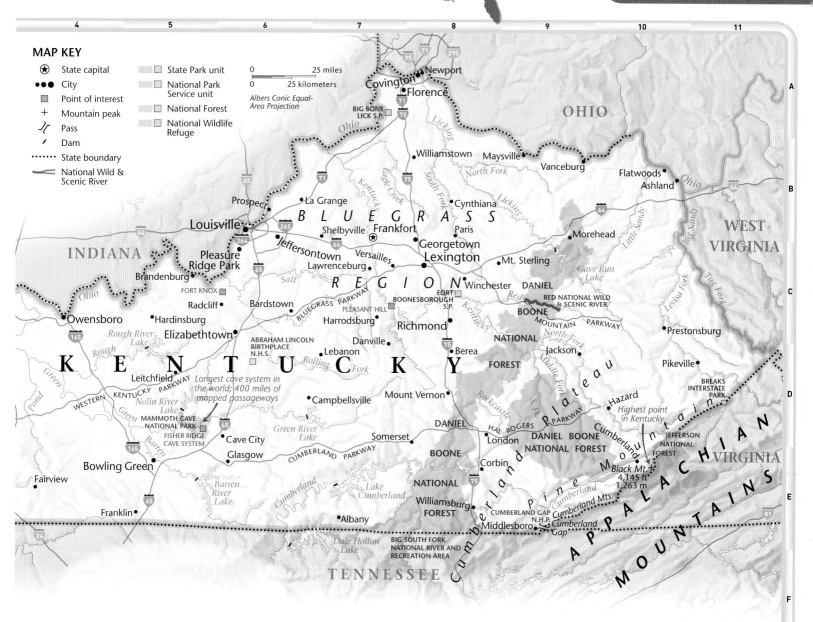

MAP KEY

- ⍟ State capital
- ●●● City
- ▪ Point of interest
- + Mountain peak
-)(Pass
- / Dam
- ······ State boundary
- ⮌ National Wild & Scenic River

- ▨ State Park unit
- ▨ National Park Service unit
- ▨ National Forest
- ▨ National Wildlife Refuge

0 ___ 25 miles
0 ___ 25 kilometers
Albers Conic Equal-Area Projection

4   5   6   7   8   9   10   11

OHIO

Newport
Covington
Florence
BIG BONE LICK S.P.

Williamstown   Maysville
Vanceburg
Flatwoods
Ashland

Ohio
Licking
North Fork
Eagle Creek
South Fork
Kentucky
Licking

WEST VIRGINIA

Prospect
La Grange
Cynthiana
Paris
BLUEGRASS
Morehead

Louisville
Shelbyville   Frankfort
Jeffersontown   Versailles   Georgetown
Lawrenceburg   Lexington
Mt. Sterling
Cave Run Lake

INDIANA
REGION
Winchester
DANIEL

Pleasure Ridge Park
Brandenburg
FORT KNOX
Bardstown
BLUEGRASS PARKWAY
PLEASANT HILL
BOONESBOROUGH S.P.
FORT BOONESBOROUGH S.P.
RED NATIONAL WILD & SCENIC RIVER
BOONE
MOUNTAIN
PARKWAY
Prestonsburg

Radcliff
Harrodsburg
Richmond
NATIONAL
Jackson
Pikeville

Owensboro
Hardinsburg
Elizabethtown
Danville
Berea
FOREST
North Fork
Middle Fork

Rough River Lake
ABRAHAM LINCOLN BIRTHPLACE N.H.S.
Lebanon
Rolling Fork
BREAKS INTERSTATE PARK

KENTUCKY
Leitchfield
Longest cave system in the world; 400 miles of mapped passageways
Campbellsville
Mount Vernon
Rockcastle
Plateau
Hazard
Highest point in Kentucky

Green
Rough
Pond
WESTERN
KENTUCKY PARKWAY
Nolin River Lake
MAMMOTH CAVE NATIONAL PARK
FISHER RIDGE CAVE SYSTEM
Green River Lake
DANIEL
HAL ROGERS PARKWAY
DANIEL BOONE NATIONAL FOREST
Cumberland Mountain
JEFFERSON NATIONAL FOREST
VIRGINIA

Green
Cave City
Glasgow
CUMBERLAND PARKWAY
Somerset
London
BOONE
Corbin
Pine
Black Mt.
4,145 ft
1,263 m
APPALACHIAN

Fairview
Bowling Green
Barren
Barren River Lake
Lake Cumberland
NATIONAL
Williamsburg
FOREST
Cumberland Gap
CUMBERLAND GAP N.H.P.
Cumberland Mts.
MOUNTAINS

Franklin
Cumberland
Dale Hollow Lake
Albany
Middlesboro
Cumberland Gap

TENNESSEE
BIG SOUTH FORK NATIONAL RIVER AND RECREATION AREA

◗ **STRUMMING A TUNE.** Music is an important part of Kentucky's cultural heritage, especially in remote mountain areas, where a banjo can become the focus of a family gathering.

BENEATH THE SURFACE

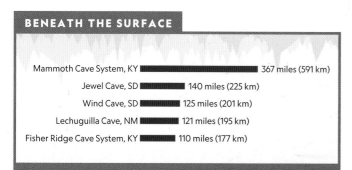

Mammoth Cave System, KY	367 miles (591 km)
Jewel Cave, SD	140 miles (225 km)
Wind Cave, SD	125 miles (201 km)
Lechuguilla Cave, NM	121 miles (195 km)
Fisher Ridge Cave System, KY	110 miles (177 km)

Caves, natural openings in Earth's surface extending beyond the reach of sunlight, are often created by water dissolving limestone.

Louisiana

Louisiana's Native American heritage is evident in place-names such as Natchitoches and Opelousas. Spanish sailors explored the area in 1528, but the French, traveling down the Mississippi River, established permanent settlements in the mid-17th century and named the region for King Louis XIV. The United States gained possession of the territory as part of the Louisiana Purchase in 1803, and Louisiana became the 18th state in 1812. The Port of South Louisiana, located near the delta of the Mississippi River, and New Orleans are Louisiana's main ports. Trade from the interior of the United States moves through these ports and out to world markets. Oil and gas are drilled in the Mississippi Delta area and Gulf of Mexico. The explosion of an offshore oil rig in 2010 brought serious environmental damage to coastal areas still recovering from Hurricane Katrina. This massive storm roared in off the Gulf in 2005, flooding towns, breaking through levees, and changing the lives of everyone in southern Louisiana.

⬭ **TASTY HARVEST.** The Gulf region, led by Louisiana, produces more than 200 million pounds (90 million t) of shrimp—more than three-quarters of the country's annual catch.

BASICS

Statehood
April 30, 1812;
18th state

**Total area
(land and water)**
52,378 sq mi
(135,659 sq km)

Land area
43,204 sq mi
(111,898 sq km)

Population
4,659,978

Capital
Baton Rouge
Population 221,599

Largest city
New Orleans
Population 391,006

Racial/ethnic groups
63.0% white; 32.6% African American; 1.9% Asian; 0.8% Native American; 5.2% Hispanic (any race)

Foreign born
4.2%

Urban population
73.2%

Population density
107.9 per sq mi (41.6 per sq km)

GEO WHIZ

The magnolia, Louisiana's state flower, is the oldest flowering plant in the world. Some species are believed to be 100 million years old.

Cajuns are people whose French-speaking ancestors were exiled by the British from Acadia, in what is now Canada. They live primarily in the bayou region of Louisiana.

MAGNOLIA
BROWN PELICAN

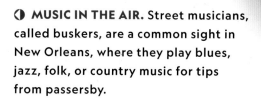

◑ **MUSIC IN THE AIR.** Street musicians, called buskers, are a common sight in New Orleans, where they play blues, jazz, folk, or country music for tips from passersby.

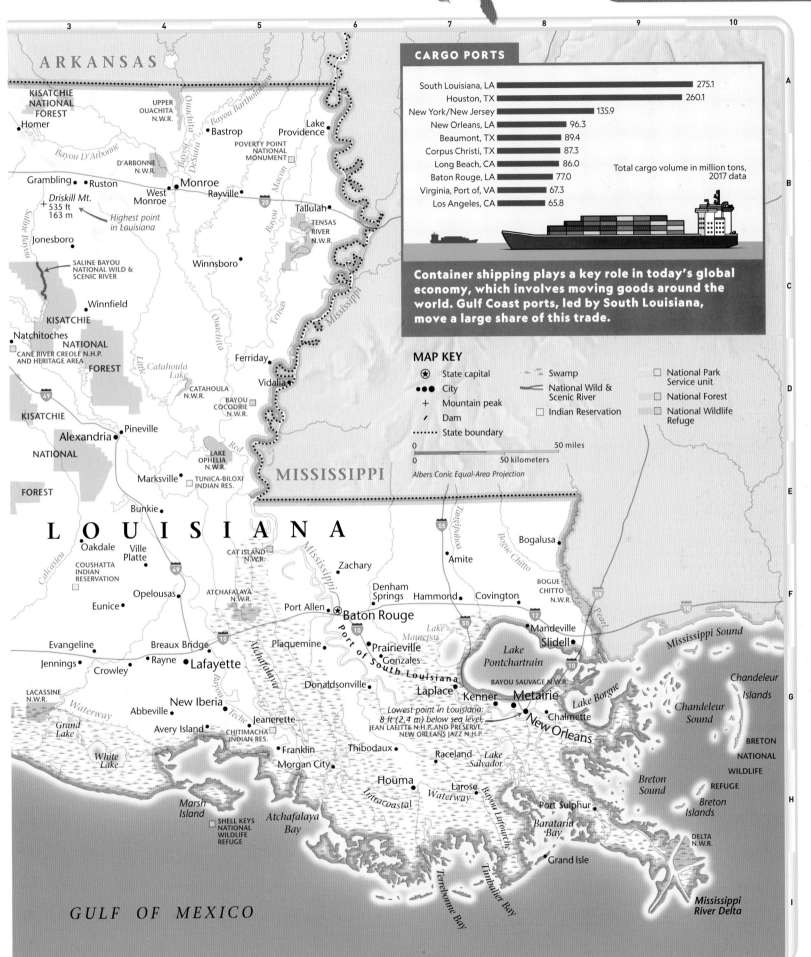

ARKANSAS

KISATCHIE
NATIONAL
FOREST

Homer

UPPER
OUACHITA
N.W.R.

Bastrop

Lake
Providence

POVERTY POINT
NATIONAL
MONUMENT

D'ARBONNE
N.W.R.

Bayou D'Arbonne

Grambling • Ruston

Driskill Mt.
+ 535 ft
163 m
Highest point
in Louisiana

West
Monroe

Monroe

Rayville •

Tallulah

20

TENSAS
RIVER
N.W.R.

Jonesboro

Winnsboro

SALINE BAYOU
NATIONAL WILD &
SCENIC RIVER

Winnfield

Natchitoches

CANE RIVER CREOLE N.H.P.
AND HERITAGE AREA

KISATCHIE
NATIONAL

FOREST

Catahoula
Lake

Ferriday

CATAHOULA
N.W.R.

Vidalia

BAYOU
COCODRIE
N.W.R.

49

KISATCHIE

Alexandria

Pineville

NATIONAL

LAKE
OPHELIA
N.W.R.

Red

MISSISSIPPI

FOREST

Marksville

TUNICA-BILOXI
INDIAN RES.

Bunkie

L O U I S I A N A

Oakdale

Ville
Platte

CAT ISLAND
N.W.R.

Zachary

49

COUSHATTA
INDIAN
RESERVATION

Opelousas

ATCHAFALAYA
N.W.R.

Denham
Springs

Hammond

Covington

BOGUE
CHITTO
N.W.R.

Amite

Bogalusa

55

59

10

Eunice

Port Allen

Baton Rouge

Mandeville

Evangeline

Breaux Bridge

10

Plaquemine

Prairieville

Slidell

Mississippi Sound

Jennings • Crowley

Rayne

Lafayette

Gonzales

Lake
Maurepas

Lake
Pontchartrain

10

LACASSINE
N.W.R.

Donaldsonville

Laplace

Kenner

Metairie

Lake Borgne

Chandeleur
Islands

Abbeville

New Iberia

Jeanerette

Lowest point in Louisiana:
8 ft (2.4 m) below sea level,
JEAN LAFITTE N.H.P. AND PRESERVE,
NEW ORLEANS JAZZ N.H.P.

Laplace

New Orleans

Chalmette

Chandeleur
Sound

Grand
Lake

Avery Island

CHITIMACHA
INDIAN RES.

Franklin

Morgan City

Thibodaux

Raceland

Lake
Salvador

Breton
Sound

BRETON

NATIONAL

White
Lake

Houma

Larose

WILDLIFE

Marsh
Island

SHELL KEYS
NATIONAL
WILDLIFE
REFUGE

Atchafalaya
Bay

Intracoastal

Waterway

Port Sulphur

Barataria
Bay

Breton
Islands

REFUGE

DELTA
N.W.R.

Grand Isle

GULF OF MEXICO

Terrebonne Bay

Timbalier Bay

Mississippi
River Delta

CARGO PORTS

Port	Cargo volume
South Louisiana, LA	275.1
Houston, TX	260.1
New York/New Jersey	135.9
New Orleans, LA	96.3
Beaumont, TX	89.4
Corpus Christi, TX	87.3
Long Beach, CA	86.0
Baton Rouge, LA	77.0
Virginia, Port of, VA	67.3
Los Angeles, CA	65.8

Total cargo volume in million tons,
2017 data

Container shipping plays a key role in today's global
economy, which involves moving goods around the
world. Gulf Coast ports, led by South Louisiana,
move a large share of this trade.

MAP KEY

★ State capital
●●● City
+ Mountain peak
⌐ Dam
•••• State boundary

Swamp
National Wild &
Scenic River
☐ Indian Reservation

☐ National Park
Service unit
☐ National Forest
☐ National Wildlife
Refuge

0   50 miles
0   50 kilometers
Albers Conic Equal-Area Projection

BASICS

Statehood
December 10, 1817; 20th state

Total area (land and water)
48,432 sq mi (125,438 sq km)

Land area
46,923 sq mi (121,531 sq km)

Population
2,986,530

Capital
Jackson
Population 164,422

Largest city
Jackson
Population 164,422

Racial/ethnic groups
59.2% white; 37.8% African American; 1.1% Asian; 0.6% Native American; 3.2% Hispanic (any race)

Foreign born
2.3%

Urban population
49.4%

Population density
63.6 per sq mi (24.6 per sq km)

GEO WHIZ

The Marine Life Oceanarium in Gulfport was almost completely destroyed by Hurricane Katrina in 2005. Eight of its 14 bottlenose dolphins were swept into the Gulf of Mexico by a 40-foot (12-m) wave. These animals and two sea lions named Splash and Elliot were eventually rescued. Others were not so lucky.

Greenville is the birthplace of Jim Henson, creator of Kermit the Frog, Miss Piggy, Big Bird, and other famous *Sesame Street* Muppets.

Mississippi

Mississippi is named for the river that forms its western boundary. The name comes from the Chippewa words *mici zibi,* meaning "great river." Indeed it is a great river, draining much of the interior United States and providing a trade artery to the world. Explored by the Spanish in 1540 and claimed by the French in 1699, the territory of Mississippi passed to the United States in 1783 and became the 20th state in 1817. For more than a hundred years following statehood, Mississippi was the center of U.S. cotton production and trade. The fertile soils and mild climate of the delta region in northwestern Mississippi provided a perfect environment for cotton, a crop that depended on slave labor. When the Civil War broke out, Mississippi joined the Confederacy. The war took a heavy toll on the state's economy. Today, poverty, especially in rural areas, is a major challenge for the state, where agriculture, including poultry, cotton, soybeans, and rice, is still the base of the economy.

⬤ **SINGING THE BLUES.** The Gateway to the Blues Museum in Tunica traces the blues, a uniquely American music form, to Mississippi's cotton fields where West Africans, brought on slave ships, toiled in the 1800s.

MOCKINGBIRD

MAGNOLIA

⬤ **BIG WHEEL TURNING.** Now popular with tourists, paddleboats made the Mississippi River a major artery for trade and travel in the 19th century.

GONE FISHIN'

Total sales, 2017 data

Mississippi	$196,745,000
Alabama	$114,029,000
Arkansas	$18,144,000
Texas	$15,540,000

The Southeast, especially Mississippi, is the leading producer of pond-raised catfish. Mississippi also tops all other states in revenue from catfish sales.

MAP KEY

- ⭐ State capital
- •• City
- + Mountain peak
- ╱ Dam
- ⋯⋯ State boundary
- ⌇⌇ National Wild & Scenic River
- Indian Reservation
- National Park Service unit
- National Forest
- National Wildlife Refuge

0   50 miles
0   50 kilometers

Albers Conic Equal-Area Projection

TENNESSEE

Corinth

Southaven
Horn Lake
Arkabutla Lake
Woodall Mt.
806 ft; 246 m +
Iuka
Pickwick Lake
Highest point in Mississippi

Tunica
Holly Springs
HOLLY SPRINGS NATIONAL FOREST
Ripley
Booneville
Tennessee

Senatobia
Sardis Lake
New Albany
Baldwyn

ARKANSAS

Little Tallahatchie
Oxford
BRICES CROSS ROADS N.B.S.

Batesville
Enid Lake
Yocona
Pontotoc
Tupelo
Fulton
TUPELO N.B.

Clarksdale
COLDWATER RIVER N.W.R.
Water Valley
HOLLY SPRINGS N.F.
TOMBIGBEE NATIONAL FOREST
Okolona
Amory

Shelby
Tallahatchie
TALLAHATCHIE N.W.R.
Grenada Lake
Houston
Aberdeen

Cleveland
DAHOMEY N.W.R.
Ruleville
Grenada
Yalobusha

West Point
Tombigbee

Leland
Indianola
Greenwood
Winona
Starkville
Columbus

Greenville
MATHEWS BRAKE N.W.R.
SAM D. HAMILTON NOXUBEE N.W.R.

Hollandale
Yazoo
MORGAN BRAKE N.W.R.
TOMBIGBEE NATIONAL FOREST
Noxubee

YAZOO N.W.R.
HILLSIDE N.W.R.
Kosciusko
Louisville

PANTHER SWAMP N.W.R.
MISSISSIPPI

DELTA NATIONAL FOREST
Yazoo City
MISSISSIPPI
CHOCTAW
Philadelphia

Vaughan
Carthage
INDIAN
Okatibbee Lake

Canton
Pearl
RESERVATION

VICKSBURG N.M.P.
Ridgeland
Ross Barnett Reservoir
BIENVILLE
Meridian
ALABAMA

Vicksburg
Clinton
Pearl
Forest
NATIONAL
Newton

Jackson
Brandon
FOREST

Port Gibson
Crystal Springs
Strong
Quitman

NATCHEZ TRACE PARKWAY
Hazlehurst
Magee
Leaf
MISSISSIPPI CHOCTAW I.R.

NATCHEZ N.H.P.
Laurel
Waynesboro

Natchez
HOMOCHITTO
Collins
Ellisville

ST. CATHERINE CREEK N.W.R.
NATIONAL
DE SOTO
Chickasawhay

Brookhaven
Pearl
Petal

FOREST
Columbia
Hattiesburg
Tallahala Cr.
Tombigbee

Homochitto
McComb

Centreville
NATIONAL

LOUISIANA
BLACK CREEK NATIONAL WILD & SCENIC RIVER
Lucedale

Mississippi
Poplarville
Wiggins
FOREST
Black Creek
Pascagoula

Bogue Chitto
BOGUE CHITTO N.W.R.
Picayune
Ocean Springs
MISSISSIPPI SANDHILL CRANE N.W.R.

Gulfport
Biloxi
Moss Point

Long Beach
Pascagoula

Bay St. Louis
MISSISSIPPI CHOCTAW I.R.
Mississippi Sound

GULF ISLANDS NATIONAL SEASHORE

GULF OF MEXICO

⬦ **FISH FARMS.** Raising catfish in large man-made ponds is the leading aquaculture industry in Mississippi and in the U.S.

North Carolina

Early attempts by English colonists to settle the area that would become North Carolina met with strong resistance from Native American groups already living there. Despite ongoing tensions, in 1663 King Charles II approved establishment of the Carolina colony, which included present-day North Carolina, South Carolina, and part of Georgia. In 1789 North Carolina became the 12th state, but in 1861 it joined the Confederacy and supplied more men and equipment to the Civil War than any other southern state. In 1903 the Wright brothers piloted the first successful airplane near Kitty Hawk, foreshadowing the change and growth coming to the Tar Heel State. Traditional industries included agriculture, textiles, and furniture making. Today, these, plus high-tech industries and education in the Raleigh-Durham Research Triangle area, as well as banking and finance in Charlotte, are important to the economy.

BASICS

Statehood
November 21, 1789; 12th state

Total area (land and water)
53,819 sq mi (139,391 sq km)

Land area
48,618 sq mi (125,920 sq km)

Population
10,383,620

Capital
Raleigh
Population 469,298

Largest city
Charlotte
Population 872,498

Racial/ethnic groups
70.8% white; 22.2% African American; 3.1% Asian; 1.6% Native American; 9.5% Hispanic (any race)

Foreign born
7.8%

Urban population
66.1%

Population density
213.6 per sq mi
(82.5 per sq km)

GEO WHIZ

The University of North Carolina at Chapel Hill, dating to 1795, is the oldest public university in the U.S.

At 208 feet (63 m) high, Cape Hatteras Lighthouse is the tallest lighthouse in the U.S.

CARDINAL

FLOWERING DOGWOOD

◑ FAVORITE PASTIME. With four of the state's schools represented in the powerful Atlantic Coast Conference, basketball is a popular sport whether on the court or in the driveway.

◑ TAKING FLIGHT. The Wright Brothers Memorial on Kill Devil Hill, near Kitty Hawk on the Outer Banks, marks the site of the first successful airplane flight in 1903.

VIRGINIA

NORTH CAROLINA

CAROLINA

ATLANTIC OCEAN

MAP KEY

⭐ State capital
●●● City
▣ Point of interest
＋ Mountain peak
／ Dam
·········· State boundary
- - - - Trail
⌁ Swamp

National Wild & Scenic River
▦ Indian Reservation
▦ National Park Service unit
▦ National Forest
▦ National Wildlife Refuge

0 ——————— 50 miles
0 ——————— 50 kilometers
Albers Conic Equal-Area Projection

◉ **SKILLED ARTISAN.** A Cherokee woman sews a beaded belt in Oconaluftee Indian Village in western North Carolina. Cherokee in this region are descendants of tribal members who hid in the mountains to avoid the forced removal known as the Trail of Tears. This living history site preserves traditional 18th-century crafts and customs.

REGIONAL GIANTS

West:
Denali, (Mt. McKinley), AK
20,310 feet (6,190 m)

Southwest:
Wheeler Peak, NM
13,161 feet (4,011 m)

Midwest:
Harney Peak, SD
7,242 feet (2,207 m)

Southeast:
Mt. Mitchell, NC
6,684 feet (2,037 m)

Northeast:
Mt. Washington, NH
6,288 feet (1,917 m)

Mount Mitchell in the Southeast is the highest peak east of the Mississippi, but young mountains in the West and Southwest tower above older eastern peaks.

South Carolina

Attempts in the 16th century by the Spanish and the French to colonize the area that would become South Carolina met fierce resistance from local Native American tribes. But in 1670 the English became the first to establish a permanent European settlement at present-day Charleston. The colony prospered by relying on slave labor to produce first cotton, then rice and indigo. South Carolina became the eighth state in 1788 and the first to leave the Union just months before the first shots of the Civil War were fired on Fort Sumter in 1861. After the war South Carolina struggled to rebuild its economy. Early in the 20th century, textile mills introduced new jobs. Today, agriculture remains important, manufacturing and high-tech industries are expanding along interstate highway corridors, and tourists and retirees are drawn to the state's Atlantic coastline. But these coastal areas are not without risk. In 1989 Hurricane Hugo's 135-mile-an-hour (217-km/h) winds left a trail of destruction.

⬕ **GLOW OF DAWN.** The rising sun reflects off the water along the Atlantic coast. Beaches attract visitors year-round, contributing to tourism, the state's largest industry.

YELLOW JESSAMINE
CAROLINA WREN

BASICS

Statehood
May 23, 1788; 8th state

Total area
(land and water)
32,020 sq mi
(82,933 sq km)

Land area
30,061 sq mi
(77,857 sq km)

Population
5,084,127

Capital
Columbia
Population 133,451

Largest city
Charleston
Population 136,208

Racial/ethnic groups
68.5% white; 27.3% African American; 1.7% Asian; 0.5% Native American; 5.7% Hispanic (any race)

Foreign born
4.9%

Urban population
66.3%

Population density
158.8 per sq mi
(61.3 per sq km)

GEO WHIZ

The loggerhead sea turtle, which is the state reptile of South Carolina, is threatened throughout its range.

Sweetgrass basketmaking, a traditional African art form, has been a part of the Mount Pleasant community for more than 300 years.

TRADE PARTNERS

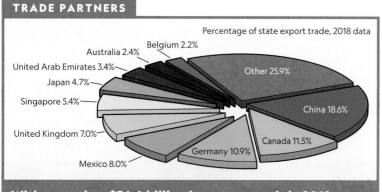

Percentage of state export trade, 2018 data

- Other 25.9%
- China 18.6%
- Canada 11.5%
- Germany 10.9%
- Mexico 8.0%
- United Kingdom 7.0%
- Singapore 5.4%
- Japan 4.7%
- United Arab Emirates 3.4%
- Australia 2.4%
- Belgium 2.2%

With more than $34.6 billion in export goods in 2018, export industries are an important source of employment in South Carolina. Transportation equipment is the leading manufactured export.

Highest point in South Carolina

Sassafras Mt.
3,560 ft
1,085 m

CHATTOOGA NATIONAL WILD & SCENIC RIVER

SUMTER NATIONAL FOREST

Lake Keowee

Greenville
Easley • Gantt

Seneca •

• Clemson

Belton

Hartwell Lake

Anderson

Richard B. Russell Lake

Abbeville

Blue Ridge

Tugaloo

Savannah

SHOWING OFF. A male wild turkey struts through Francis Beidler Forest, a wildlife sanctuary and virgin cypress-tupelo swamp forest.

NORTH CAROLINA

COWPENS N.B.
Gaffney
Greer • Spartanburg
Taylors
York
Rock Hill
KINGS MOUNTAIN N.M.P.
Wylie Lake
Fort Mill
CATAWBA I.R.
Mauldin
Simpsonville
Union
Chester
Lancaster
Cheraw
Bennettsville
SUMTER NATIONAL FOREST
CAROLINA SANDHILLS N.W.R.
Laurens
Clinton
Winnsboro
Wateree Lake
Hartsville
Dillon
Greenwood
Newberry
Camden
Darlington
Florence
Mullins
Lake Murray
Saluda
NINETY SIX N.H.S.
SUMTER
SOUTH
Irmo
Forest Acres
Columbia
Sumter
Lake City
Loris
NATIONAL
West Columbia
Cayce
Conway
North Myrtle Beach
FOREST
Edgefield
CONGAREE NATIONAL PARK
Manning
WACCAMAW N.W.R.
Myrtle Beach
J. Strom Thurmond Reservoir
CAROLINA
Kingstree
Socastee
Surfside Beach
Garden City
Aiken
Clearwater
Orangeburg
SANTEE N.W.R.
SANTEE DAM
Georgetown
Long Bay
North Augusta
Williston
Lake Marion
Lake Moultrie
North Island
ATLANTIC
GEORGIA
Bamberg
Barnwell
FRANCIS BEIDLER FOREST
Moncks Corner
FRANCIS MARION NATIONAL FOREST
Cape Island
OCEAN
Allendale
Summerville
Goose Creek
Hanahan
CAPE ROMAIN N.W.R.
Walterboro
Ladson
North Charleston
CHARLES PINCKNEY N.H.S.
Hampton
Charleston
Mt. Pleasant
FT. SUMTER NAT. MON.
ERNEST F. HOLLINGS ACE BASIN N.W.R.
Edisto Island
Burton
Beaufort
St. Helena Sound
Port Royal
St. Helena Island
SEA ISLANDS
SAVANNAH NATIONAL WILDLIFE REFUGE
PINCKNEY ISLAND N.W.R.
Parris Island
Hilton Head Island
Port Royal Sound
Hilton Head Island
Daufuskie Island

Broad
Catawba
Great Pee Dee
Wateree
Congaree
Lynches
Black
Little Pee Dee
Great Pee Dee
Waccamaw
Santee
Cooper
Ashley
Edisto
S. Fork Edisto
N. Fork Edisto
Savannah
Coosawhatchie
Combahee
Intracoastal Waterway

SOUTHERN CHARM. Established in 1670, Charleston is famous for its stately antebellum homes. The city is an important port, located where the Ashley and Cooper Rivers merge before flowing to the Atlantic Ocean.

MAP KEY

⭐ State capital
•• City
▪ Point of interest
+ Mountain peak
∕ Dam
••••• State boundary
Swamp
National Wild & Scenic River
Indian Reservation
National Park Service unit
National Forest
National Wildlife Refuge

0 ——— 25 miles
0 ——— 25 kilometers
Albers Conic Equal-Area Projection

BASICS

Statehood
June 1, 1796; 16th state

Total area (land and water)
42,144 sq mi (109,153 sq km)

Land area
41,235 sq mi (106,798 sq km)

Population
6,770,010

Capital
Nashville/Davidson County
Population 669,053

Largest city
Nashville/Davidson County
Population 669,053

Racial/ethnic groups
78.6% white; 17.1% African American; 1.9% Asian; 0.5% Native American; 5.5% Hispanic (any race)

Foreign born
5.0%

Urban population
66.4%

Population density
160.6 per sq mi
(62.0 per sq km)

GEO WHIZ

Great Smoky Mountains National Park has earned the title Salamander Capital of the World in recognition of the 30 species of salamanders that live there, including the five-foot (1.5-m)-long hellbender.

The New Madrid Earthquakes of 1811–1812, some of the largest earthquakes in U.S. history, created Reelfoot Lake in northwestern Tennessee. It is the state's only large, natural lake; others were created by damming waterways.

The Tennessee-Tombigbee Waterway is a 234-mile (376-km) artificial waterway that connects the Tennessee and Tombigbee Rivers. This water transportation route provides inland ports with an outlet to the Gulf of Mexico.

Tennessee

Following the last ice age, ancestors of today's Native Americans moved onto the fertile lands of Tennessee. The earliest Europeans in Tennessee were Spanish explorers who passed through in 1541. In 1673 both the English and French made claims on the land, hoping to develop trade with the powerful Cherokee, whose town, called Tanasi, gave the state its name. Originally part of North Carolina, Tennessee was ceded to the federal government and became the 16th state in 1796. Tennessee was the last state to join the Confederacy and endured years of hardship after the war. Beginning in the 1930s, the federally funded Tennessee Valley Authority (TVA) set a high standard in water management in the state, and the hydropower that it generated supported major industrial development. Tennessee played a key role in the civil rights movement of the 1960s. Today, visitors to Tennessee are drawn to national parks, Nashville's country music, and the mournful sound of the blues in Memphis.

MOCKINGBIRD

IRIS

◑ OUT FOR A STROLL.
Black bear cubs are usually born in January and remain with their mother for about 18 months. Great Smoky Mountains National Park is one of the few remaining natural habitats for black bears in the eastern United States.

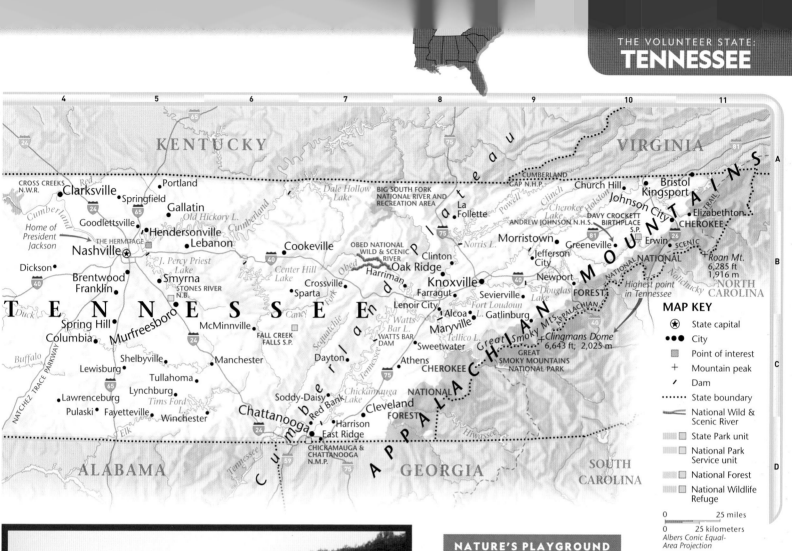

KENTUCKY

VIRGINIA

CROSS CREEKS N.W.R.
Clarksville
Springfield
Portland
Dale Hollow Lake
BIG SOUTH FORK NATIONAL RIVER AND RECREATION AREA
La Follette
CUMBERLAND GAP N.H.P.
Church Hill
Bristol
Kingsport
Johnson City
Elizabethton
CHEROKEE

Gallatin
Goodlettsville
Hendersonville
Lebanon
Old Hickory L.
Cumberland
Cherokee Lake
Holston
DAVY CROCKETT BIRTHPLACE S.P.
ANDREW JOHNSON N.H.S.
Morristown
Greeneville
Erwin
SCENIC

Home of President Jackson
THE HERMITAGE
Nashville
Cookeville
OBED NATIONAL WILD & SCENIC RIVER
Clinton
Oak Ridge
Norris L.
Jefferson City
Newport
NATIONAL
Roan Mt. 6,285 ft 1,916 m
Highest point in Tennessee
NORTH CAROLINA

Dickson
J. Percy Priest Lake
Harriman
Knoxville
Farragut
Sevierville
Douglas Lake
FOREST

Brentwood
Franklin
Smyrna
STONES RIVER N.B.
Center Hill Lake
Crossville
Sparta
Lenoir City
Alcoa
L. Gatlinburg
APPALACHIAN

Spring Hill
Columbia
Murfreesboro
McMinnville
FALL CREEK FALLS S.P.
Caney Fork
Watts Bar L.
WATTS BAR DAM
Maryville
Tellico L.
Fort Loudoun
Clingmans Dome 6,643 ft; 2,025 m

Buffalo
Duck
Shelbyville
Manchester
Dayton
Sweetwater
GREAT SMOKY MOUNTAINS NATIONAL PARK
Great Smoky Mts.

Lewisburg
Tullahoma
Athens
CHEROKEE

Lawrenceburg
Lynchburg
Tims Ford L.
Soddy-Daisy
Chickamauga Lake
Cleveland
NATIONAL

Pulaski
Fayetteville
Winchester
Chattanooga
Red Bank
Harrison
East Ridge
FOREST

ALABAMA
CHICKAMAUGA & CHATTANOOGA N.M.P.
GEORGIA
SOUTH CAROLINA
Hiwassee

MAP KEY

- ⊛ State capital
- ●●● City
- ◻ Point of interest
- + Mountain peak
- ⁄ Dam
- ⋯ State boundary
- National Wild & Scenic River
- State Park unit
- National Park Service unit
- National Forest
- National Wildlife Refuge

0 — 25 miles
0 — 25 kilometers
Albers Conic Equal-Area Projection

NATURE'S PLAYGROUND

🚶 One million national park visitors, 2017 data

Park	Visitors
Great Smoky Mountains N.P.	11.39
Grand Canyon N.P.	6.25
Zion N.P.	4.50
Rocky Mountain N.P.	4.44
Yosemite N.P.	4.37

Great Smoky Mountains National Park, on the Tennessee-North Carolina border, attracts more visitors than any other U.S. national park.

⬬ **WATER POWER.** Watts Bar Dam is one of nine TVA dams built on the Tennessee River to aid navigation and flood control and to supply power. The large reservoir behind the dam provides a recreation area that attracts millions of vacationers each year. Without the dam, cities such as Chattanooga would face devastating floods.

◗ **SOUTHERN TRADITION.** Nashville's Grand Ole Opry is the home of country music. Originally a 1925 radio show called WSM Barn Dance, the Opry now occupies a theater that seats 4,400. The Opry is the longest running radio show in the U.S. Country music, using mainly stringed instruments, evolved from traditional folk tunes of the Appalachians.

BASICS

Statehood
June 25, 1788; 10th state

Total area (land and water)
42,775 sq mi (110,787 sq km)

Land area
39,490 sq mi (102,279 sq km)

Population
8,517,685

Capital
Richmond
Population 228,783

Largest city
Virginia Beach
Population 450,189

Racial/ethnic groups
69.7% white; 19.8% African American; 6.8% Asian; 0.5% Native American; 9.4% Hispanic (any race)

Foreign born
12.1%

Urban population
75.5%

Population density
215.7 per sq mi (83.3 per sq km)

GEO WHIZ

In the early 1700s, the bustling port of Hampton was a major target for pirates, including the notorious Blackbeard. Today, the city hosts the Blackbeard Festival each spring, complete with pirate reenactors, live music, games, and fireworks.

During the Battle of Hampton Roads in 1862, the ships U.S.S. *Monitor* and the C.S.S. *Virginia* (a rebuilt version of the U.S.S. *Merrimack*) met in one of the most famous naval engagements in U.S. history. The battle marked the dawn of a new era of naval warfare.

Virginia

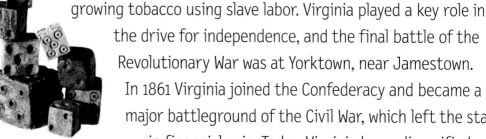

Long before Europeans arrived in present-day Virginia, Native Americans populated the area. Early Spanish attempts to establish a colony failed, but in 1607 merchants established the first permanent English settlement in North America at Jamestown. Virginia became a prosperous colony, growing tobacco using slave labor. Virginia played a key role in the drive for independence, and the final battle of the Revolutionary War was at Yorktown, near Jamestown. In 1861 Virginia joined the Confederacy and became a major battleground of the Civil War, which left the state in financial ruin. Today, Virginia has a diversified economy. Farmers still grow tobacco, along with other crops. The Hampton Roads area, near the mouth of

○ **EARLY ENTERTAINMENT.** Dice made of bone, ivory, and lead, dating to 1607, were excavated at Jamestown.

Chesapeake Bay, is a center for shipbuilding and home to major U.S. naval bases. Northern Virginia, across the Potomac River from Washington, D.C., boasts federal government offices and high-tech businesses. The state's natural beauty and many historic sites attract tourists from around the world.

KENTUCKY

TENNESSEE

Bluefield
Tazewell
Richlands
APPALACHIAN
Norton
Lebanon
Clinch
Mountain
Wytheville
CUMBERLAND
GAP
N.H.P.
Big
Stone
Gap
JEFFERSON
NATIONAL
FOREST
Powell
Clinch
North Fork
Marion
Abingdon
Bristol
Mt. Rogers
+5,729 ft
1,746 m
Holston
S. Fork
New
Highest point
in Virginia

FLOWERING
DOGWOOD

CARDINAL

◑ **NATURAL WONDER.** Winding under the Appalachian Mountains, Luray Caverns were formed as water dissolved limestone rocks and deposited minerals to form dramatic stalactites and stalagmites.

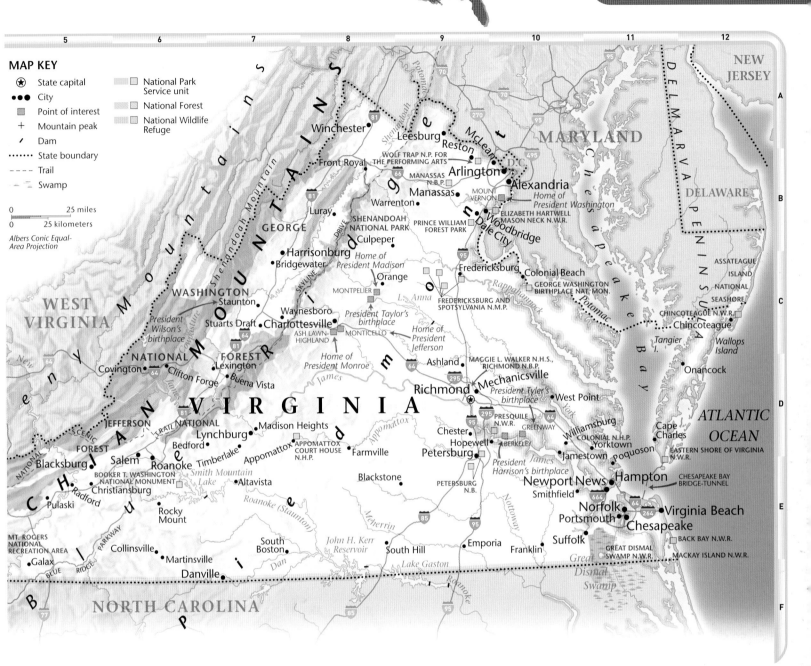

MAP KEY

⭐ State capital
●●● City
▪ Point of interest
+ Mountain peak
/ Dam
···· State boundary
---- Trail
⌐ Swamp

▢ National Park Service unit
▨ National Forest
▨ National Wildlife Refuge

0 ___ 25 miles
0 ___ 25 kilometers

Albers Conic Equal-Area Projection

NEW JERSEY

MARYLAND

DELAWARE

DELMARVA PENINSULA

WEST VIRGINIA

Winchester
Leesburg
Reston
McLean
WOLF TRAP N.P. FOR THE PERFORMING ARTS
Front Royal
Arlington
D.C.
Alexandria
MANASSAS N.B.P.
Manassas
MOUNT VERNON
Home of President Washington
Warrenton
Luray
ELIZABETH HARTWELL MASON NECK N.W.R.
Woodbridge
PRINCE WILLIAM FOREST PARK
Dale City
SHENANDOAH NATIONAL PARK
GEORGE
Harrisonburg
Home of President Madison
Bridgewater
Fredericksburg
Colonial Beach
Orange
GEORGE WASHINGTON BIRTHPLACE NAT. MON.
MONTPELIER
FREDERICKSBURG AND SPOTSYLVANIA N.M.P.
WASHINGTON
Staunton
President Wilson's birthplace
Waynesboro
L. Anna
Stuarts Draft
President Taylor's birthplace
Charlottesville
ASH LAWN-HIGHLAND
MONTICELLO
Home of President Jefferson
NATIONAL
Covington
Clifton Forge
Lexington
Buena Vista
Home of President Monroe
Ashland
MAGGIE L. WALKER N.H.S., RICHMOND N.B.P.
FOREST
Richmond
Mechanicsville
President Tyler's birthplace
West Point
JEFFERSON
Madison Heights
Lynchburg
Chester
PRESQUILE N.W.R.
GREENWAY
Williamsburg
Cape Charles
ATLANTIC OCEAN
Bedford
Appomattox
APPOMATTOX COURT HOUSE N.H.P.
Farmville
Hopewell
BERKELEY
COLONIAL N.H.P.
Yorktown
Jamestown
Poquoson
EASTERN SHORE OF VIRGINIA N.W.R.
Blacksburg
Salem
Roanoke
Timberlake
Petersburg
President Harrison's birthplace
Newport News
Hampton
CHESAPEAKE BAY BRIDGE-TUNNEL
BOOKER T. WASHINGTON NATIONAL MONUMENT
Christiansburg
Smith Mountain Lake
Blackstone
PETERSBURG N.B.
Smithfield
Norfolk
Virginia Beach
Radford
Altavista
Portsmouth
Chesapeake
Pulaski
Rocky Mount
Suffolk
BACK BAY N.W.R.
MT. ROGERS NATIONAL RECREATION AREA
Collinsville
South Boston
South Hill
Emporia
Franklin
GREAT DISMAL SWAMP N.W.R.
MACKAY ISLAND N.W.R.
Galax
Martinsville
Danville
John H. Kerr Reservoir
Lake Gaston
Great Dismal Swamp

NORTH CAROLINA

ASSATEAGUE ISLAND NATIONAL SEASHORE
CHINCOTEAGUE N.W.R.
Chincoteague
Tangier I.
Wallops Island
Onancock

CHESAPEAKE BAY
Potomac
Rappahannock
James
Appomattox
Roanoke (Staunton)
Dan
Meherrin
Nottoway

MOUNTAINS
SHENANDOAH
BLUE RIDGE
APPALACHIAN MOUNTAINS
ALLEGHENY MOUNTAINS

🔘 **DEFENSE CENTRAL.** The Pentagon, located just outside of Washington, D.C., in Arlington, Virginia, is the world's largest office building, with 17.5 miles (28.2 km) of corridors. It is the headquarters of the U.S. Department of Defense.

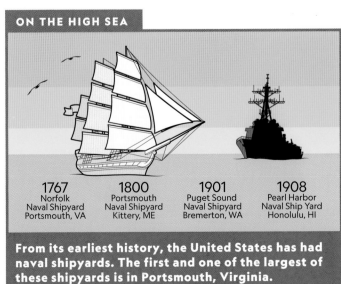

ON THE HIGH SEA

1767	1800	1901	1908
Norfolk Naval Shipyard Portsmouth, VA	Portsmouth Naval Shipyard Kittery, ME	Puget Sound Naval Shipyard Bremerton, WA	Pearl Harbor Naval Ship Yard Honolulu, HI

From its earliest history, the United States has had naval shipyards. The first and one of the largest of these shipyards is in Portsmouth, Virginia.

West Virginia

West Virginia was first settled by Native Americans who favored the wooded region for hunting. The first Europeans to settle in what originally was an extension of Virginia were Germans and Scotch-Irish, who came through mountain valleys in Pennsylvania in the early 1700s. Because farms in West Virginia were not dependent on slave labor, residents opposed secession during the Civil War and broke away from Virginia, becoming the 35th state in 1863. In the early 1800s, West Virginia harvested forest products and mined salt, but it was the discovery of vast coal deposits that brought industrialization to the state. Coal fueled steel mills, steamboats, and trains, and jobs in the mines attracted immigrants from far and near to the state. However, poor work conditions resulted in a legacy of poverty, illness, and environmental degradation— problems the state continues to face. Today, the state is working to build a tourist industry based on its natural beauty as well as its mountain crafts and culture.

BASICS

Statehood
June 20, 1863; 35th state

Total area (land and water)
24,230 sq mi (62,756 sq km)

Land area
24,038 sq mi (62,259 sq km)

Population
1,805,832

Capital
Charleston
Population 47,215

Largest city
Charleston
Population 47,215

Racial/ethnic groups
93.6% white; 3.6% African American; 0.8% Asian; 0.2% Native American; 1.6% Hispanic (any race)

Foreign born
1.6%

Urban population
48.7%

Population density
75.1 per sq mi (29.0 per sq km)

GEO WHIZ

Weirton, the only U.S. city that sits in one state and borders two others, is nestled in West Virginia's panhandle between Ohio and Pennsylvania.

The first rural free mail delivery in the U.S. started in Charles Town on October 1, 1896.

⬤ **HARD LABOR.** Coal miners work under difficult conditions—some in underground mines; others in surface mines.

CARDINAL

RHODODENDRON

O H I O

Point Pleasant

Kanawha

Ohio

Hurricane

Huncington 64

Kenova

Big Sandy

Guyandotte

Tug Fork

Logan

Williamson

KENTUCKY

◑ **STRATEGIC LOCATION.** Harpers Ferry, established at the site of a ferry crossing over the Shenandoah River, was the target of John Brown's historic 1859 raid on the town's U.S. military arsenal. This anti-slavery movement was a precursor to the Civil War.

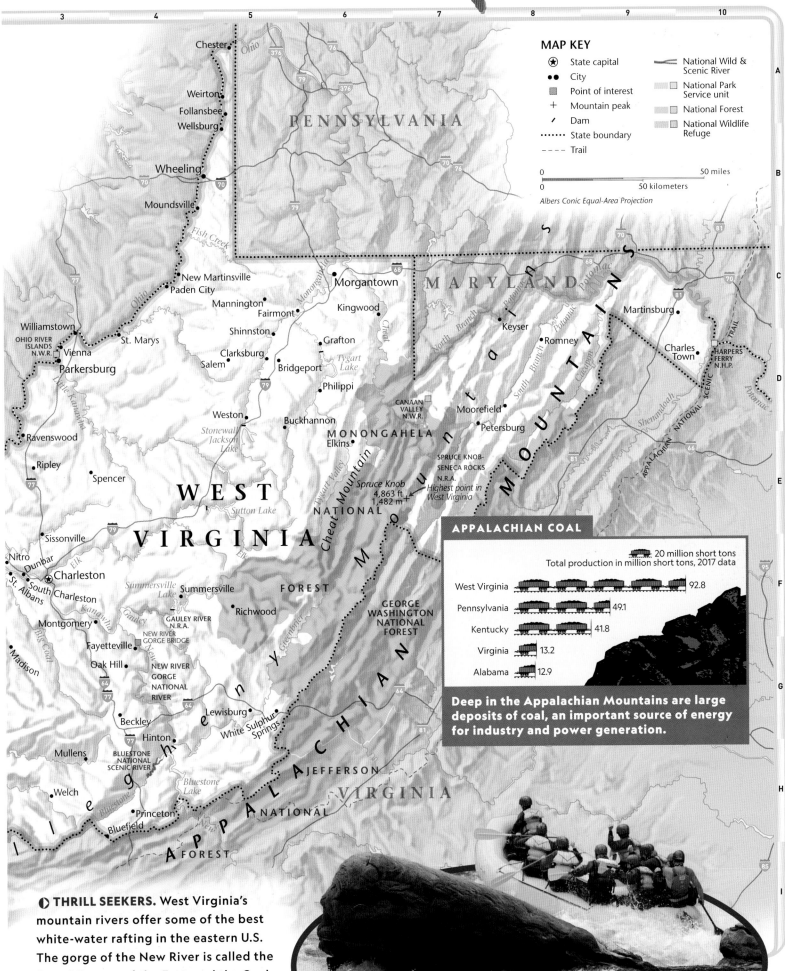

MAP KEY

★ State capital

•• City

■ Point of interest

+ Mountain peak

⟋ Dam

⋯ State boundary

--- Trail

〰 National Wild & Scenic River

▦ National Park Service unit

▦ National Forest

▦ National Wildlife Refuge

0 _____ 50 miles
0 _____ 50 kilometers

Albers Conic Equal-Area Projection

PENNSYLVANIA

MARYLAND

VIRGINIA

WEST VIRGINIA

Chester
Weirton
Follansbee
Wellsburg
Wheeling
Moundsville
New Martinsville
Paden City
Mannington
Fairmont
Morgantown
Kingwood
Williamstown
OHIO RIVER ISLANDS N.W.R.
Vienna
St. Marys
Shinnston
Clarksburg
Salem
Bridgeport
Grafton
Tygart Lake
Keyser
Romney
Martinsburg
Charles Town
HARPERS FERRY N.H.P.
Parkersburg
Philippi
CANAAN VALLEY N.W.R.
Moorefield
Petersburg
Ravenswood
Weston
Buckhannon
Stonewall Jackson Lake
MONONGAHELA
Elkins
Ripley
Spencer
SPRUCE KNOB-SENECA ROCKS N.R.A.
Spruce Knob 4,863 ft 1,482 m + Highest point in West Virginia
Sutton Lake
NATIONAL
Sissonville
Cheat Mountain
Nitro
Dunbar
Charleston
St. Albans
South Charleston
Summersville Lake
Summersville
FOREST
Richwood
GEORGE WASHINGTON NATIONAL FOREST
Montgomery
GAULEY RIVER N.R.A.
NEW RIVER GORGE BRIDGE
Fayetteville
NEW RIVER GORGE NATIONAL RIVER
Oak Hill
Madison
Beckley
Lewisburg
Hinton
White Sulphur Springs
Mullens
BLUESTONE NATIONAL SCENIC RIVER
Welch
Bluestone Lake
Princeton
Bluefield
JEFFERSON
NATIONAL
FOREST
APPALACHIAN

APPALACHIAN COAL

🚃 20 million short tons
Total production in million short tons, 2017 data

	Production
West Virginia	92.8
Pennsylvania	49.1
Kentucky	41.8
Virginia	13.2
Alabama	12.9

Deep in the Appalachian Mountains are large deposits of coal, an important source of energy for industry and power generation.

◗ **THRILL SEEKERS.** West Virginia's mountain rivers offer some of the best white-water rafting in the eastern U.S. The gorge of the New River is called the Grand Canyon of the East, and the Gauley River is called the Beast of the East.

THE REGION

PHYSICAL

Total area (land and water)
821,726 sq mi
(2,128,257 sq km)

Highest point
Harney Peak, SD
7,242 ft (2,207 m)

Lowest point
St. Francis River, MO
230 ft (70 m)

Longest rivers
Mississippi, Missouri,
Arkansas, Ohio

Largest lakes
Superior, Michigan,
Huron, Erie

Vegetation
Grassland; broadleaf,
needleleaf, and mixed forest

Climate
Continental to mild, ranging
from cold winters and cool
summers in the north to mild
winters and humid summers
in the south

POLITICAL

Total population
68,308,744

States (12):
Illinois, Indiana, Iowa, Kansas, Michigan,
Minnesota, Missouri, Nebraska, North
Dakota, Ohio, South Dakota, Wisconsin

Largest state
Michigan: 96,714 sq mi (250,487 sq km)

Smallest state
Indiana: 36,420 sq mi
(94,326 sq km)

Most populous state
Illinois: 12,741,080

Least populous state
North Dakota: 760,077

Largest city proper
Chicago, IL: 2,705,994

THE MIDWEST

PHYSICAL MAP

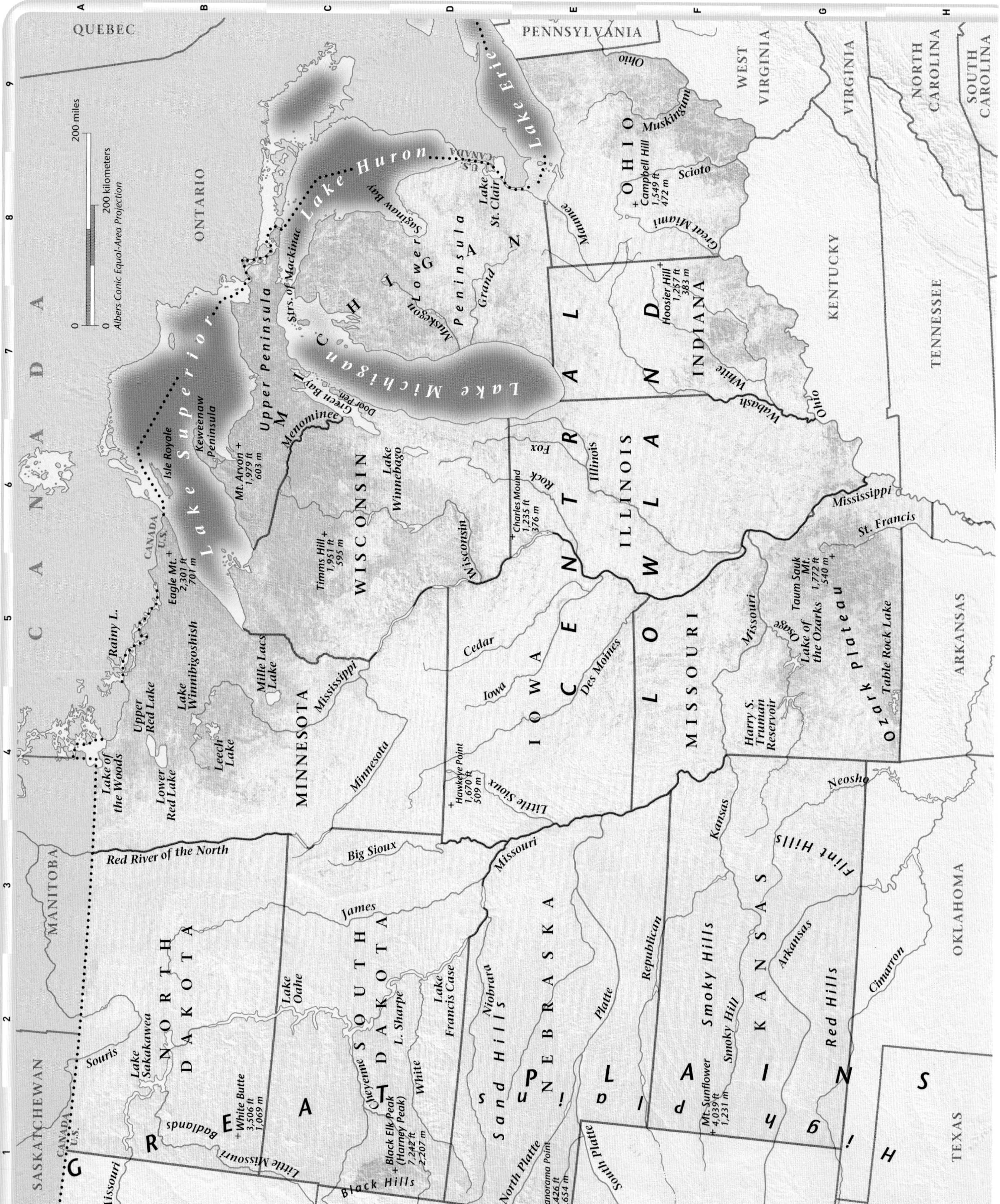

QUEBEC
PENNSYLVANIA
ONTARIO
CANADA
MANITOBA
SASKATCHEWAN
MONTANA
WYOMING
COLORADO
NEW MEXICO
TEXAS
OKLAHOMA
ARKANSAS
TENNESSEE
KENTUCKY
WEST VIRGINIA
VIRGINIA
NORTH CAROLINA
SOUTH CAROLINA
200 miles
200 kilometers
Albers Conic Equal-Area Projection
GREAT PLAINS
HIGH PLAINS
CENTRAL LOWLAND
NORTH DAKOTA
SOUTH DAKOTA
NEBRASKA
KANSAS
MINNESOTA
IOWA
MISSOURI
WISCONSIN
ILLINOIS
MICHIGAN
INDIANA
OHIO
Lake Superior
Lake Michigan
Lake Huron
Lake Erie
Lake St. Clair
Saginaw Bay
Green Bay
Door Pen.
Strs. of Mackinac
Upper Peninsula
Lower Peninsula
Keweenaw Peninsula
Isle Royale
Mt. Arvon 1,979 ft 603 m
Eagle Mt. 2,301 ft 701 m
Timms Hill 1,951 ft 595 m
Charles Mound 1,235 ft 376 m
Hawkeye Point 1,670 ft 509 m
Hoosier Hill 1,257 ft 383 m
Campbell Hill 1,549 ft 472 m
Taum Sauk Mt. 1,772 ft 540 m
Mt. Sunflower 4,039 ft 1,231 m
Panorama Point 5,426 ft 1,654 m
Black Elk Peak (Harney Peak) 7,242 ft 2,207 m
White Butte 3,506 ft 1,069 m
Lake of the Woods
Rainy L.
Upper Red Lake
Lower Red Lake
Lake Winnibigoshish
Leech Lake
Mille Lacs Lake
Lake Winnebago
Lake Sakakawea
Lake Oahe
L. Sharpe
Lake Francis Case
Lake of the Ozarks
Harry S. Truman Reservoir
Table Rock Lake
Ozark Plateau
Black Hills
Badlands
Sand Hills
Smoky Hills
Red Hills
Flint Hills
Red River of the North
Souris
Missouri
Little Missouri
Cheyenne
White
Niobrara
James
Big Sioux
Little Sioux
Minnesota
Mississippi
Wisconsin
Menominee
Cedar
Iowa
Des Moines
Rock
Fox
Illinois
Wabash
Ohio
Muskingum
Scioto
Great Miami
Maumee
Muskegon
Grand
Platte
North Platte
South Platte
Republican
Smoky Hill
Kansas
Arkansas
Cimarron
Neosho
Osage
St. Francis
U.S.

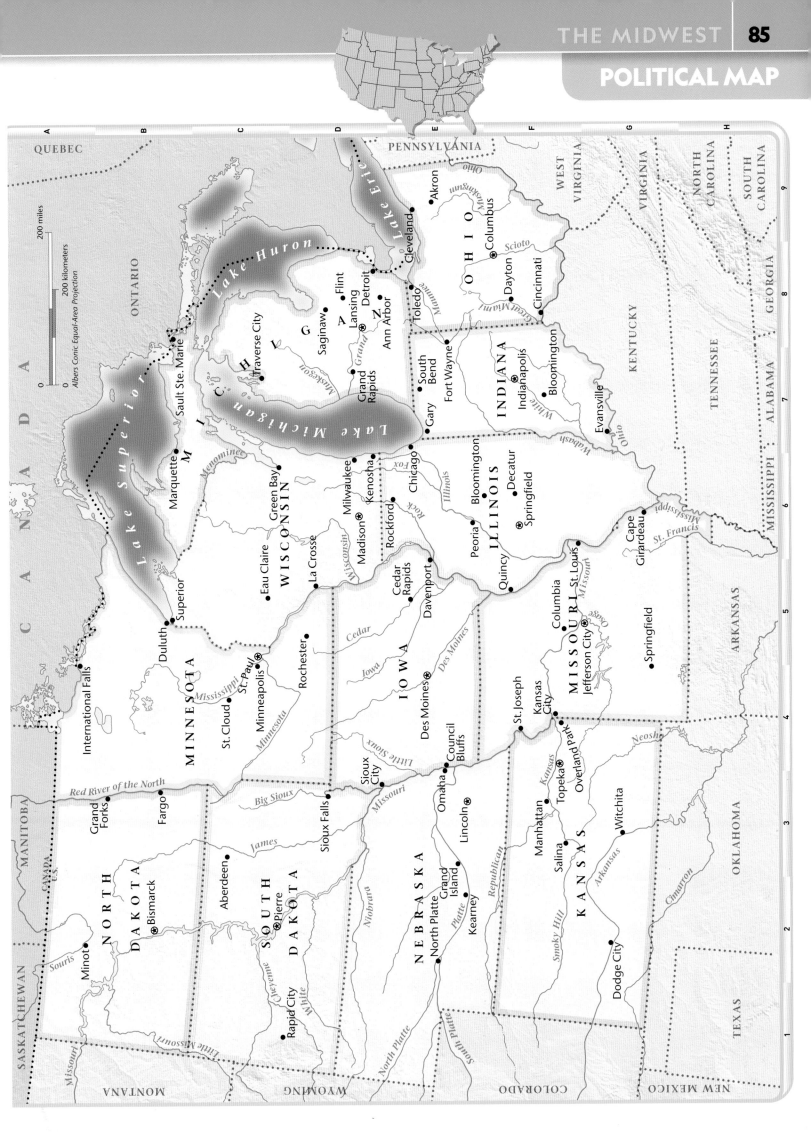

200 miles
200 kilometers
Albers Conic Equal-Area Projection

QUEBEC
PENNSYLVANIA

ONTARIO

CANADA

Lake Superior

Lake Huron

Lake Erie

Lake Michigan

Cleveland
Akron
Ohio
OHIO
Columbus
Scioto
Muskingum
WEST VIRGINIA
VIRGINIA
NORTH CAROLINA
SOUTH CAROLINA

Flint
Detroit
Lansing
Ann Arbor
M I C H I G A N
Saginaw
Grand
Traverse City
Grand Rapids
Dayton
Cincinnati
Great Miami

Sault Ste. Marie
Marquette
Menominee

South Bend
Fort Wayne
INDIANA
Indianapolis
Bloomington
White
Evansville
Ohio
KENTUCKY
TENNESSEE
GEORGIA
ALABAMA

Gary

Green Bay
Milwaukee
Kenosha
Chicago
Fox
Rockford
Illinois
Bloomington
ILLINOIS
Decatur
Springfield
Wabash
MISSISSIPPI

Eau Claire
WISCONSIN
La Crosse
Madison
Wisconsin
Rock
Peoria
Quincy
Mississippi
St. Francis
Cape Girardeau

Superior
Duluth

MINNESOTA
St. Cloud
St. Paul
Minneapolis
Rochester
Mississippi
Cedar Rapids
Davenport
Cedar
IOWA
Iowa
Des Moines
Des Moines
MISSOURI
Columbia
St. Louis
Missouri
Jefferson City
Osage
Springfield
ARKANSAS

International Falls

MANITOBA
Red River of the North
Grand Forks
Fargo
Big Sioux
Sioux Falls
Sioux City
Council Bluffs
Omaha
St. Joseph
Kansas City
Overland Park
Topeka
Neosho

James
Aberdeen
NORTH DAKOTA
Bismarck
SOUTH DAKOTA
Pierre
Missouri
Little Sioux
Minnesota
Manhattan
Salina
KANSAS
Witchita
Arkansas
OKLAHOMA

Minot
Souris
SASKATCHEWAN
CANADA
U.S.
Cheyenne
White
Rapid City
Niobrara
NEBRASKA
North Platte
Grand Island
Kearney
Lincoln
Republican
Smoky Hill
Dodge City
Cimarron

MONTANA
WYOMING
North Platte
Little Missouri
Missouri
South Platte
Platte
COLORADO
NEW MEXICO
TEXAS

Toledo
Maumee

ABOUT THE
MIDWEST

The Midwest

GREAT LAKES, GREAT RIVERS

◖ FIERCE GIANT. This *Tyrannosaurus rex* at Chicago's Field Museum roamed North America 65 million years ago.

The Midwest's early white settlers arrived from eastern U.S. states or Europe, but recent immigrants come from all parts of the world. Hispanics, for example, are settling in communities large and small throughout the region, and many Arabs reside in Detroit and Dearborn, Michigan. Drained by three mighty rivers—the Mississippi, Missouri, and Ohio—the Midwest's lowlands and plains are one of the world's most bountiful farmlands. Though the number of farmers has declined, new technologies and equipment have made farms larger and more productive. Meanwhile, industrial cities of the Rust Belt are adjusting to an economy focused more on information and services than on manufacturing.

◖ CROP CIRCLES. Much of the western part of the region receives less than 20 inches (50 cm) of rain yearly—not enough to support agriculture. Large, circular, center-pivot irrigation systems draw water from underground reserves called aquifers to provide life-giving water to crops.

◖ DAIRY HEARTLAND. Dairy cows, such as these in Wisconsin, are sometimes treated with growth hormones to increase milk production. These animals play an important role in the economy of the Midwest, which supplies much of the country's milk, butter, and cheese.

MIDWEST URBAN HUB. Chicago, the third largest metropolitan area in the U.S., is the economic and cultural core of the Midwest.

PROUD LEADER.
A statue of Menominee Chief Oshkosh stands near Lake Winnebago in Oshkosh, Wisconsin, which was named for him.

NATURE'S MOST VIOLENT STORMS.
Parts of the midwestern U.S. have earned the nickname Tornado Alley because these destructive, swirling storms, which develop in association with thunderstorms along eastward-moving cold fronts, occur here more than any other place on Earth.

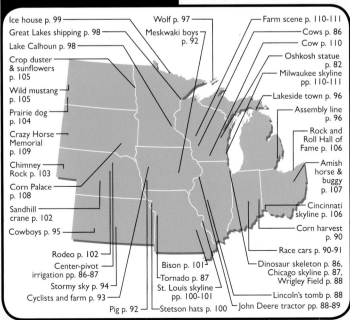

WHERE THE PICTURES ARE

Ice house p. 99
Great Lakes shipping p. 98
Lake Calhoun p. 98
Crop duster & sunflowers p. 105
Wild mustang p. 105
Prairie dog p. 104
Crazy Horse Memorial p. 109
Chimney Rock p. 103
Corn Palace p. 108
Sandhill crane p. 102
Cowboys p. 95

Wolf p. 97
Meskwaki boys p. 92

Farm scene p. 110-111
Cows p. 86
Cow p. 110
Oshkosh statue p. 82
Milwaukee skyline pp. 110-111
Lakeside town p. 96
Assembly line p. 96
Rock and Roll Hall of Fame p. 106
Amish horse & buggy p. 107
Cincinnati skyline p. 106
Corn harvest p. 90
Race cars p. 90-91
Dinosaur skeleton p. 86, Chicago skyline p. 87, Wrigley Field p. 88
Lincoln's tomb p. 88
John Deere tractor pp. 88-89

Rodeo p. 102
Center-pivot irrigation pp. 86-87
Stormy sky p. 94
Cyclists and farm p. 93
Pig p. 92

Bison p. 101
Tornado p. 87
St. Louis skyline pp. 100-101
Stetson hats p. 100

ILLINOIS

THE BASICS

Statehood
December 3, 1818; 21st state

Total area (land and water)
57,914 sq mi (149,995 sq km)

Land area
55,519 sq mi (143,793 sq km)

Population
12,741,080

Capital
Springfield
Population 114,694

Largest city
Chicago
Population 2,705,994

Racial/ethnic groups
77.1% white; 14.6% African American; 5.7% Asian; 0.6% Native American; 17.3% Hispanic (any race)

Foreign born
14.0%

Urban population
88.5%

Population density
229.5 per sq mi (88.6 per sq km)

GEO WHIZ

A giant, fossilized rainforest has been unearthed in an eastern Illinois coal mine near Danville. Scientists believe it was buried by an earthquake 300 million years ago.

The Great Chicago Fire of 1871 destroyed the city's waterworks, so firemen had to drag water in buckets from Lake Michigan and the Chicago River.

Illinois

Two rivers that now form the borders of Illinois were key to the state's early white settlement. French explorers traveled down the Mississippi in 1673, and many 19th-century settlers followed the Ohio to southern Illinois. By the 1830s many Native Americans had been forced out of Illinois. Chicago, the most populous city in the Midwest, is an economic giant and one of the country's busiest transportation hubs. Barges from Chicago's port on Lake Michigan reach the Gulf of Mexico via rivers and canals; ships reach the Atlantic Ocean via the Great Lakes and St. Lawrence Seaway. Flat terrain and fertile soils in the northern and central regions of the state help make Illinois a top producer of corn and soybeans. The more rugged, forested south has deposits of coal. Springfield, capital of the Land of Lincoln, welcomes tourists visiting the home and tomb of the country's 16th president.

⬤ **REMEMBERING A PRESIDENT.** Dedicated in 1874, the National Lincoln Monument in Springfield honors Abraham Lincoln, who was assassinated in 1865. A special vault holds the remains of the slain president, who led the country during the Civil War.

VIOLET

CARDINAL

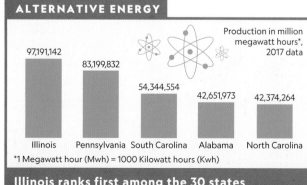

WRIGLEY FIELD
HOME OF
CHICAGO CUBS
WORLD SERIES CHAMPIONS

⬤ **PLAY BALL!** Wrigley Field, home to the Chicago Cubs baseball team, is affected by wind conditions more than any other major league park due to its location near Lake Michigan.

ALTERNATIVE ENERGY

Production in million megawatt hours*, 2017 data

Illinois	Pennsylvania	South Carolina	Alabama	North Carolina
97,191,142	83,199,832	54,344,554	42,651,973	42,374,264

*1 Megawatt hour (Mwh) = 1000 Kilowatt hours (Kwh)

Illinois ranks first among the 30 states that produce nuclear power. The state has six nuclear power plants with 11 reactors.

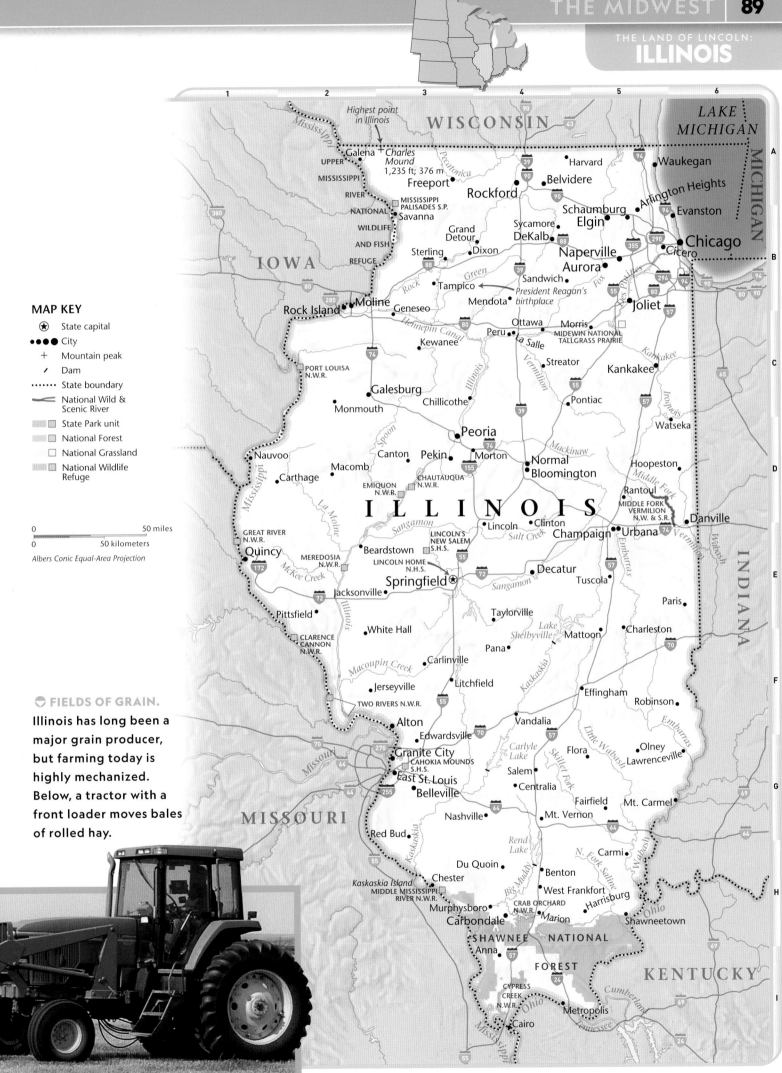

LAKE
MICHIGAN

WISCONSIN

MICHIGAN

Highest point
in Illinois

Mississippi

Galena + Charles
Mound
1,235 ft; 376 m

UPPER

Harvard

Waukegan

MISSISSIPPI

Freeport

Belvidere

Arlington Heights

RIVER

Rockford

Schaumburg

Evanston

NATIONAL

MISSISSIPPI
PALISADES S.P.

Grand
Detour

Sycamore

Elgin

WILDLIFE

Savanna

DeKalb

Chicago

AND FISH

Sterling

Dixon

Naperville

Cicero

IOWA

REFUGE

Aurora

Sandwich

Tampico

President Reagan's
birthplace

Joliet

Rock Island

Moline

Geneseo

Mendota

Green

Fox

Rock

Hennepin Canal

Ottawa

Morris

MIDEWIN NATIONAL
TALLGRASS PRAIRIE

Peru

La Salle

Kewanee

Illinois

Streator

Kankakee

PORT LOUISA
N.W.R.

Galesburg

Chillicothe

Pontiac

Monmouth

Watseka

Peoria

ILLINOIS

Nauvoo

Canton

Pekin

Morton

Normal

Hoopeston

Macomb

Bloomington

Middle Fork

Carthage

CHAUTAUQUA
N.W.R.

EMIQUON
N.W.R.

Rantoul

MIDDLE FORK
VERMILION
N.W. & S.R.

Danville

Sangamon

Lincoln

Clinton

Champaign

Urbana

GREAT RIVER
N.W.R.

Salt Creek

LINCOLN'S
NEW SALEM
S.H.S.

Beardstown

LINCOLN HOME
N.H.S.

Quincy

MEREDOSIA
N.W.R.

Decatur

Tuscola

Jacksonville

Springfield

Sangamon

Paris

Pittsfield

Taylorville

McKee Creek

White Hall

Lake
Shelbyville

Mattoon

Charleston

CLARENCE
CANNON
N.W.R.

Pana

Carlinville

Macoupin Creek

Litchfield

Effingham

Robinson

Jerseyville

TWO RIVERS N.W.R.

Kaskaskia

Alton

Vandalia

Edwardsville

Carlyle
Lake

Flora

Olney

Granite City

CAHOKIA MOUNDS
S.H.S.

Lawrenceville

East St. Louis

Salem

MISSOURI

Belleville

Centralia

Fairfield

Mt. Carmel

Nashville

Mt. Vernon

Red Bud

Rend
Lake

Carmi

Du Quoin

Benton

Kaskaskia Island
MIDDLE MISSISSIPPI
RIVER N.W.R.

Chester

West Frankfort

Harrisburg

Murphysboro

CRAB ORCHARD
N.W.R.

Marion

Shawneetown

Carbondale

Anna

SHAWNEE   NATIONAL

FOREST

KENTUCKY

CYPRESS
CREEK
N.W.R.

Ohio

Metropolis

Cairo

INDIANA

MAP KEY

⊛ State capital
●●● City
+ Mountain peak
⟋ Dam
⋯⋯ State boundary
National Wild &
Scenic River
State Park unit
National Forest
National Grassland
National Wildlife
Refuge

0 — 50 miles
0 — 50 kilometers
Albers Conic Equal-Area Projection

⊕ FIELDS OF GRAIN.

Illinois has long been a
major grain producer,
but farming today is
highly mechanized.
Below, a tractor with a
front loader moves bales
of rolled hay.

THE BASICS

Statehood
December 11, 1816; 19th state

Total area (land and water)
36,420 sq mi (94,326 sq km)

Land area
35,826 sq mi (92,789 sq km)

Population
6,691,878

Capital
Indianapolis
Population 867,125

Largest city
Indianapolis
Population 867,125

Racial/ethnic groups
85.4% white; 9.7% African American; 2.4% Asian; 0.4% Native American; 7.0% Hispanic (any race)

Foreign born
5.0%

Urban population
72.4%

Population density
186.8 per sq mi
(72.1 per sq km)

GEO WHIZ

Every year Fort Wayne hosts the Johnny Appleseed Festival to honor John Chapman, who planted apple orchards from Pennsylvania to Illinois.

The Children's Museum of Indianapolis, the world's largest children's museum, features life-size dinosaur replicas, hands-on science labs, and much more.

Indiana

Indiana's name, meaning "Land of the Indians," honors the tribes who lived in the region before the arrival of Europeans. The first permanent white settlement was Vincennes, established by the French in the early 1700s. Following statehood in 1816, most Native Americans were forced out to make way for white settlement. Lake Michigan, in the state's northwest corner, brings economic and recreational opportunities. The lakefront city of Gary anchors a major industrial region. Nearby, the natural beauty and shifting sands of the Indiana Dunes National Lakeshore attract many visitors. Corn, soybeans, and hogs are the most important products from Indiana's many farms. True to the state motto, "The Crossroads of America," highways from all directions converge at Indianapolis. Traveling at a much higher speed are cars on that city's famed Motor Speedway, home to the Indy 500 auto race since 1911. Cheering for a favorite high school or college team is a popular pastime for many Hoosiers who catch basketball fever.

○ **START YOUR ENGINES.** The Indianapolis Motor Speedway seats up to 250,000 sports fans. Nicknamed the Brickyard, its track was once paved with 3.2 million bricks.

CARDINAL
PEONY

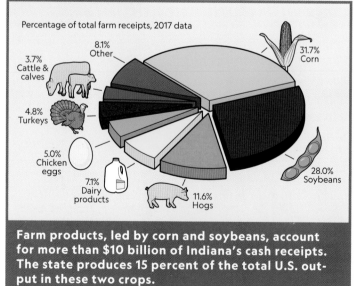

FARM TO TABLE

Percentage of total farm receipts, 2017 data

- 31.7% Corn
- 28.0% Soybeans
- 11.6% Hogs
- 8.1% Other
- 7.1% Dairy products
- 5.0% Chicken eggs
- 4.8% Turkeys
- 3.7% Cattle & calves

Farm products, led by corn and soybeans, account for more than $10 billion of Indiana's cash receipts. The state produces 15 percent of the total U.S. output in these two crops.

◖ **FUEL FARMING.** Indiana farmers grow corn for many uses—livestock feed, additives used in human food products, and production of ethanol, a non-fossil fuel energy source.

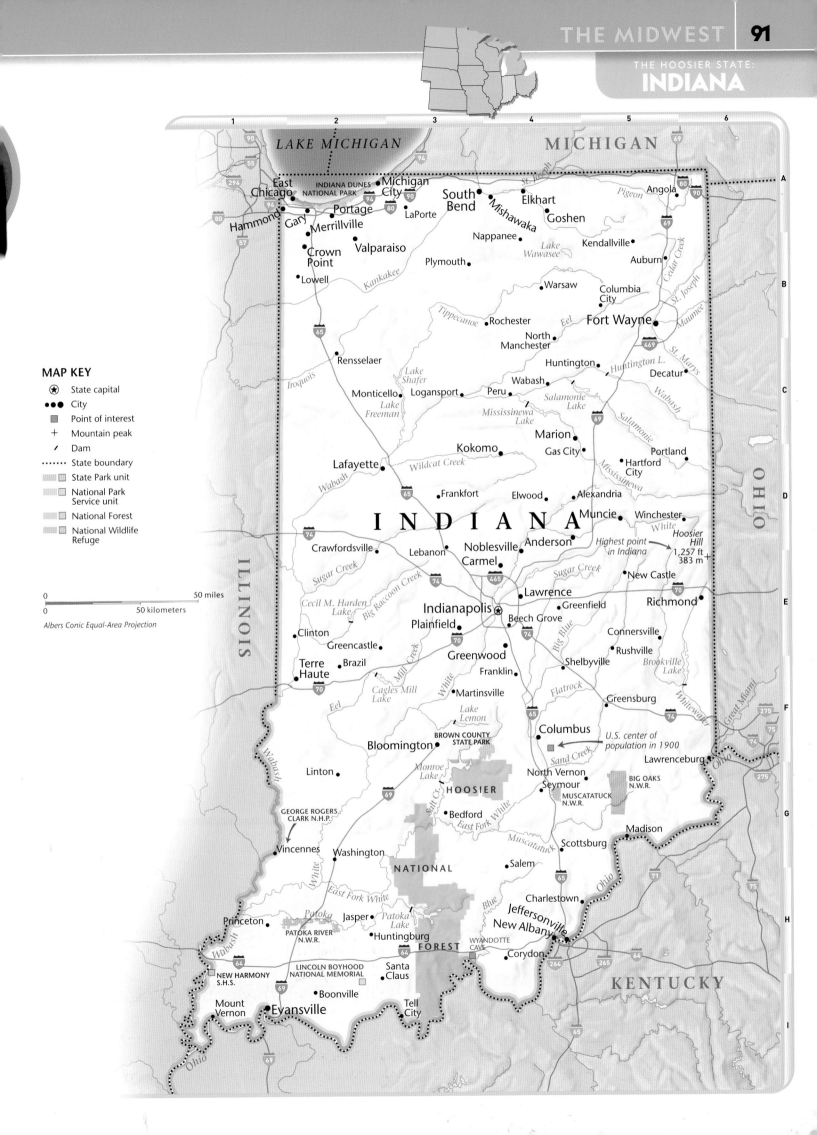

LAKE MICHIGAN

MICHIGAN

East Chicago

INDIANA DUNES NATIONAL PARK

Michigan City

South Bend

Mishawaka

Elkhart

Angola

Hammond

Portage

LaPorte

Goshen

Gary

Merrillville

Nappanee

Kendallville

Auburn

Crown Point

Valparaiso

Plymouth

Columbia City

Lowell

Warsaw

Rensselaer

Rochester

Eel

Fort Wayne

North Manchester

Huntington

Decatur

Monticello

Logansport

Peru

Wabash

Marion

Portland

Kokomo

Gas City

Hartford City

Lafayette

Frankfort

Elwood

Alexandria

Muncie

Winchester

INDIANA

Hoosier Hill 1,257 ft 383 m

Highest point in Indiana

Crawfordsville

Lebanon

Noblesville

Carmel

Anderson

New Castle

Lawrence

Greenfield

Richmond

Indianapolis

Beech Grove

Connersville

Plainfield

Clinton

Greencastle

Greenwood

Rushville

Terre Haute

Brazil

Franklin

Shelbyville

Martinsville

Greensburg

Columbus

U.S. center of population in 1900

Bloomington

BROWN COUNTY STATE PARK

Lawrenceburg

Linton

North Vernon

Seymour

BIG OAKS N.W.R.

MUSCATATUCK N.W.R.

Madison

HOOSIER

GEORGE ROGERS CLARK N.H.P.

Bedford

Scottsburg

Vincennes

Washington

Salem

NATIONAL

Charlestown

Jeffersonville

New Albany

Princeton

Jasper

Patoka Lake

FOREST

WYANDOTTE CAVE

Corydon

PATOKA RIVER N.W.R.

Huntingburg

Santa Claus

New Harmony S.H.S.

LINCOLN BOYHOOD NATIONAL MEMORIAL

Mount Vernon

Evansville

Boonville

Tell City

ILLINOIS

OHIO

KENTUCKY

MAP KEY

- ⊛ State capital
- ●●● City
- ■ Point of interest
- + Mountain peak
- / Dam
- ······ State boundary
- State Park unit
- National Park Service unit
- National Forest
- National Wildlife Refuge

0 ————— 50 miles
0 ————— 50 kilometers

Albers Conic Equal-Area Projection

IOWA

THE BASICS

Statehood
December 28, 1846; 29th state

Total area (land and water)
56,273 sq mi (145,746 sq km)

Land area
55,857 sq mi (144,669 sq km)

Population
3,156,145

Capital
Des Moines
Population 216,853

Largest city
Des Moines
Population 216,853

Racial/ethnic groups
91.1% white; 3.8% African American; 2.6% Asian; 0.5% Native American; 6.0% Hispanic (any race)

Foreign born
5.0%

Urban population
64.0%

Population density
56.5 per sq mi (21.8 per sq km)

GEO WHIZ

One of America's most famous houses is in Eldon. It was immortalized in Grant Wood's famous painting "American Gothic." The pitchfork-holding man and his wife shown in the art were not farmers at all. Wood's dentist and his sister posed for the painting.

Effigy Mounds National Monument, in northeast Iowa, is the only place in the country with such a large collection of mounds in the shapes of birds, mammals, and reptiles. Eastern Woodland Indians built these mounds from about 500 B.C. to A.D. 1300.

Iowa ranks second, after Texas, among U.S. wind energy producers.

WILD ROSE

AMERICAN
GOLDFINCH

Iowa

Iowa's earliest inhabitants built earthen mounds—some shaped like birds and bears—that are visible in the state's northeast. Nineteenth-century white settlers found rolling prairies covered by a sea of tall grasses that soon yielded to the plow. A decade after statehood in 1846, a group of religious German immigrants established the Amana Colonies, a communal society that still draws visitors. Blessed with ample precipitation and rich soils, Iowa is the heart of one of the world's most productive farming regions. The state is a major producer of corn, soybeans, hogs, and eggs. Much of the grain crop feeds livestock destined to reach dinner plates throughout the United States and around the world. An increasing amount of corn is used to make ethanol, which is mixed with gasoline to fuel cars and trucks. Two of the state's biggest industries are food processing and the manufacture of machinery. Des Moines, the capital and largest city, is a center of insurance and publishing.

◒ **PIG BUSINESS.**
Hogs outnumber people more than seven to one in Iowa. The state is the leading hog producer in the U.S.

◖ **CELEBRATING CULTURE.**
Young Meskwaki boys dance at a powwow near Tama. Such gatherings allow Native Americans to preserve their traditions.

SOUTH DAKOTA

Hawkeye Point +
1,670 ft
509 m
Highest point in Iowa

Sioux Center • Sheldon

Orange City •

Le Mars •

Big Sioux

Floyd

Missouri

Sioux City •

Little Sioux

• Onawa

NEBRASKA

DESOTO N.W.R.

Platte

680

680

Council Bluffs

80

Glenwood •

Missouri

1   2

THE HAWKEYE STATE:
IOWA

MINNESOTA

WISCONSIN

Spirit Lake
West Okoboji L.
East Okoboji Lake
Estherville
Spencer
Cherokee
Storm Lake

UNION SLOUGH N.W.R.
Forest City
Emmetsburg
Algona
Humboldt
Fort Dodge
Clear Lake
Mason City
Hampton
Webster City
Eldora

Winnebago
Iowa

Osage
Charles City
Waverly
Oelwein
Iowa Falls
Cedar Falls
Waterloo
Independence

Cresco
Decorah
Waukon
New Hampton

Shell Rock
Cedar
Wapsipinicon

Upper Iowa
Mississippi

EFFIGY MOUNDS N.M.

UPPER MISSISSIPPI RIVER NATIONAL WILDLIFE AND FISH REFUGE

Turkey
Manchester
Dyersville
Dubuque
ILLINOIS

Maquoketa
Monticello
Anamosa
Maquoketa
Clinton
De Witt
Bettendorf
Davenport

Central City
Marion
Cedar Rapids

Vinton
SAC AND FOX/ MESKWAKI INDIAN RESERVATION
Tama

AMANA COLONIES

Cedar
Iowa

HERBERT HOOVER N.H.S.
Coralville
Iowa City
Muscatine

PORT LOUISA N.W.R.

I O W A

Carroll
Denison
Jefferson
Story City
Boone
Ames
Nevada
Perry
Ankeny
Urbandale
Windsor Heights
West Des Moines
Des Moines
Newton
Grinnell
Marshalltown

NEAL SMITH N.W.R.

Harlan
Atlantic
Winterset
Indianola
Knoxville
Pella
Oskaloosa
Washington
Lake Red Rock

Red Oak
Creston
Osceola
Chariton
Ottumwa
Eldon
Fairfield
Mount Pleasant
Rathbun Lake
Chariton
Des Moines

Shenandoah
Clarinda
Blanchard
Bedford
Centerville
Bloomfield
Fort Madison
Burlington

Keokuk

MISSOURI

North Raccoon
Boyer
E. Nodaway
Thompson

Des Moines

MAP KEY

⭐ State capital
●●● City
⬛ Point of interest
＋ Mountain peak
／ Dam
···· State boundary
▨ Indian Reservation
▨ National Park Service unit
▨ National Wildlife Refuge

0 ———— 25 miles
0 ———— 25 kilometers
Albers Conic Equal-Area Projection

GREEN ENERGY

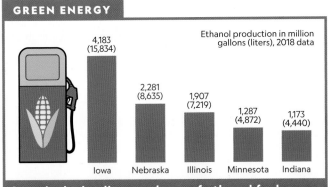

Ethanol production in million gallons (liters), 2018 data

4,183 (15,834) — Iowa
2,281 (8,635) — Nebraska
1,907 (7,219) — Illinois
1,287 (4,872) — Minnesota
1,173 (4,440) — Indiana

Iowa is the leading producer of ethanol fuel, a clean-burning, renewable, non-fossil fuel energy source made mainly from corn.

⬭ **FITNESS RALLY.** Cyclists pass a farm community during the Annual Great Bicycle Ride Across Iowa. Begun in 1973, it is the oldest and longest recreational bicycle event in the world.

KANSAS

THE BASICS

Statehood
January 29, 1861; 34th state

Total area (land and water)
82,278 sq mi (213,100 sq km)

Land area
81,759 sq mi (211,754 sq km)

Population
2,911,505

Capital
Topeka
Population 125,904

Largest city
Wichita
Population 389,255

Racial/ethnic groups
86.5% white; 6.2% African
American; 3.1% Asian; 1.2%
Native American; 11.9%
Hispanic (any race)

Foreign born
7.0%

Urban population
74.2%

Population density
35.6 per sq mi (13.7 per sq km)

GEO WHIZ

**Plesiosaur skeletons and
many other marine reptile
fossils have been unearthed
in Kansas.**

**The Tallgrass Prairie National
Preserve, one of the last great
expanses of tallgrass prairie, is
in the Flint Hills.**

**Lindsborg is proud of its
Swedish heritage and the fact
that it is home to the Anatoly
Karpov International School
of Chess, named for the
Russian who succeeded
American Bobby Fischer
as world champion in 1975.**

SUNFLOWER

WESTERN MEADOWLARK

Kansas

Considered by the government to be unsuitable for settlement, Kansas was made part of Indian Territory—a vast tract of land between Missouri and the Rockies—in the 1830s. By the 1850s white settlers were fighting Native Americans for more land and among themselves over the issue of slavery. In 1861 Kansas entered the Union as a free state. After the Civil War, cowboys drove Texas cattle to the Wild West railroad towns of Abilene and Dodge City, where waiting trains hauled cattle to slaughterhouses in the East. Today, the state remains a major producer of beef, oil and natural gas wells dot the landscape, and factories in Wichita make aircraft equipment. Heading west toward the High Plains and the Rockies in neighboring Colorado, the elevation gradually increases, and the climate becomes drier. Threats of fierce thunderstorms accompanied by tornadoes have many Kansans keeping an eye on the sky.

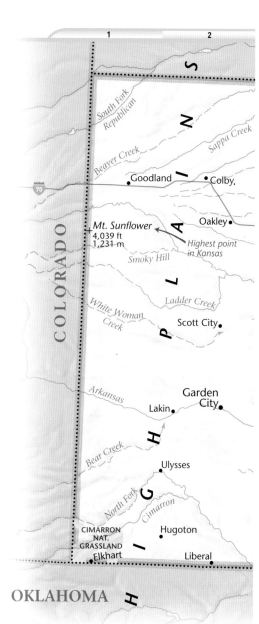

◗ **OMINOUS SKY.** Lightning splits the sky as black clouds of a thunderstorm roll across a field of wheat. Such storms bring heavy rain and often spawn dangerous tornadoes.

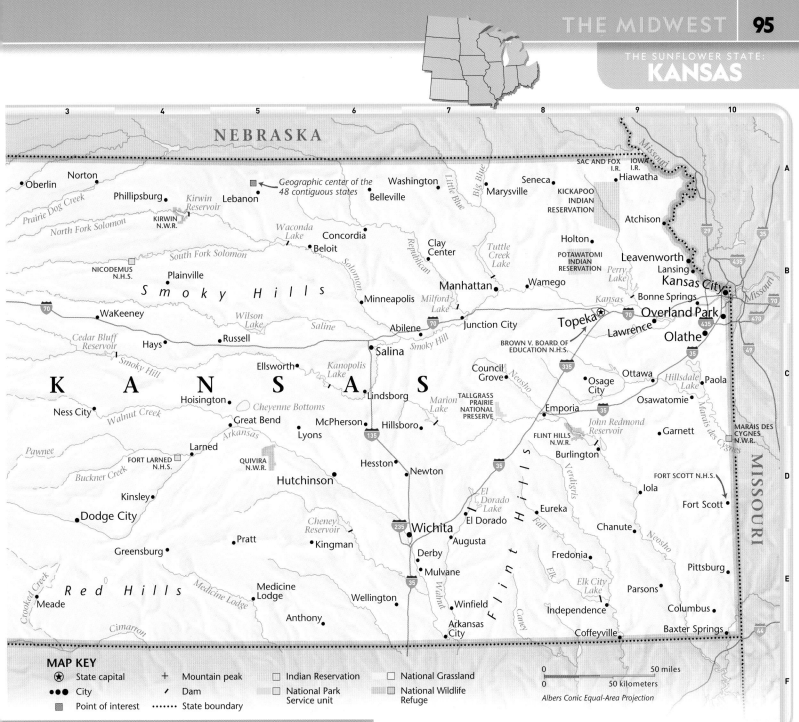

NEBRASKA

3   4   5   6   7   8   9   10

Oberlin • Norton • Washington • Seneca • SAC AND FOX I.R. • IOWA I.R. • Hiawatha

Phillipsburg • Kirwin Reservoir • Lebanon • Belleville • Marysville • KICKAPOO INDIAN RESERVATION • Atchison

Geographic center of the 48 contiguous states

Prairie Dog Creek

KIRWIN N.W.R.

North Fork Solomon

Waconda Lake • Concordia • Beloit • Clay Center • Tuttle Creek Lake • Holton • POTAWATOMI INDIAN RESERVATION • Leavenworth • Lansing

South Fork Solomon

NICODEMUS N.H.S. • Plainville • Manhattan • Wamego • Perry Lake • Kansas City

S m o k y   H i l l s

WaKeeney • Wilson Lake • Minneapolis • Milford Lake • Kansas • Bonne Springs • Overland Park

Cedar Bluff Reservoir • Hays • Russell • Saline • Abilene • Junction City • Topeka • Lawrence • Olathe

Smoky Hill • BROWN V. BOARD OF EDUCATION N.H.S.

K A N S A S • Salina • Ellsworth • Kanopolis Lake • Council Grove • Osage City • Ottawa • Hillsdale Lake • Paola

Ness City • Walnut Creek • Hoisington • Cheyenne Bottoms • Lindsborg • Marion Lake • TALLGRASS PRAIRIE NATIONAL PRESERVE • Emporia • Osawatomie

Pawnee • Great Bend • McPherson • Hillsboro • FLINT HILLS N.W.R. • Garnett • MARAIS DES CYGNES N.W.R.

Arkansas • Lyons • John Redmond Reservoir

Larned • QUIVIRA N.W.R. • Hesston • Newton • Burlington • FORT SCOTT N.H.S.

FORT LARNED N.H.S. • Iola • Fort Scott

Buckner Creek • Kinsley • Hutchinson • El Dorado Lake • Eureka • Chanute

Dodge City • Cheney Reservoir • Wichita • El Dorado • Fredonia • Pittsburg

Greensburg • Pratt • Kingman • Augusta • Derby • Independence • Parsons • Columbus

R e d   H i l l s • Medicine Lodge • Mulvane • Elk City Lake

Meade • Medicine Lodge • Wellington • Winfield • Coffeyville • Baxter Springs

Cimarron • Anthony • Arkansas City

F l i n t   H i l l s

Verdigris • Neosho • Fall • Walnut • Elk • Caney

MISSOURI

MAP KEY
- ⊛ State capital
- ●●● City
- ▣ Point of interest
- + Mountain peak
- ⟋ Dam
- ▢ Indian Reservation
- ▢ National Park Service unit
- ▢ National Grassland
- ▣ National Wildlife Refuge
- •••••• State boundary

0 — 50 miles
0 — 50 kilometers
Albers Conic Equal-Area Projection

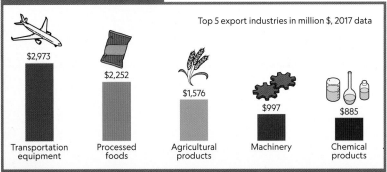

Top 5 export industries in million $, 2017 data

- Transportation equipment — $2,973
- Processed foods — $2,252
- Agricultural products — $1,576
- Machinery — $997
- Chemical products — $885

Participation in the global economy earns Kansas more than $11 billion each year. Top markets are Canada and Mexico. Aircraft and processed meat products make up much of its export sales.

◑ **MODERN-DAY COWBOYS.** Dodge City traces its history to Fort Dodge, built on the Santa Fe Trail in 1865 to protect pioneer wagon trains and the mail service from attacks by outlaws or bands of Native Americans. The town, frequented by cattle herders and bison hunters, was known for its lawlessness.

THE BASICS

Statehood
January 26, 1837; 26th state

Total area (land and water)
96,714 sq mi (250,487 sq km)

Land area
56,539 sq mi (146,435 sq km)

Population
9,995,915

Capital
Lansing
Population 118,427

Largest city
Detroit
Population 672,662

Racial/ethnic groups
79.4% white; 14.1% African American; 3.2% Asian; 0.7% Native American; 5.1% Hispanic (any race)

Foreign born
6.6%

Urban population
74.6%

Population density
176.8 per sq mi (68.3 per sq km)

GEO WHIZ

Researchers at the Seney National Wildlife Refuge on the Upper Peninsula have discovered that loons change their call as they move to different territories.

The Great Lakes, which contain 20 percent of Earth's freshwater, are at risk due to industrial and municipal dumping and agricultural runoff.

Michigan

Native Americans had friendly relations with early French fur traders who came to what is now Michigan, but they waged battles with the British who later assumed control. Completion of New York's Erie Canal in 1825 made it easier for settlers to reach the area, and statehood came in 1837. Michigan consists of two large peninsulas that border four of the five Great Lakes—Erie, Huron, Michigan, and Superior. Most of the population is on the state's Lower Peninsula, while the Upper Peninsula, once a productive mining area, now is popular among vacationing nature lovers. The five-mile (8-km)-long Mackinac Bridge has linked the peninsulas since 1957. In the 20th century Michigan became the center of the American auto industry, and the state's fortunes have risen and fallen with those of major car companies. Though it remains a big producer of cars and trucks, the state is working to diversify its economy. Michigan's farms grow crops ranging from grains to fruits and vegetables.

⊝ **ASSEMBLY LINE.** For more than 100 years the Ford Motor Company's Rouge Complex in Dearborn has been a leader in motor vehicle production, which is a major part of the state economy. Today, the plant turns out a truck every 53 seconds.

APPLE BLOSSOM

ROBIN

DRIVING FORCE

$39,283

Top 5 manufacturing sectors in million $, 2016 data

$7,823 $7,789 $7,524 $6,156

Motor vehicles & parts   Machinery   Fabricated metal products   Chemical products   Food, beverage, & tobacco products

Once the main hub of automotive production in the U.S., Michigan is still among the top auto manufacturing states.

⊝ **REFLECTION OF THE PAST.** Victorian-style summer homes, built on Mackinac Island in the late 19th century by wealthy railroad families, now welcome vacationers to the island. To protect the environment, cars are not allowed.

THE GREAT LAKE STATE:
MICHIGAN

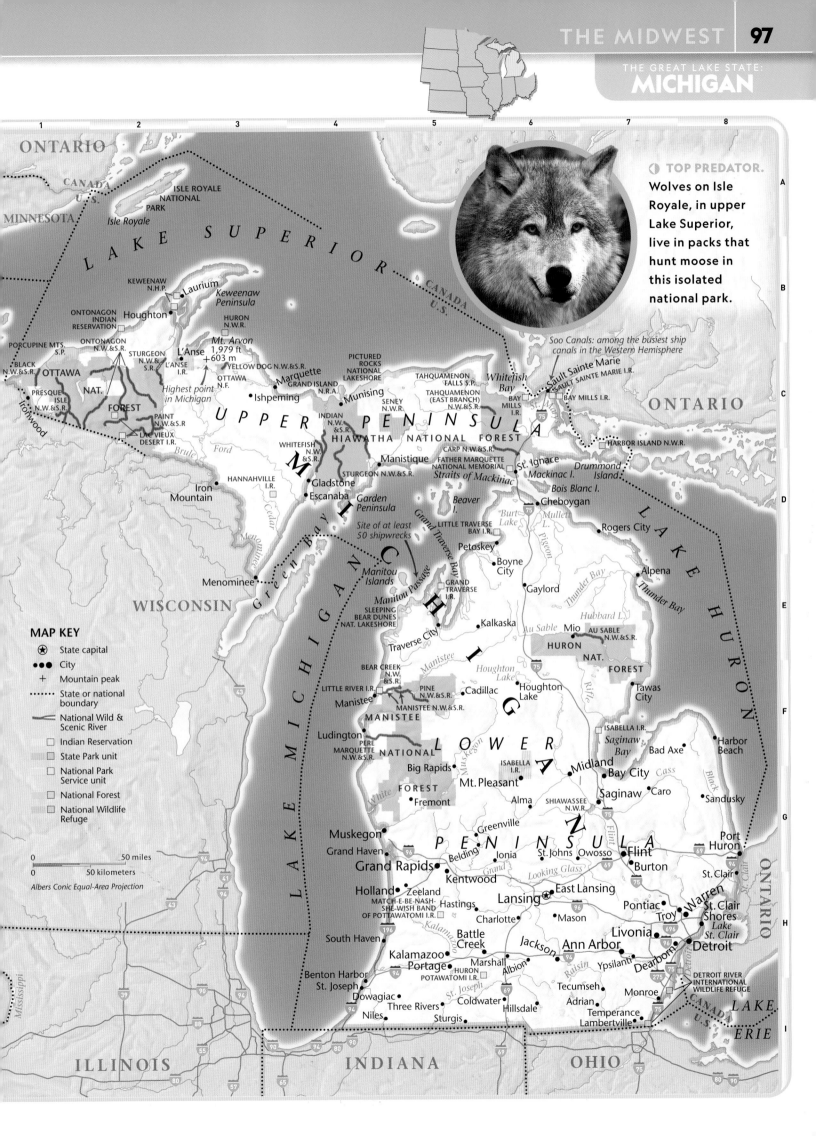

ONTARIO

CANADA
U.S.

MINNESTA

LAKE SUPERIOR

ISLE ROYALE
NATIONAL
PARK

Isle Royale

KEWEENAW
N.H.P. • Laurium
ONTONAGON   Keweenaw
INDIAN   • Houghton   Peninsula
RESERVATION
HURON
PORCUPINE MTS.   N.W.R.
S.P.   ONTONAGON
N.W.&S.R.   Mt. Arvon
BLACK   STURGEON   1,979 ft
N.W.&S.R. OTTAWA N.W.&   L'Anse +603 m
S.R. • L'Anse
N.W.&S.R.   I.R.
PRESQUE   NAT.   OTTAWA   Highest point
ISLE   N.F.   in Michigan
N.W.&S.R.   FOREST
Ironwood   PAINT
N.W.&S.R. WHITEFISH
LAC VIEUX   N.W.
DESERT I.R. &S.R.

TOP PREDATOR.

Wolves on Isle
Royale, in upper
Lake Superior,
live in packs that
hunt moose in
this isolated
national park.

Soo Canals: among the busiest ship
canals in the Western Hemisphere

PICTURED
ROCKS
NATIONAL
LAKESHORE
• Marquette
GRAND ISLAND   TAHQUAMENON
N.R.A.   SENEY   FALLS S.P.   Whitefish
• Ishpeming • Munising   N.W.R.   TAHQUAMENON   Bay
INDIAN   (EAST BRANCH)   BAY
N.W.   N.W.&S.R.   MILLS   Sault Sainte Marie
&S.R.   I.R.   SAULT SAINTE MARIE I.R.
CARP N.W.&S.R.   St. BAY MILLS I.R.

UPPER PENINSULA
HIAWATHA NATIONAL FOREST   FATHER MARQUETTE
NATIONAL MEMORIAL   St. Ignace
HANNAHVILLE   • Manistique   Straits of Mackinac   Mackinac I.
I.R.   STURGEON N.W.&S.R.   Bois Blanc I.
• Gladstone   Beaver
Iron   • Escanaba   Garden   I.
Mountain   Peninsula
Site of at least   LITTLE TRAVERSE
50 shipwrecks   BAY I.R.   Burt
Manitou   L.
Islands   Petoskey
Menominee • GREEN BAY   Manitou   Boyne
Passage   GRAND   City
WISCONSIN   Manitou   TRAVERSE
Islands   I.R.   Gaylord
SLEEPING
BEAR DUNES
NAT. LAKESHORE
Kalkaska
Traverse City   Au Sable   Mio
HURON
BEAR CREEK   Houghton NAT.
N.W.   Manistee   Lake   FOREST
&S.R.   PINE
LITTLE RIVER I.R. N.W.   Cadillac Houghton
Manistee •   &S.R.   Lake
MANISTEE N.W.&S.R.
MANISTEE
Ludington •
PERE   LOWER
MARQUETTE   NATIONAL
N.W.&S.R.
Big Rapids •   ISABELLA
Mt. Pleasant • I.R.   Midland
FOREST   Alma •
Fremont •   SHIAWASSEE
N.W.R.
Greenville •
Muskegon •
Grand Haven •   Belding •   Ionia   St. Johns Owosso
Grand Rapids •   PENINSULA
Kentwood •   Grand
Holland • Zeeland •
MATCH-E-BE-NASH-   Hastings •   Lansing
SHE-WISH BAND
OF POTTAWATOMI I.R.   Charlotte •   • Mason
South Haven •   Battle   Jackson
Kalamazoo • Creek
Portage •   Marshall • Albion
Benton Harbor •   HURON
St. Joseph • POTAWATOMI I.R.
Dowagiac •
Three Rivers • Coldwater • Hillsdale
Niles •   Sturgis •

Rogers City •

Alpena •
LAKE HURON
Thunder Bay
Thunder Bay
Hubbard L.
AU SABLE
N.W.&S.R.
Tawas
City •
ISABELLA I.R.
Saginaw
Bay   Bad Axe •   Harbor
Beach •
Bay City •
Saginaw • Caro •
• Sandusky
Port
Flint • Huron •
Burton •
East Lansing   St. Clair •
Pontiac • St. Clair
Troy •   Shores
Livonia • Warren •
Ypsilanti •   Troy • St. Clair
Ann Arbor •   Dearborn • Detroit •
Tecumseh • Monroe •
Adrian •   DETROIT RIVER
INTERNATIONAL
Lambertville • WILDLIFE REFUGE
Temperance •

DRUMMOND
Island
HARBOR ISLAND N.W.R.
ONTARIO

ONTARIO

LAKE
ST. CLAIR

CANADA
U.S.
LAKE
ERIE

MAP KEY

★ State capital
••• City
+ Mountain peak
····· State or national
boundary
National Wild &
Scenic River
▫ Indian Reservation
▫ State Park unit
▫ National Park
Service unit
▫ National Forest
▫ National Wildlife
Refuge

0   50 miles
0   50 kilometers
Albers Conic Equal-Area Projection

ILLINOIS   INDIANA   OHIO

THE BASICS

Statehood
May 11, 1858; 32nd state

Total area (land and water)
86,936 sq mi (225,163 sq km)

Land area
79,627 sq mi (206,232 sq km)

Population
5,611,179

Capital
St. Paul
Population 307,695

Largest city
Minneapolis
Population 425,403

Racial/ethnic groups
84.4% white; 6.5% African American; 5.1% Asian; 1.4% Native American; 5.4% Hispanic (any race)

Foreign born
8.2%

Urban population
73.3%

Population density
70.5 per sq mi (27.2 per sq km)

GEO WHIZ

The Mayo Clinic, a world-famous medical research center, is in Rochester.

The Boundary Waters Canoe Area Wilderness was the first U.S. wilderness area set aside for canoeing.

COMMON LOON
SHOWY LADY'S SLIPPER

Minnesota

French fur traders began arriving in present-day Minnesota in the mid-17th century. Statehood was established in 1858, and most remaining Native Americans were forced from the state after a decisive battle in 1862. During the late 1800s, large numbers of Scandinavians, Germans, and other immigrants settled a land rich in wildlife, timber, minerals, and fertile soils. Today, farming is concentrated in the south and west. In the northeast, the Mesabi Range's open-pit mines make the state the country's leading source of iron ore. Most of the ore is shipped from Duluth. Both Duluth and nearby Superior in Wisconsin (see page 111) are leading Great Lakes ports. From these ports, ships can reach the Atlantic Ocean via the St. Lawrence Seaway. Scattered across the state's landscape are thousands of lakes—ancient footprints of retreating glaciers—that draw anglers and canoeists. One of those lakes, Lake Itasca, is the source of the mighty Mississippi River, which flows through the Twin Cities of Minneapolis and St. Paul.

◯ SUMMER FUN. Lake Calhoun, also known by its Dakota name Bde Maka Ska, which means "White Earth Lake," is surrounded by a Minneapolis city park that is popular with bikers and pedestrians.

SHOPPER'S PARADISE

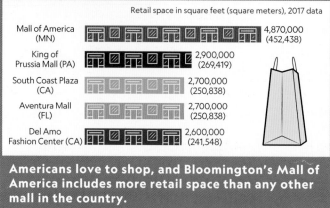

Retail space in square feet (square meters), 2017 data

Mall		Retail space
Mall of America (MN)		4,870,000 (452,438)
King of Prussia Mall (PA)		2,900,000 (269,419)
South Coast Plaza (CA)		2,700,000 (250,838)
Aventura Mall (FL)		2,700,000 (250,838)
Del Amo Fashion Center (CA)		2,600,000 (241,548)

Americans love to shop, and Bloomington's Mall of America includes more retail space than any other mall in the country.

◖ INLAND PORT. Duluth, on the northern shore of Lake Superior, is the westernmost deep-water port on the St. Lawrence Seaway. Barges and container ships move products such as iron ore and grain along the Great Lakes to the Atlantic Ocean and to markets around the world.

1 2 3 4 5 6 7 8

The "Northwest Angle" is the northernmost point in the 48 contiguous states

MANITOBA

CANADA
U.S.

RED LAKE
INDIAN RES.

Lake of the Woods

Rainy Lake

ONTARIO

• Hallock   • Roseau

Roseau

Baudette

International Falls

Rainy

Namakan Lake

VOYAGEURS NATIONAL

PARK

RED LAKE INDIAN RES.

Big Fork

BOIS FORTE (NETT LAKE) I.R.

Vermilion Lake

Highest point in Minnesota

AGASSIZ N.W.R.

Mud Lake

Upper Red Lake

BOUNDARY WATERS CANOE AREA WILDERNESS

CANADA
U.S.

• Warren

RED LAKE INDIAN RESERVATION

Eagle Mt. + 2,301 ft 701 m

GRAND PORTAGE I.R.

GRAND PORTAGE NAT. MON.

Thief River Falls

Red Lake

Lower Red Lake

BOIS FORTE (VERMILION LAKE) I.R.

Ely SUPERIOR

• East Grand Forks

Crookston

RYDELL N.W.R.

Red Lake

BOIS FORTE (DEER CREEK) I.R.

Grand Marais

GLACIAL RIDGE N.W.R.

Source of the Mississippi River

Red Lake

Winnibigoshish Lake

CHIPPEWA

Mesabi Range

NATIONAL

• Virginia

Chisholm

LAKE SUPERIOR

• Bemidji

WHITE EARTH INDIAN RESERVATION

Lake Itasca

NATIONAL

LEECH LAKE INDIAN RES.

Mississippi

Hibbing

FOREST

• Grand Rapids

HAMDEN SLOUGH N.W.R.

TAMARAC N.W.R.

Walker

Leech Lake

FOREST

St. Louis

Two Harbors

MICHIGAN

Moorhead

• Detroit Lakes

Park Rapids

MILLE LACS I.R.

FOND DU LAC I.R.

Duluth

• Menahga

Mississippi

Superior

Pelican Rapids

• Perham

Crow Wing

RICE LAKE N.W.R.

Cloquet Proctor

• Wadena

Aitkin

Mille Lacs Lake

MINNESOTA

Fergus Falls

Otter Tail Lake

• Brainerd

Otter Tail

Sandstone

ST. CROIX

MILLE LACS I.R.

St. Croix

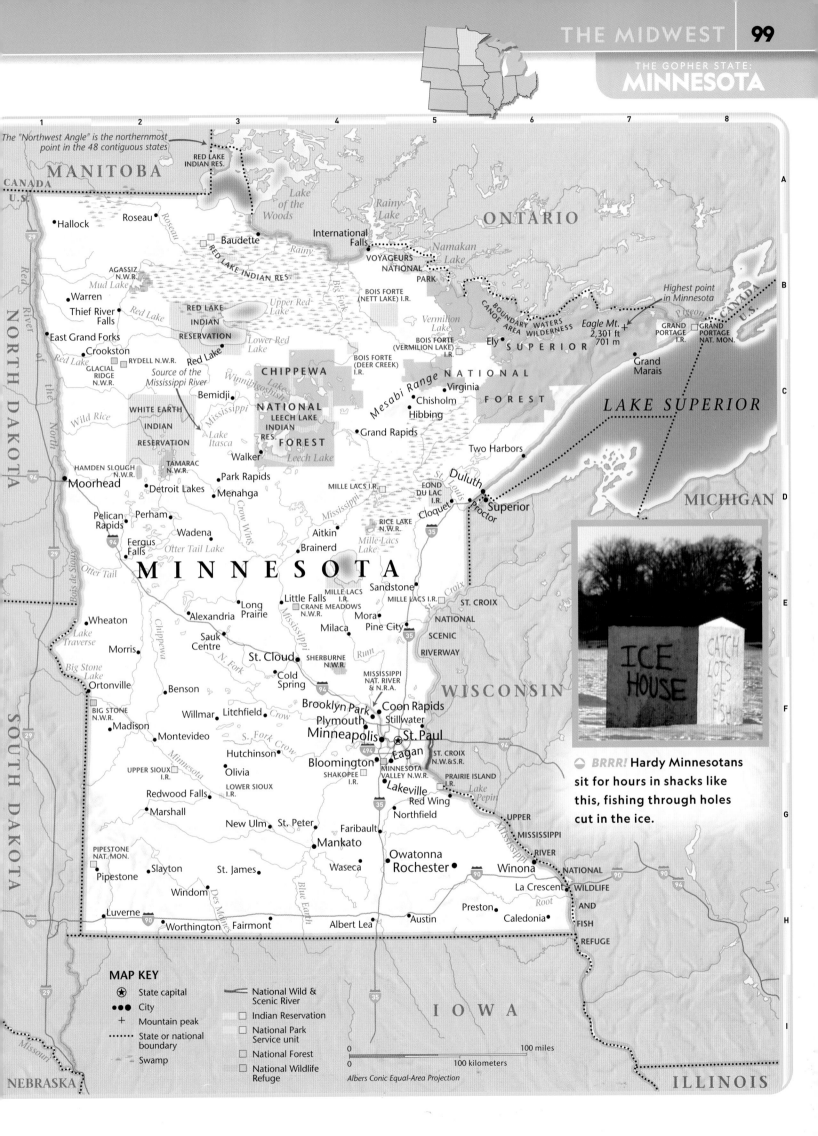

• Wheaton

Long Prairie

Little Falls

MILLE LACS I.R.

ST. CROIX

• Alexandria

CRANE MEADOWS N.W.R.

Mora

NATIONAL

Lake Traverse

• Morris

Sauk Centre

Milaca

Pine City

SCENIC

Big Stone Lake

St. Cloud

SHERBURNE N.W.R.

Rum

RIVERWAY

• Ortonville

Benson

Cold Spring

MISSISSIPPI NAT. RIVER & N.R.A.

WISCONSIN

BIG STONE N.W.R.

• Willmar

Litchfield

Crow

Brooklyn Park Coon Rapids

• Madison

Plymouth

Stillwater

ICE HOUSE CATCH LOTS OF FISH

Montevideo

Hutchinson

Minneapolis **St. Paul**

S. Fork Crow

Eagan

ST. CROIX N.W.&S.R.

UPPER SIOUX I.R.

Olivia

Bloomington

MINNESOTA VALLEY N.W.R.

Minnesota

SHAKOPEE I.R.

PRAIRIE ISLAND I.R.

Redwood Falls

LOWER SIOUX I.R.

Lakeville

Lake Pepin

• Marshall

New Ulm

St. Peter

Red Wing

UPPER

PIPESTONE NAT. MON.

Faribault

Northfield

MISSISSIPPI

• Slayton

St. James

Mankato

RIVER

Pipestone

Waseca

Owatonna

Windom

Blue Earth

Rochester

Winona

NATIONAL

Des Moines

La Crescent

WILDLIFE

• Luverne

Preston

Caledonia

AND

Worthington Fairmont

Albert Lea

Austin

Root

FISH

SOUTH DAKOTA

NORTH DAKOTA

REFUGE

🛑 **BRRR!** Hardy Minnesotans sit for hours in shacks like this, fishing through holes cut in the ice.

MAP KEY

⭐ State capital
●●● City
+ Mountain peak
•••• State or national boundary
〰 Swamp

⎯ National Wild & Scenic River
▢ Indian Reservation
▢ National Park Service unit
▢ National Forest
▢ National Wildlife Refuge

0   100 miles
0   100 kilometers

Albers Conic Equal-Area Projection

NEBRASKA   **IOWA**   **ILLINOIS**

Missouri

TALL HATS. Since its founding in 1865 in St. Joseph, the Stetson Company has been associated with Western hats worn by men and women around the world.

The Osage people were among the largest Native American tribes in present-day Missouri when the French began establishing permanent settlements in the 1700s. The United States obtained the territory as part of the 1803 Louisiana Purchase, and Lewis and Clark began exploring the vast wilderness by paddling up the Missouri River from the St. Louis area. Missouri entered the Union as a slave state in 1821. Though it remained in the Union during the Civil War, sympathies were split between the North and South. For much of the 1800s the state was the staging ground for pioneers traveling to western frontiers on the Santa Fe and Oregon Trails. Today, Missouri leads the country in lead mining. Farmers raise cattle, hogs, poultry, corn, and soybeans. Cotton and rice are grown in the southeastern Bootheel region. Cross-state riverport rivals St. Louis and Kansas City are centers of transportation, manufacturing, and finance. Scenic views, lakes, caves, and Branson's country music shows bring many tourists to the Ozarks.

THE BASICS

Statehood
August 10, 1821; 24th state

Total area (land and water)
69,707 sq mi (180,540 sq km)

Land area
68,742 sq mi (178,040 sq km)

Population
6,126,452

Capital
Jefferson City
Population 42,838

Largest city
Kansas City
Population 491,918

Racial/ethnic groups
83.1% white; 11.8% African American; 2.1% Asian; 0.6% Native American; 4.2% Hispanic (any race)

Foreign born
4.0%

Urban population
70.4%

Population density
89.1 per sq mi (34.4 per sq km)

GEO WHIZ

Camp Wood, near St. Louis, was the starting point for Lewis and Clark's Corps of Discovery, commissioned by President Thomas Jefferson to seek a water route to the Pacific. Along the way they encountered hundreds of new plants and animal species, nearly 50 native tribes, and the Rocky Mountains.

In Ash Grove, near Springfield, Father Moses Berry has turned his family history into a museum for slavery education. The museum is the only one of its kind in the Ozark region.

EASTERN BLUEBIRD

HAWTHORN

NATIONAL LANDMARK. Named a national historic landmark in 1987, the steel and concrete Gateway Arch is the tallest arch in the world. Here it frames St. Louis and the Mississippi River.

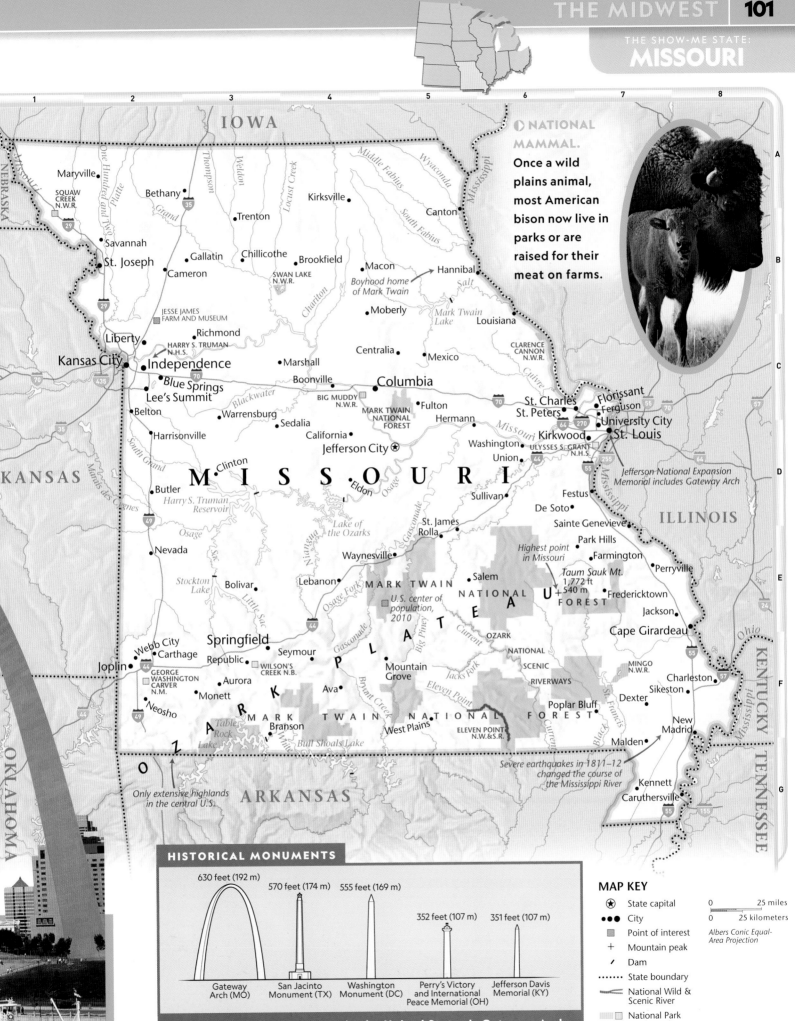

IOWA
NEBRASKA
KANSAS
OKLAHOMA
ARKANSAS
ILLINOIS
KENTUCKY
TENNESSEE

MISSOURI

Maryville
SQUAW CREEK N.W.R.
Bethany
Trenton
Kirksville
Canton
Savannah
Gallatin
Chillicothe
Brookfield
Macon
Hannibal
St. Joseph
Cameron
SWAN LAKE N.W.R.
JESSE JAMES FARM AND MUSEUM
Boyhood home of Mark Twain
Moberly
Louisiana
Liberty
Richmond
HARRY S. TRUMAN N.H.S.
CLARENCE CANNON N.W.R.
Kansas City
Independence
Marshall
Centralia
Mexico
Blue Springs
Boonville
Columbia
St. Charles
Florissant
Lee's Summit
BIG MUDDY N.W.R.
Fulton
St. Peters
Ferguson
Belton
Warrensburg
Sedalia
MARK TWAIN NATIONAL FOREST
Hermann
University City
Harrisonville
California
Washington
Kirkwood
St. Louis
Jefferson City
Union
ULYSSES S. GRANT N.H.S.
Clinton
Eldon
Sullivan
Jefferson National Expansion Memorial includes Gateway Arch
Butler
Harry S. Truman Reservoir
Festus
De Soto
Lake of the Ozarks
St. James
Sainte Genevieve
Nevada
Rolla
Park Hills
Highest point in Missouri
Farmington
Perryville
Stockton Lake
Bolivar
Lebanon
Waynesville
Salem
Taum Sauk Mt. 1,772 ft +540 m
Fredericktown
U.S. center of population, 2010
NATIONAL
Jackson
Springfield
Seymour
Mountain Grove
OZARK
Cape Girardeau
Webb City
Carthage
Republic
WILSON'S CREEK N.B.
NATIONAL SCENIC RIVERWAYS
MINGO N.W.R.
Joplin
GEORGE WASHINGTON CARVER N.M.
Aurora
Ava
Charleston
Sikeston
Monett
MARK TWAIN NATIONAL FOREST
Dexter
Neosho
Table Rock Lake
Branson
West Plains
ELEVEN POINT N.W.&S.R.
Poplar Bluff
New Madrid
Bull Shoals Lake
Malden
Severe earthquakes in 1811–12 changed the course of the Mississippi River
Kennett
Only extensive highlands in the central U.S.
Caruthersville

MISSOURI PLATEAU
Current
Jacks Fork
Eleven Point
Bryant Creek
St. Francis
Black
Ohio
Mississippi

○ NATIONAL MAMMAL.
Once a wild plains animal, most American bison now live in parks or are raised for their meat on farms.

HISTORICAL MONUMENTS

630 feet (192 m) — Gateway Arch (MO)
570 feet (174 m) — San Jacinto Monument (TX)
555 feet (169 m) — Washington Monument (DC)
352 feet (107 m) — Perry's Victory and International Peace Memorial (OH)
351 feet (107 m) — Jefferson Davis Memorial (KY)

The tallest of all monuments in the United States is Gateway Arch in St. Louis, which was the departure point for westward-bound pioneers during the 19th century.

MAP KEY

⍟ State capital
●●● City
▪ Point of interest
+ Mountain peak
⟋ Dam
······· State boundary
～ National Wild & Scenic River
▨ National Park Service unit
▨ National Forest
▨ National Wildlife Refuge

0   25 miles
0   25 kilometers
Albers Conic Equal-Area Projection

THE BASICS

Statehood
March 1, 1867; 37th state

Total area (land and water)
77,348 sq mi (200,330 sq km)

Land area
**76,824 sq mi
(198,974 sq km)**

Population
1,929,268

Capital
**Lincoln
Population 287,401**

Largest city
**Omaha
Population 468,262**

Racial/ethnic groups
**88.6% white; 5.1% African
American; 2.6% Asian; 1.5%
Native American; 11.0%
Hispanic (any race)**

Foreign born
6.9%

Urban population
73.1%

Population density
25.1 per sq mi (9.7 per sq km)

GEO WHIZ

**Many of Nebraska's early
white settlers were called
sodbusters because they cut
chunks of the grassy prairie
(sod) to build their houses.
These building blocks became
known as "Nebraska marble."**

**Nebraska's state fossil is the
mammoth. The state estimates
that as many as 10 of these
prehistoric elephants are
buried beneath an average
square mile of territory.**

**Boys Town, a village-style
community founded near
Omaha in 1917 as a home
for troubled boys, has
provided a haven for girls,
too, since 1979.**

GOLDENROD

WESTERN
MEADOWLARK

Nebraska

For thousands of westbound pioneers on the Oregon and California Trails, Scotts Bluff and Chimney Rock were unforgettable landmarks, towering above the North Platte River. Much of the Nebraska Territory was reserved by the U.S. government for Native Americans, who hunted bison and farmed there, but in 1854 Nebraska was opened to settlers from the East. Following statehood in 1867, ranchers clashed with farmers in an unsuccessful bid to preserve open rangelands. Today, farms and ranches cover nearly all of the state. Ranchers graze beef cattle on the grass-covered Sand Hills, and farmers grow corn, soybeans, and wheat elsewhere. The vast underground Ogallala Aquifer feeds center-pivot irrigation systems needed to water crops in areas that do not receive enough rain. Processing the state's farm products, especially meatpacking, is a big part of the economy. Omaha, which sits along the Missouri River, is a center of finance, insurance, and agribusiness. Lincoln, the state capital, has the only unicameral, or one-house, legislature in the country.

◒ TAKING FLIGHT.
**Migratory sandhill
cranes pass through
in late winter, stop-
ping in the Platte
River Valley to feed
and rest.**

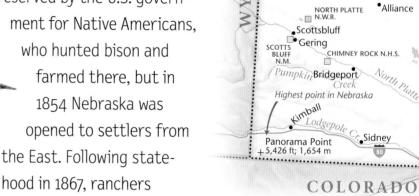

**◐ RIDER DOWN. The
Big Rodeo is an annual
event in tiny Burwell
(population 1,191) in
Nebraska's Sand Hills.
The town, sometimes
called "the place where
the Wild West meets
the 21st century," has
hosted the rodeo for
more than 80 years.**

MAP KEY

⊛	State capital
••••	City
■	Point of interest
+	Mountain peak
⫻	Dam
⋯⋯	State boundary
〜	National Wild & Scenic River
☐	Indian Reservation
☐	State Park unit
☐	National Park Service unit
☐	National Forest
☐	National Grassland
☐	National Wildlife Refuge

0 ____ 25 miles
0 ____ 25 kilometers
Albers Conic Equal-Area Projection

SOUTH DAKOTA

Gordon
Rushville
Valentine
FORT NIOBRARA N.W.R.
NIOBRARA NATIONAL SCENIC RIVER
SAMUEL R. McKELVIE NATIONAL FOREST
Ainsworth
Atkinson
O'Neill
Hartington
SANTEE INDIAN RES.
South Sioux City
VALENTINE N.W.R.
JOHN W. AND LOUISE SEIER N.W.R.
20,000 square miles of grass-covered dunes, the largest such area in North America
Holt Creek
Wayne
WINNEBAGO I.R.
Neligh
Pender
OMAHA I.R.
Mullen
Norfolk
Calamus Reservoir
Madison
West Point
CRESCENT LAKE N.W.R.
NEBRASKA NAT. FOREST
Dismal
Burwell
Tekamah
Blair
DE SOTO N.W.R.
BOYER CHUTE N.W.R.
NEBRASKA
Ord
Albion
Schuyler
Columbus
Fremont
Broken Bow
Wild West Show began in 1883
St. Paul
Fullerton
David City
Wahoo
Omaha
President Ford's birthplace
Lake C.W. McConaughy
North Platte
Central City
Papillion
Bellevue
Plattsmouth
Ogallala
BUFFALO BILL S.H.P.
Ravenna
Grand Island
Aurora
York
Seward
Ashland
Waverly
Grant
Gothenburg
Cozad
Gibbon
NINE-MILE PRAIRIE
Lincoln
Nebraska City
Largest mammoth fossil ever found, 1922
Lexington
Kearney
Milford
IOWA
Imperial
Hugh Butler Lake
Hastings
Crete
Minden
Holdrege
Geneva
Wilber
Auburn
Cambridge
HOMESTEAD NAT. MON. OF AMERICA
Beatrice
McCook
Hebron
Fairbury
Falls City
Swanson Res.
Alma
Harlan County Lake
Red Cloud
Superior
SAC AND FOX I.R.
IOWA I.R.

MISSOURI

KANSAS

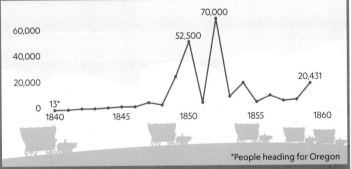

WESTWARD BOUND

70,000
60,000
52,500
40,000
20,000
20,431
0
13*
1840   1845   1850   1855   1860

*People heading for Oregon

Pioneers crossed Nebraska during the 19th century on their way to Oregon. Traffic varied due to cholera epidemics and conflicts with Native Americans.

◖ **THE WAY WEST.** Longhorn cattle and a bison stand knee-deep in grass below Chimney Rock, which rises more than 300 feet (91 m) above western Nebraska's rolling landscape. An important landmark on the Oregon Trail for 19th-century westbound pioneers and now a national historic site, the formation is being worn away by forces of erosion.

THE BASICS

Statehood
November 2, 1889; 39th state

Total area (land and water)
70,698 sq mi
(183,108 sq km)

Land area
69,001 sq mi
(178,711 sq km)

Population
760,077

Capital
Bismarck
Population 73,112

Largest city
Fargo
Population 124,844

Racial/ethnic groups
87.5% white; 3.1% African
American; 1.6% Asian; 5.5%
Native American; 3.7%
Hispanic (any race)

Foreign born
3.6%

Urban population
59.9%

Population density
11.0 per sq mi (4.3 per sq km)

GEO WHIZ

The state's largest reservoir is named in honor of Sacagawea (also known as Sakakawea), the young Shoshone guide who joined the Lewis and Clark expedition in the spring of 1805.

Devils Lake has earned the title Perch Capital of the World for the large number of walleye— a kind of perch—caught there.

North Dakota's landscape boasts some of the world's largest outdoor animal sculptures, including Salem Sue, the world's largest Holstein cow; a giant grasshopper; and a snowmobiling turtle.

WILD PRAIRIE ROSE

WESTERN
MEADOWLARK

North Dakota

During the winter of 1804–05 Lewis and Clark camped at a Mandan village where they met Sacagawea, the young Shoshone woman who helped guide them through the Rockies and on to the Pacific Ocean. White settlement of the vast grassy plains coincided with the growth of railroads, and statehood was gained in 1889. The geographic center of North America is southwest of Rugby. The state's interior location helps give it a huge annual temperature range: A record low temperature of -60°F (-51°C) and record high of 121°F (49°C) were recorded in 1936. Fargo, located on the northward flowing Red River of the North, is the state's largest city. Garrison Dam, on the Missouri River, generates electricity and provides water for irrigation. The state is a major producer of flaxseed, canola, sunflowers, and barley, but it is wheat, cattle, and soybeans that provide the greatest income. Oil and lignite coal are important in the western part of the state.

🔊 **ALERT LOOKOUT.**
A black-tailed prairie dog watches for signs of danger. This member of the squirrel family lives in burrows in the Great Plains.

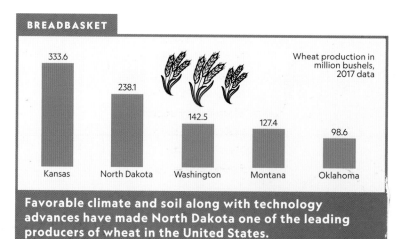

BREADBASKET

Wheat production in million bushels, 2017 data

333.6	238.1	142.5	127.4	98.6
Kansas	North Dakota	Washington	Montana	Oklahoma

Favorable climate and soil along with technology advances have made North Dakota one of the leading producers of wheat in the United States.

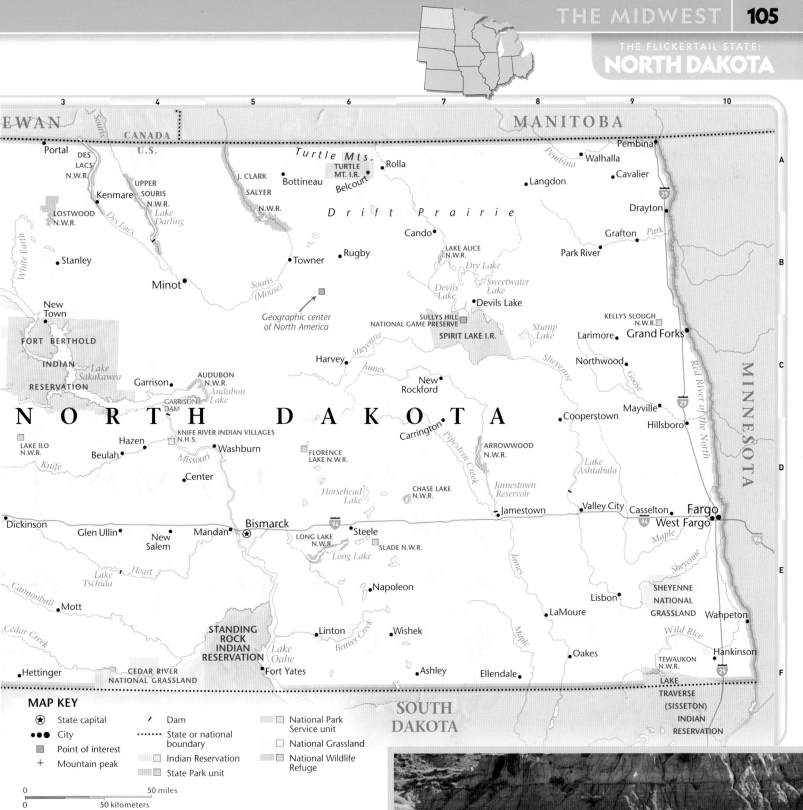

3   4   5   6   7   8   9   10

EWAN   **MANITOBA**

CANADA
U.S.

Portal
DES
LACS
N.W.R.

UPPER
SOURIS
N.W.R.

Souris

Turtle Mts.

Pembina
Walhalla

Cavalier

Langdon

TURTLE
MT. I.R.
Belcourt

Rolla

J. CLARK
SALYER
N.W.R.

Bottineau

Drift Prairie

Kenmare

Lake
Darling

Des Lacs

LOSTWOOD
N.W.R.

Drayton

Grafton   Park

Stanley

White Earth

Cando

LAKE ALICE
N.W.R.

Park River

Towner   Rugby

Dry Lake

Sweetwater
Lake

Minot

Souris
(Mouse)

Devils
Lake

Devils Lake

KELLYS SLOUGH
N.W.R.

Larimore   Grand Forks

New
Town

Geographic center
of North America

SULLYS HILL
NATIONAL GAME PRESERVE

SPIRIT LAKE I.R.

Stump
Lake

Northwood

Goose

Red River of the North

FORT BERTHOLD

INDIAN

RESERVATION

Lake
Sakakawea

Garrison

AUDUBON
N.W.R.

Audubon
Lake

Harvey

Sheyenne

James

New
Rockford

Sheyenne

Cooperstown

Mayville

Hillsboro

MINNESOTA

NORTH   DAKOTA

GARRISON
DAM

KNIFE RIVER INDIAN VILLAGES
N.H.S.

Carrington

Pipestem Creek

ARROWWOOD
N.W.R.

Lake
Ashtabula

LAKE ILO
N.W.R.

Hazen

Washburn

FLORENCE
LAKE N.W.R.

Beulah

Knife

Missouri

Center

Horsehead
Lake

CHASE LAKE
N.W.R.

Jamestown
Reservoir

Valley City   Casselton   Fargo

Dickinson

Glen Ullin

New
Salem

Mandan

Bismarck

Steele

LONG LAKE
N.W.R.

SLADE N.W.R.

Long Lake

Jamestown

94

94   West Fargo

Maple

94

Sheyenne

Lake
Tschida

Heart

Napoleon

James

Lisbon

SHEYENNE
NATIONAL
GRASSLAND

Cannonball

Mott

STANDING
ROCK
INDIAN
RESERVATION

Linton

Beaver Creek

Wishek

LaMoure

Maple

Wild Rice

Wahpeton

Cedar Creek

Hettinger

CEDAR RIVER
NATIONAL GRASSLAND

Lake
Oahe

Fort Yates

Ashley

Ellendale

Oakes

TEWAUKON
N.W.R.

Hankinson

29

LAKE
TRAVERSE
(SISSETON)
INDIAN
RESERVATION

SOUTH
DAKOTA

A

B

C

D

E

F

MAP KEY

⭑ State capital
●●● City
▢ Point of interest
+ Mountain peak
╱ Dam
······· State or national boundary
▤▢ Indian Reservation
▥▢ State Park unit
▢ National Park Service unit
▢ National Grassland
▥▢ National Wildlife Refuge

0 ———————— 50 miles
0 ———————— 50 kilometers
Albers Conic Equal-Area Projection

◗ **RUNNING FREE.**
A wild horse runs through a landscape eroded by the Little Missouri River in Theodore Roosevelt National Park in North Dakota's Badlands region.

◖ **GOLDEN HARVEST.** A crop duster, spraying for insects, flies low over a field of sunflowers in the Red River Valley in eastern North Dakota. In the valley's fertile soil, farmers grow sunflowers mainly for the oil in their seeds.

THE BUCKEYE STATE:
OHIO

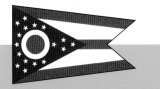

THE BASICS

Statehood
March 1, 1803; 17th state

Total area (land and water)
44,826 sq mi (116,098 sq km)

Land area
40,861 sq mi (105,829 sq km)

Population
11,689,442

Capital
Columbus
Population 892,533

Largest city
Columbus
Population 892,533

Racial/ethnic groups
82.2% white; 12.9% African American; 2.3% Asian; 0.3% Native American; 3.8% Hispanic (any race)

Foreign born
4.3%

Urban population
77.9%

Population density
286.1 per sq mi
(110.5 per sq km)

GEO WHIZ

Cedar Point Amusement Park, in Sandusky, is known as the Roller Coaster Capital of the World. Top Thrill Dragster has a maximum speed of 120 miles an hour (193 km/h).

Ohio's state tree is the buckeye, so called because the nut it produces resembles the eye of a male deer, or buck.

Ohio

Ohio and the rest of the land north and west of the Ohio River became part of the United States after the Revolutionary War. The movement of white settlers into the region led to conflicts with Native Americans until 1794, when the native people were defeated at Fallen Timbers. Ohio entered the Union nine years later. Lake Erie in the north and the Ohio River in the south, along with canals and railroads, provided transportation links that spurred early immigration and commerce. The state became an industrial giant, producing steel, machinery, rubber, and glass. From 1869 to 1923, seven of twelve U.S. presidents were Ohioans. With 18 electoral votes, the seventh highest number in the country, Ohio is still a big player in presidential elections. Education, government, and finance employ many people in Columbus, the capital and largest city. Manufacturing in Cleveland, Toledo, Cincinnati, and other cities remains a vital segment of the state's economy. Farmers on Ohio's western plains, which were created by glaciers, grow soybeans and corn, the two largest cash crops.

⬤ **INLAND URBAN CENTER.**
Cincinnati's skyline sparkles in the red glow of twilight. Founded in 1788, the modern city boasts education and medical centers as well as headquarters for companies such as Procter & Gamble.

SCARLET CARNATION

CARDINAL

TRADITIONAL CULTURE

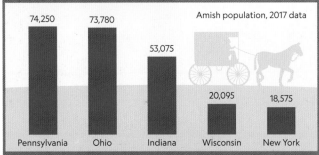

Amish population, 2017 data

Pennsylvania	Ohio	Indiana	Wisconsin	New York
74,250	73,780	53,075	20,095	18,575

The Amish, who migrated to the United States from Europe beginning in the mid-1700s, observe simple lifestyles and hold conservative values.

ROCK AND ROLL HALL OF

⬤ **SOUND OF MUSIC.** Colorful guitars mark the entrance to the Rock and Roll Hall of Fame in downtown Cleveland. The museum, through its Rockin' the Schools program, attracts thousands of students annually to experience the sounds of rock and roll music and learn about its history.

THE BUCKEYE STATE:
OHIO

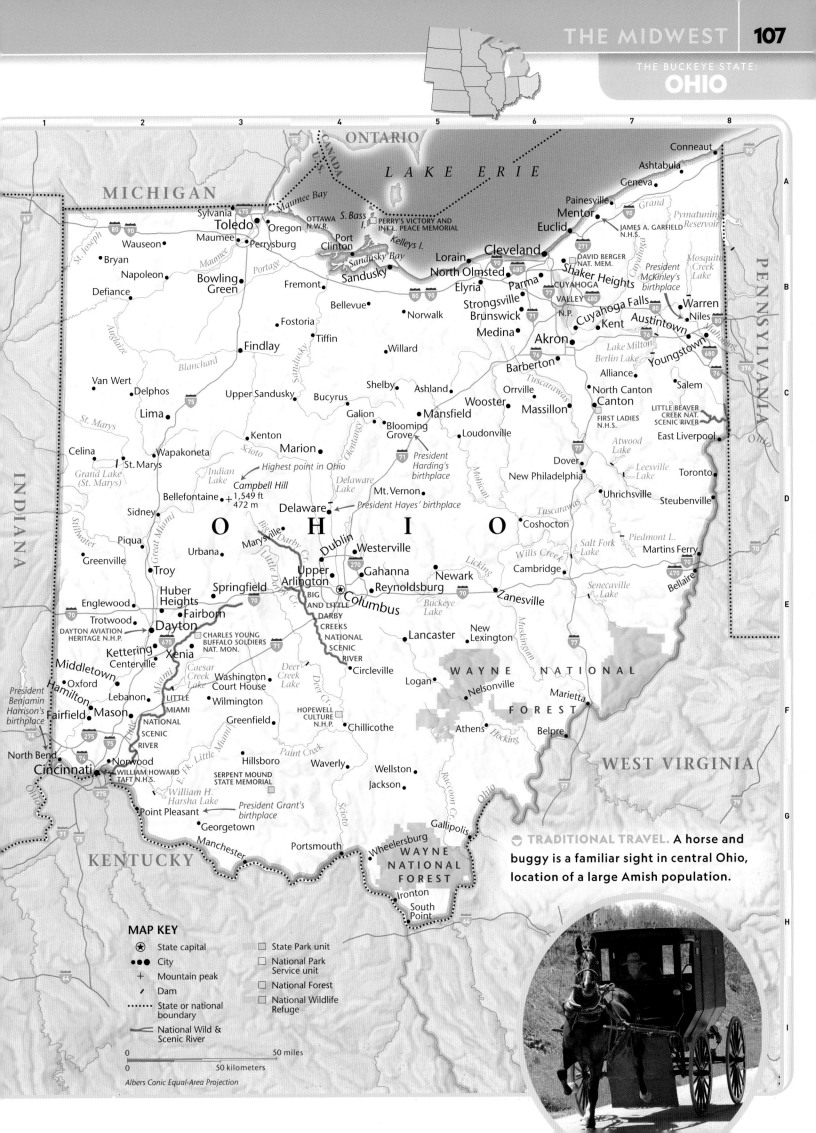

TRADITIONAL TRAVEL. A horse and buggy is a familiar sight in central Ohio, location of a large Amish population.

South Dakota

THE BASICS

Statehood
November 2, 1889; 40th state

Total area (land and water)
77,116 sq mi (199,729 sq km)

Land area
75,811 sq mi (196,350 sq km)

Population
882,235

Capital
Pierre
Population 13,980

Largest city
Sioux Falls
Population 181,883

Racial/ethnic groups
84.9% white; 2.1% African American; 1.5% Asian; 9.0% Native American; 3.8% Hispanic origin (any race)

Foreign born
3.3%

Urban population
56.7%

Population density
11.6 per sq mi (4.5 per sq km)

GEO WHIZ

Thanks to captive breeding programs, the world's largest population of wild black-footed ferrets is thriving in a blacktailed prairie dog colony in south-central South Dakota.

Sometimes known as the Shrine of Democracy, Mount Rushmore National Monument features the faces of four presidents: Washington, Jefferson, Lincoln, and Theodore Roosevelt.

After the discovery of Black Hills gold in 1874, prospectors poured in and established lawless mining towns such as Deadwood. Native Americans fought this invasion but were defeated, and statehood came in 1889. Today, South Dakota has several reservations, and 9 percent of the state's people are Native Americans. The Missouri River flows through the center of the state, creating two distinct regions: To the east, farmers grow corn and soybeans on the fertile, rolling prairie; to the west, where it is too dry for most crops, farmers grow wheat and graze cattle and sheep on the vast plains. In the southwest the Black Hills, named for the dark coniferous trees blanketing their slopes, are still a rich source of gold. Millions of tourists visit the area to see Mount Rushmore and a giant sculpture of Lakota leader Crazy Horse, which has been in the works since 1948. Nearby, the fossil-rich Badlands, a region of eroded buttes and pinnacles, dominates the landscape.

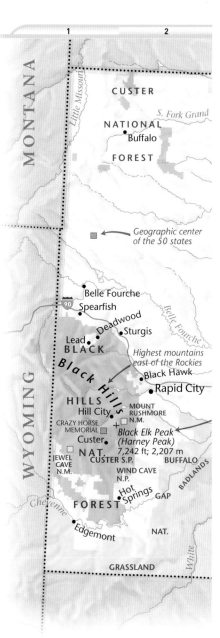

PASQUEFLOWER

RING-NECKED PHEASANT

◖ HONORING AGRICULTURE.
The face of the Corn Palace in Mitchell is renewed each year using thousands of bushels of grain to create pictures depicting the role of agriculture in the state's history.

NORTH DAKOTA

STANDING ROCK

GRAND
RIVER
NATIONAL
GRASSLAND

Lemmon
McIntosh
INDIAN
RESERVATION

POCASSE N.W.R.

Eureka

SAND
LAKE
N.W.R.

Britton

TRAVERSE
(SISSETON)
Sisseton
INDIAN

Lake
Traverse

MINNESOTA

Bison

Mobridge

Selby

Leola

Ipswich

Aberdeen

Groton

RES.

WAUBAY
N.W.R.

Milbank

Big
Stone
Lake

Timber Lake

Waubay L.

Webster

CHEYENNE RIVER

Lake
Oahe

INDIAN

Gettysburg

Faulkton

Clark

Watertown

Clear
Lake

Dupree

RESERVATION

Redfield

Lake Poinsett

Moreau

Okobojo Creek

Onida

Sulphur Creek

Cherry Creek

Highmore

Miller

De Smet

Brookings
Volga

S O U T H   D A K O T A

Cheyenne

Fort Pierre ★ Pierre

Huron

FLANDREAU
I.R.

Missouri

Lake
Sharpe

CROW
CREEK
INDIAN
RESERVATION

Wessington
Springs

Woonsocket

Madison

Flandreau

MINUTEMAN
MISSILE
N.H.S.

Philip

Bad

FORT PIERRE
NATIONAL
GRASSLAND

LOWER
BRULE
INDIAN
RESERVATION

Howard

Highest
point
in South
Dakota

Wall

BUFFALO GAP

Murdo

Kennebec

Fort Thompson

Crow Creek

NATIONAL   PARK

Kadoka

White

Chamberlain

Salem

GRASSLAND

Huge rock barrier sculptured into
pinnacles and gullies by running water

White River

Plankinton

Mitchell

Alexandria

Sioux Falls

PINE RIDGE

Last major conflict of the
Indian Wars, December 1890

Winner

Lake
Francis
Case

Platte

Parkston

Freeman

Parker

Lennox
Canton

INDIAN RESERVATION

Rosebud

Armour

WOUNDED KNEE
MASSACRE SITE

Martin

ROSEBUD
INDIAN
RESERVATION

Gregory

Burke

YANKTON
Lake Andes

LAKE ANDES
N.W.R.

Beresford

LACREEK
N.W.R.

Keya Paha

INDIAN
RES.

Wagner

Tyndall

IOWA

Pine Ridge

Lewis and Clark
Lake

Yankton

NEBRASKA

MISSOURI

NATIONAL

RECREATIONAL

RIVER

Vermillion

Elk Point
N. Sioux
City

Missouri

⬤ **CARVED IN STONE. Begun in 1948, the
Crazy Horse Memorial in the Black Hills honors
the culture, tradition, and living heritage of Native
Americans. In the background, sculptors are re-creating
the statue of the Lakota leader and his horse.**

MAP KEY

★ State capital
●●● City
▣ Point of interest
+ Mountain peak
⟋ Dam

▪▪▪▪▪ State boundary
▥ Indian Reservation
▤ State Park unit
▢ National Park
    Service unit

▨ National Forest
▢ National Grassland
▦ National Wildlife
    Refuge

0   25 miles
0   25 kilometers
Albers Conic Equal-Area Projection

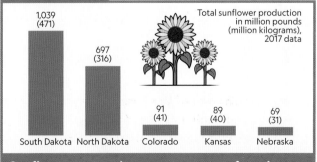

EDIBLE SEEDS

Total sunflower production
in million pounds
(million kilograms),
2017 data

South Dakota	North Dakota	Colorado	Kansas	Nebraska
1,039 (471)	697 (316)	91 (41)	89 (40)	69 (31)

**Sunflowers are an important source of seeds
and edible oil, which is obtained by crushing
the seeds of the flower.**

WISCONSIN

1848

THE BASICS

Statehood
May 29, 1848; 30th state

Total area (land and water)
65,496 sq mi (169,635 sq km)

Land area
54,158 sq mi (140,268 sq km)

Population
5,813,568

Capital
Madison
Population 258,054

Largest city
Milwaukee
Population 592,025

Racial/ethnic groups
87.3% white; 6.7% African American; 2.9% Asian; 1.2% Native American; 6.9% Hispanic (any race)

Foreign born
4.9%

Urban population
70.2%

Population density
107.3 per sq mi (41.4 per sq km)

GEO WHIZ

The Indian Community School in Milwaukee has courses in numerous native languages, history, and rituals, all stressing seven core values: bravery, love, truth, wisdom, humility, loyalty, and respect.

Bogs left by retreating ice-age glaciers provide excellent conditions for raising cranberries. Wisconsin leads the country in harvesting this fruit.

Wisconsin's nickname—Badger State—comes not from the animal but from miners who dug living spaces by burrowing like badgers into the hillsides during the 1820s.

Wisconsin

Frenchman Jean Nicolet was the first European to reach present-day Wisconsin when he landed on the shore of Green Bay in 1634. As more settlers arrived, tensions with the region's Native Americans increased, but the Black Hawk War in 1832 brought an end to most conflicts. Wisconsin became a state in 1848. Although health care and other services have increased in importance, food processing and the manufacture of machinery and metal products remain significant for the state economy. More than one million dairy cows graze in America's Dairyland, as the state is often called, and Wisconsin leads the country in cheese production. It is second only to California in the production of milk and butter. Farmers also grow crops ranging from corn and soybeans to potatoes and cranberries. Northern Wisconsin is sparsely populated but heavily forested and is an important source of paper and paper products.

CITY BY THE LAKE. Milwaukee derives its name from the Algonquian word for "beautiful land." Known for brewing and manufacturing, the city also has a growing service sector.

TASTY GRAZING.
The largest concentration of Brown Swiss cows in the United States is in Wisconsin. The milk of this breed is prized by cheese manufacturers.

254

RURAL ECONOMY. The dairy industry is an important part of Wisconsin's rural economy, and dairy farmers control most of the state's farmland.

WOOD VIOLET

ROBIN

DAIRY HEARTLAND

Cheese production in million lb (million kg), 2017 data

Wisconsin	California	Idaho	New York	New Mexico
3400 (1500)	2500 (1100)	959 (435)	861 (391)	766 (347)

Wisconsin, with more than 1.27 million dairy cows, is known for dairy products and leads the country in cheese production.

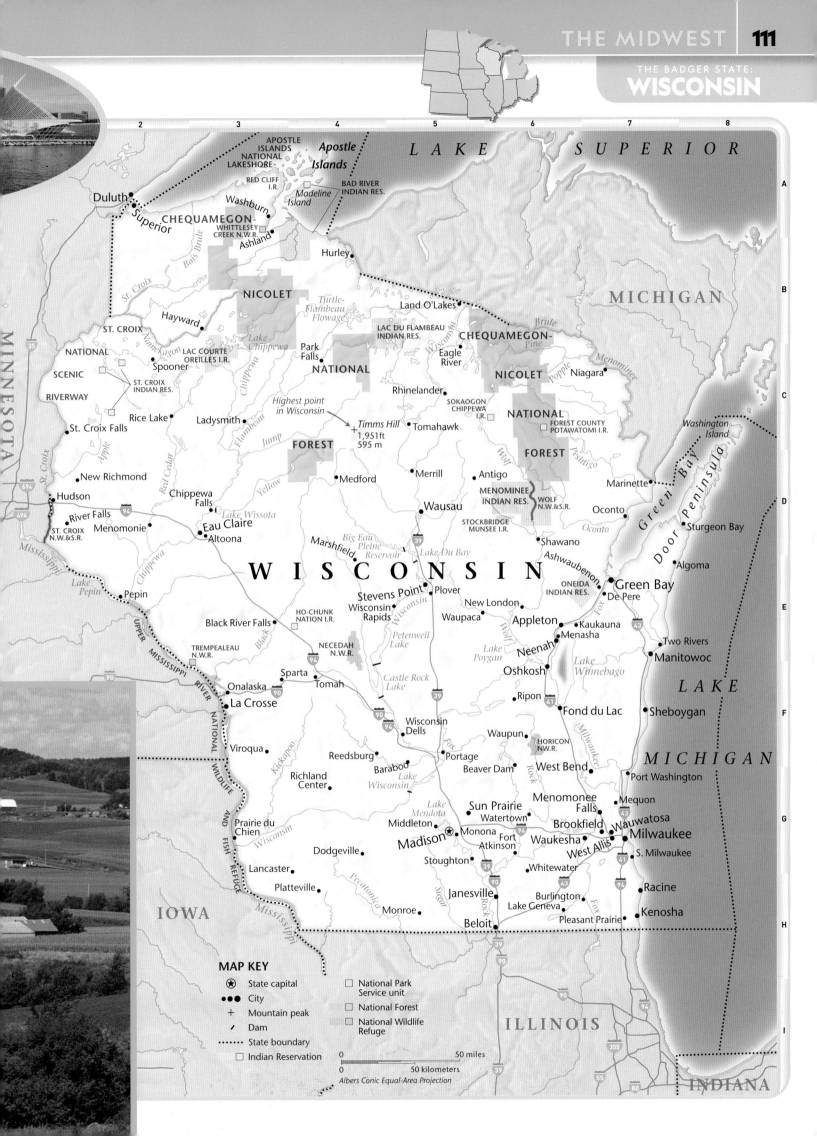

THE REGION

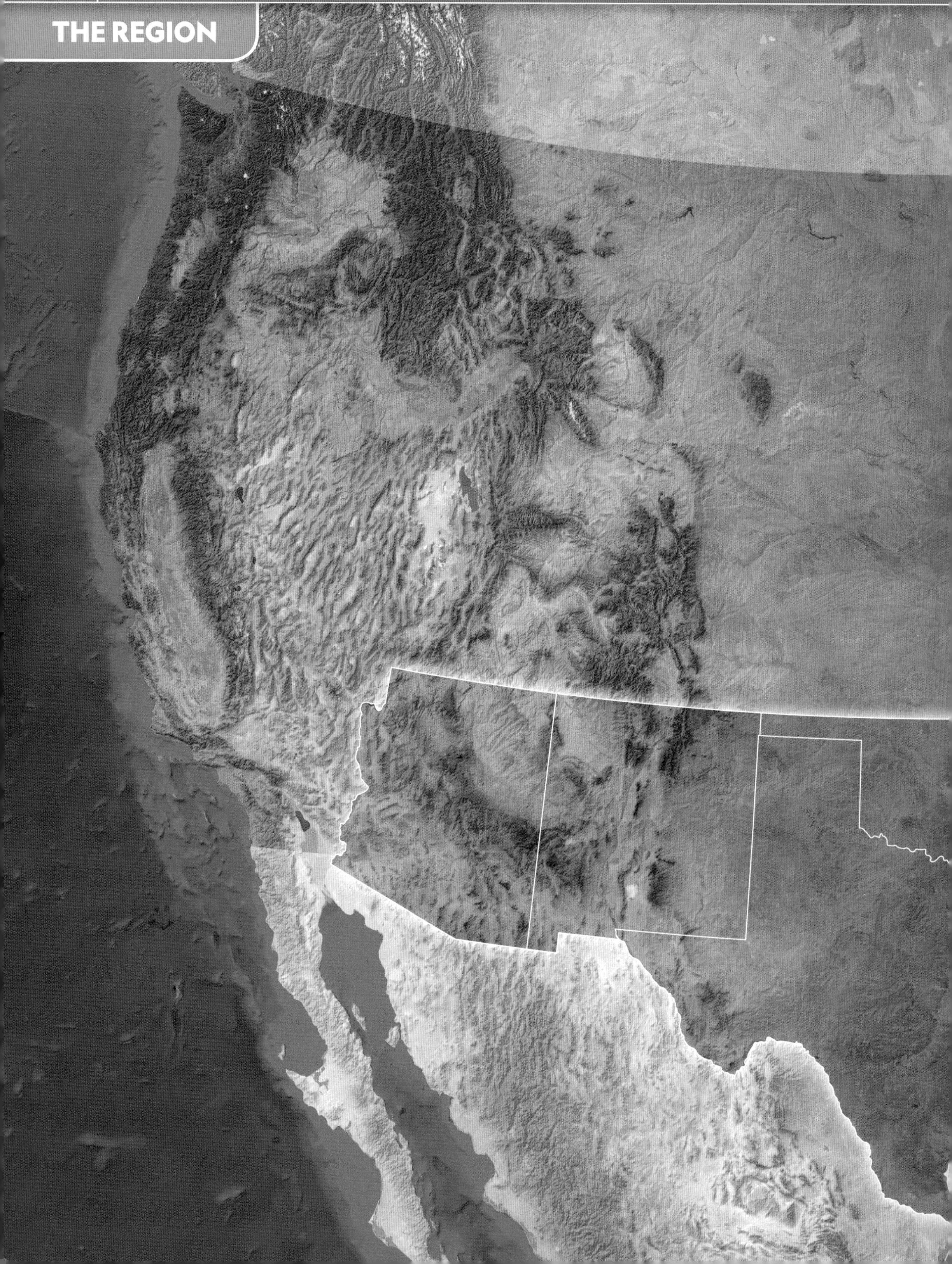

THE REGION

THE SOUTHWEST

PHYSICAL

Total area (land and water)
574,075 sq mi
(1,486,850 sq km)

Highest point
Wheeler Peak, NM
13,161 ft (4,011 m)

Lowest point
Sea level, shores of the
Gulf of Mexico

Longest rivers
Rio Grande, Arkansas,
Colorado

Largest lakes
Toledo Bend, Sam Rayburn,
Eufaula (all reservoirs)

Vegetation
Mixed, broadleaf, and needleleaf forest; grassland; desert

Climate
Humid subtropical, semiarid
and arid, with warm to hot
summers and cool winters

POLITICAL

Total population
41,911,998

States (4):
Arizona, New Mexico, Oklahoma, Texas

Largest state
Texas: 268,596 sq mi
(695,662 sq km)

Smallest state
Oklahoma: 69,899 sq mi
(181,037 sq km)

Most populous state
Texas: 28,701,845

Least populous state
New Mexico: 2,095,428

Largest city proper
Houston, TX: 2,325,502

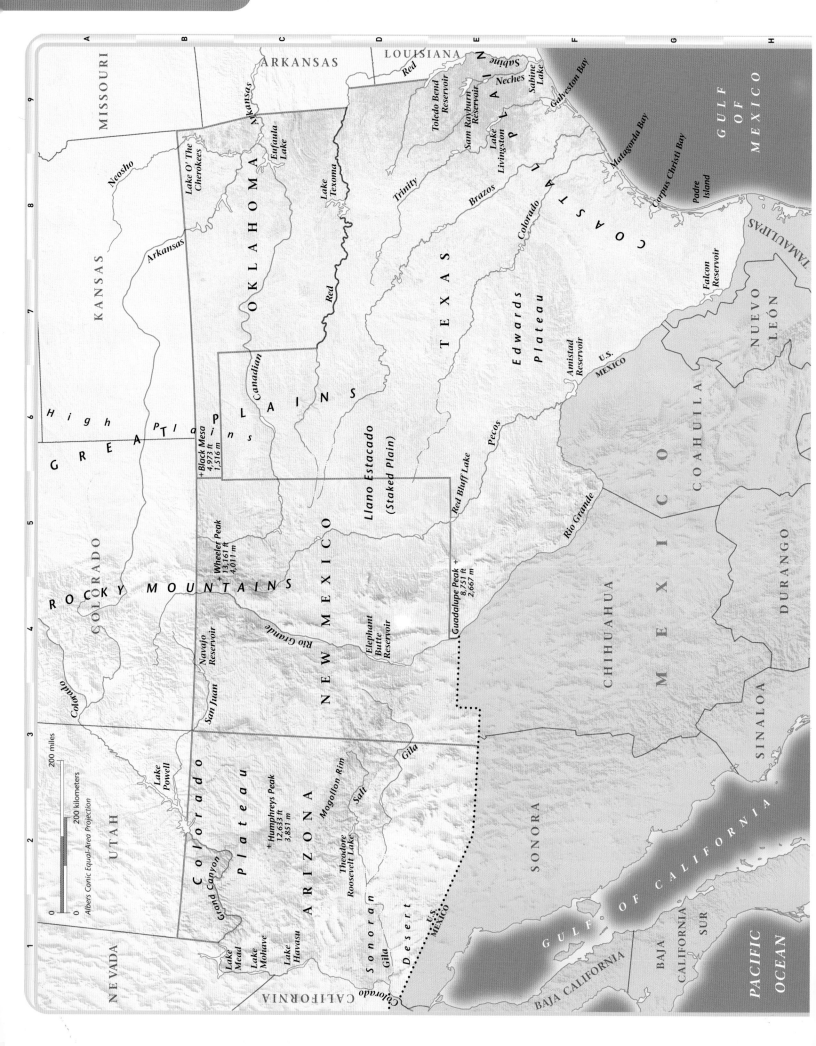

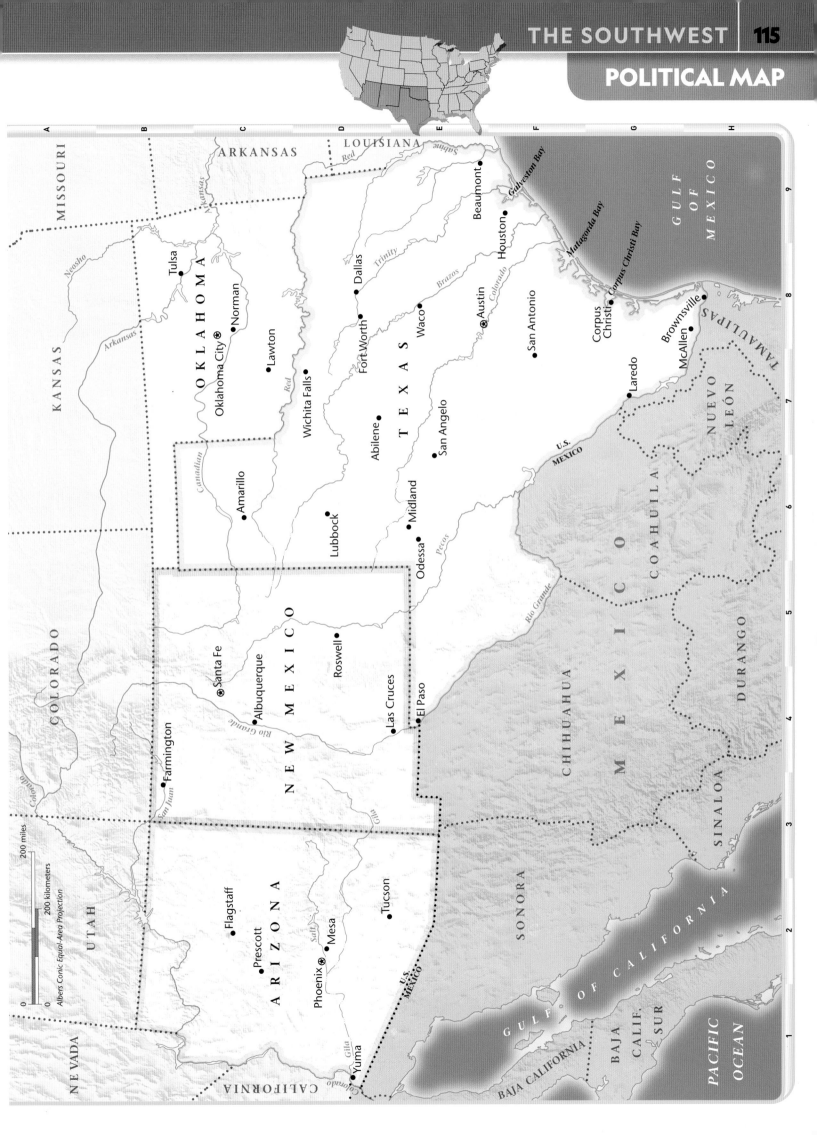

MISSOURI

ARKANSAS

LOUISIANA

KANSAS

OKLAHOMA

Tulsa

Norman

Oklahoma City ⊗

Lawton

Amarillo

Wichita Falls

Dallas

Fort Worth

Waco

Abilene

San Angelo

Midland

Lubbock

Odessa

TEXAS

Austin ⊗

San Antonio

Beaumont

Houston

Galveston Bay

Matagorda Bay

Corpus Christi Bay

Corpus Christi

Laredo

Brownsville

McAllen

TAMAULIPAS

NUEVO LEÓN

COAHUILA

DURANGO

SINALOA

MEXICO

CHIHUAHUA

SONORA

U.S.
MEXICO

COLORADO

NEW MEXICO

Santa Fe ⊗

Albuquerque

Roswell

Las Cruces

El Paso

Farmington

San Juan

Rio Grande

Pecos

Gila

ARIZONA

Flagstaff

Prescott

Phoenix ⊗

Mesa

Tucson

Yuma

Salt

Gila

Colorado

UTAH

NEVADA

CALIFORNIA

BAJA CALIFORNIA

BAJA CALIF. SUR

GULF OF CALIFORNIA

PACIFIC OCEAN

GULF OF MEXICO

Neosho

Arkansas

Red

Canadian

Trinity

Brazos

Colorado

Sabine

U.S.
MEXICO

200 miles

200 kilometers

Albers Conic Equal-Area Projection

ABOUT THE
SOUTHWEST

The Southwest

FROM CANYONS TO GRASSLANDS

◗ SKY STONE. According to Pueblo legend, turquoise stole its color from the sky. This Zuni woman is wearing turquoise rings and bracelets for a festival in Phoenix.

I n the 1500s, legendary cities of gold lured Spanish conquistadors to the Southwest—land inhabited by ancestors of present-day Native Americans. Today, the promise of economic opportunities brings people from other states as well as immigrants from countries south of the border. This part of the Sunbelt region boasts future-oriented cities while preserving Wild West tales and Native American traditions. Its climate ranges from humid subtropical along the Gulf Coast to arid in Arizona's deserts, and the landscape ranges from sprawling plains in the east to plateaus cut by dramatic canyons in the west. Water is a major concern in the Southwest, one of the country's fastest-growing regions.

⬤ HIGH SOCIETY. A young woman participates in the Society of Martha Washington pageant in Laredo, Texas. This event presents daughters of wealthy and long-established Hispanic families to the local community.

MODERN METROPOLIS. Towering skyscrapers tell a story of success and wealth. Although incorporated as a town in 1856, it was not until 1930 that Dallas, Texas, experienced explosive growth and prosperity due to the discovery of oil. Today, the city is a center of the U.S. oil industry and a leader in technology-based industries.

DEADLY VIPER. Shaking the rattles on the tip of its tail, this diamondback rattlesnake—coiled for attack—warns intruders to stay away. Common throughout the arid Southwest, the snake eats mainly small rodents.

STANDING TALL. The saguaro cactus, which often rises more than 30 feet (9 m) above the shrubs of the Sonoran Desert, frequently has several branches and produces creamy-white flowers that bloom at night. The Sonoran, the hottest desert in North America, is located in the borderlands of southern Arizona and California and extends into northern Mexico.

WHERE THE PICTURES ARE

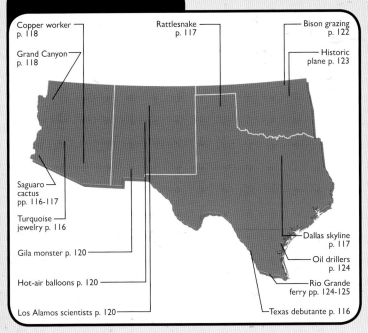

Copper worker p. 118

Grand Canyon p. 118

Rattlesnake p. 117

Bison grazing p. 122

Historic plane p. 123

Saguaro cactus pp. 116-117

Turquoise jewelry p. 116

Gila monster p. 120

Hot-air balloons p. 120

Los Alamos scientists p. 120

Dallas skyline p. 117

Oil drillers p. 124

Rio Grande ferry pp. 124-125

Texas debutante p. 116

Arizona

The first Europeans to visit what is now Arizona were the Spanish in the 1500s. The territory passed from Spain to Mexico and then to the United States over the next three centuries. In the 1800s settlers clashed with the Apache people led by Cochise and Geronimo—and with one another in lawless towns like Tombstone. Youngest of the 48 contiguous states, Arizona achieved statehood in 1912. Arizona's economy was long based on the Five C's: copper, cattle, cotton, citrus, and climate—but manufacturing and service industries have gained prominence. A fast-growing population, sprawling cities, and agricultural irrigation strain limited water supplies in this dry state, which depends on water from the Colorado River and underground aquifers. Tourists flock to the Colorado Plateau in the north to see stunning vistas of the Grand Canyon, Painted Desert, and Monument Valley. To the south, the Sonoran Desert's unique ecosystem includes the giant saguaro cactus. Reservations scattered around the state offer visitors the chance to learn about Native American history and culture.

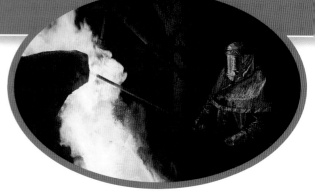

🔘 **HOT WORK.** A man in protective clothing works near a furnace that melts and refines copper ore at Magma Copper Company near Tucson. Arizona is one of the largest copper-producing regions in the world.

THE BASICS

Statehood
February 14, 1912; 48th state

Total area (land and water)
113,990 sq mi (295,234 sq km)

Land area
113,594 sq mi (294,207 sq km)

Population
7,171,646

Capital
Phoenix
Population 1,660,272

Largest city
Phoenix
Population 1,660,272

Racial/ethnic groups
83.1% white; 5.0% African American; 3.5% Asian; 5.3% Native American; 31.4% Hispanic (any race)

Foreign born
13.4%

Urban population
89.8%

Population density
63.1 per sq mi (24.4 per sq km)

GEO WHIZ

California condors, once common in the Southwest, nearly became extinct in 1987, but conservation measures have led to their reintroduction into the wild.

People have carved pictures called petroglyphs into rock cliffs near Flagstaff for thousands of years, but the meanings of most petroglyphs remain a mystery.

CACTUS WREN
SAGUARO

⬤ **NATURAL WONDER.** Carved by the rushing waters of the Colorado River, the Grand Canyon's geologic features and fossil record reveal almost two billion years of Earth's history. Archaeological evidence indicates human habitation dating back 12,000 years.

INDIAN RESERVATIONS

Number of people, 2010 data

Reservation	Number of people
Navajo AZ-NM-UT	169,321
Pine Ridge SD-NE	16,906
Fort Apache AZ	13,041
Gila River AZ	11,251
Osage OK	9,920

More than 200,000 Native Americans live on reservations in the Southwest. The Navajo Reservation in Arizona and adjoining states is the most populous.

THE GRAND CANYON STATE:
ARIZONA

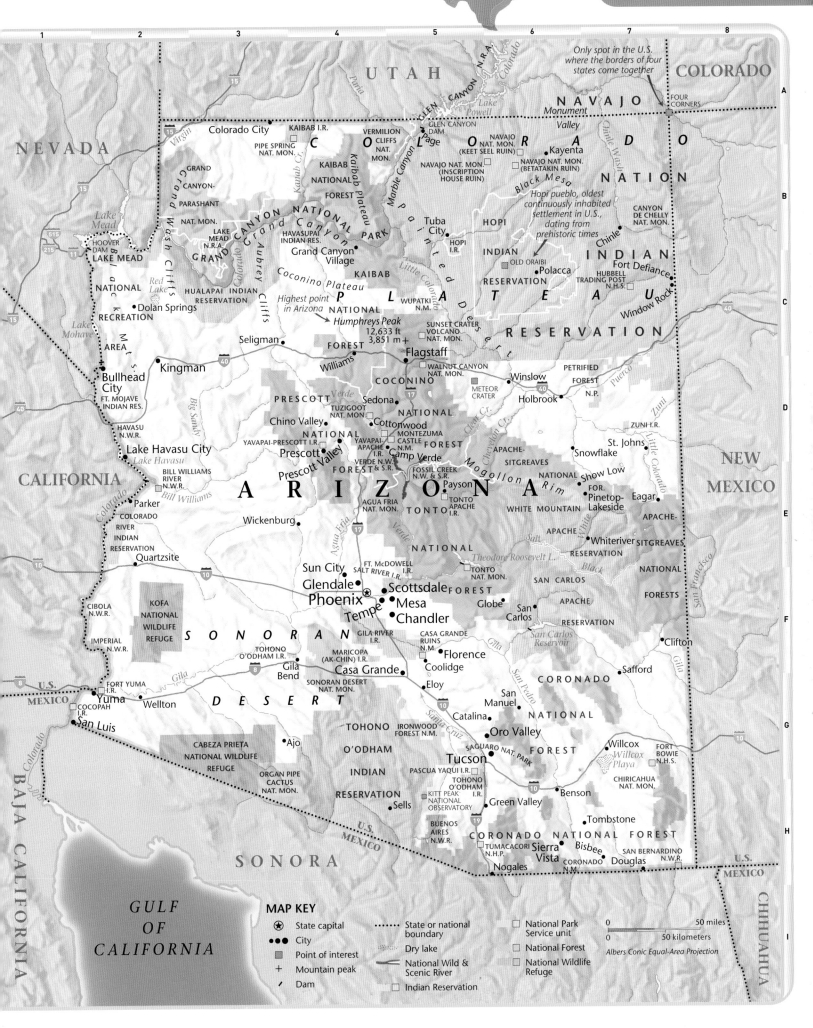

NEVADA

UTAH

COLORADO

NEW MEXICO

CALIFORNIA

MEXICO

BAJA CALIFORNIA

SONORA

CHIHUAHUA

Only spot in the U.S. where the borders of four states come together

Hopi pueblo, oldest continuously inhabited settlement in U.S., dating from prehistoric times

Highest point in Arizona
Humphreys Peak 12,633 ft 3,851 m

COLORADO PLATEAU

NAVAJO NATION

HOPI INDIAN RESERVATION

NAVAJO INDIAN RESERVATION

ARIZONA

SONORAN DESERT

GULF OF CALIFORNIA

MAP KEY

★ State capital
●●● City
▪ Point of interest
+ Mountain peak
⌐ Dam

···· State or national boundary
Dry lake
National Wild & Scenic River
▫ Indian Reservation

▫ National Park Service unit
▫ National Forest
▫ National Wildlife Refuge

0   50 miles
0   50 kilometers
Albers Conic Equal-Area Projection

Four Corners
Monument
Colorado City
Kaibab I.R.
Page
Glen Canyon Dam
Navajo Nat. Mon. (Keet Seel Ruin)
Kayenta
Navajo Nat. Mon. (Inscription House Ruin)
Navajo Nat. Mon. (Betatakin Ruin)
Pipe Spring Nat. Mon.
Vermilion Cliffs Nat. Mon.
Kaibab National Forest
Tuba City
Hopi I.R.
Old Oraibi
Polacca
Canyon de Chelly Nat. Mon.
Chinle
Fort Defiance
Hubbell Trading Post N.H.S.
Window Rock
Havasupai Indian Res.
Grand Canyon Village
Hualapai Indian Reservation
Dolan Springs
Lake Mead National Recreation Area
Hoover Dam
Lake Mohave
Seligman
Sunset Crater Volcano Nat. Mon.
Wupatki N.M.
Flagstaff
Walnut Canyon Nat. Mon.
Meteor Crater
Winslow
Petrified Forest N.P.
Holbrook
Kingman
Williams
Coconino National Forest
Sedona
Bullhead City
Ft. Mojave Indian Res.
Prescott
Tuzigoot Nat. Mon.
Chino Valley
Cottonwood
Montezuma Castle N.M.
Camp Verde
Verde N.W. & S.R.
Zuni I.R.
St. Johns
Snowflake
Show Low
Havasu N.W.R.
Lake Havasu City
Yavapai-Prescott I.R.
Prescott Valley
Yavapai-Apache I.R.
Fossil Creek N.W. & S.R.
Payson
Tonto Apache I.R.
Apache-Sitgreaves National Forest
Pinetop-Lakeside
Eagar
Bill Williams River N.W.R.
Wickenburg
Agua Fria Nat. Mon.
Whiteriver
Apache-Sitgreaves National Forests
Parker
Colorado River Indian Reservation
Theodore Roosevelt L.
Apache Reservation
Quartzsite
Tonto Nat. Mon.
San Carlos
Cibola N.W.R.
Kofa National Wildlife Refuge
Sun City
Glendale
Scottsdale
Phoenix
Mesa
Tempe
Chandler
Ft. McDowell Salt River I.R.
Globe
San Carlos
Clifton
Imperial N.W.R.
Tohono O'odham I.R.
Casa Grande Ruins N.M.
Florence
Safford
Fort Yuma I.R.
Maricopa (Ak-Chin) I.R.
Gila Bend
Casa Grande
Coolidge
Eloy
Yuma
Cocopah I.R.
Wellton
Sonoran Desert Nat. Mon.
San Manuel
Coronado National Forest
San Luis
Catalina
Willcox
Fort Bowie N.H.S.
Cabeza Prieta National Wildlife Refuge
Ajo
Oro Valley
Willcox Playa
Tohono O'odham Indian Reservation
Ironwood Forest N.M.
Saguaro Nat. Park
Chiricahua Nat. Mon.
Organ Pipe Cactus Nat. Mon.
Pascua Yaqui I.R.
Tucson
Benson
Kitt Peak National Observatory
Green Valley
Sells
Tombstone
Buenos Aires N.W.R.
Tumacacori N.H.P.
Sierra Vista
Bisbee
San Bernardino N.W.R.
Coronado N.M.
Douglas
Nogales
U.S. MEXICO
Lake Mead
Lake Havasu
Red Lake
Colorado River
Gila
Salt
Black
San Carlos Reservoir
San Pedro
Santa Cruz
San Francisco
Little Colorado
Puerco
Zuni
Mogollon Rim
Black Mesa
Painted Desert
Grand Canyon
Marble Canyon
Glen Canyon
Lake Powell
Virgin
Grand Wash Cliffs
Aubrey Cliffs
Coconino Plateau
Kaibab Plateau
Big Sandy
Bill Williams
Verde
Agua Fria
Chevelon Cr.
Clear Cr.
White

THE BASICS

Statehood
January 6, 1912; 47th state

Total area (land and water)
121,590 sq mi (314,917 sq km)

Land area
121,298 sq mi (314,161 sq km)

Population
2,095,428

Capital
Santa Fe
Population 84,612

Largest city
Albuquerque
Population 560,218

Racial/ethnic groups
82.2% white; 2.5% African
American; 1.7% Asian; 10.9%
Native American; 48.8%
Hispanic (any race)

Foreign born
9.7%

Urban population
77.4%

Population density
17.3 per sq mi (6.7 per sq km)

GEO WHIZ

Carlsbad Caverns National Park has more than a hundred caves, including the deepest limestone cavern in the U.S. From May through October thousands of Mexican free-tailed bats emerge from the caverns on their nightly search for food.

Taos Pueblo, near Taos in north-central New Mexico, has been continuously inhabited by Pueblo people for more than 1,000 years.

New Mexico

New Mexico is among the youngest states—statehood was established in 1912—but its capital city is the country's oldest. The Spanish founded Santa Fe in 1610, a decade before the *Mayflower* reached America. Beginning in the 1820s, the Santa Fe Trail brought trade and settlers, and the United States acquired the territory from Mexico by 1853. Most large cities are in the center of the state, along the Rio Grande. The Rocky Mountains divide the plains in the east from eroded mesas and canyons in the west. Cattle and sheep ranching on the plains is the chief agricultural activity, but hay, onions, and chili peppers are also important. Copper, potash, and natural gas are sources of mineral wealth. Cultural richness created by the historic interaction of Native American, Hispanic, and Anglo peoples abounds. Visitors experience this unique culture in the state's spicy cuisine, the famous art galleries of Taos, and Native American crafts.

⬭ **FLYING HIGH. Brightly colored balloons rise into a brilliant blue October sky during Albuquerque's annual International Balloon Fiesta, the largest such event in the world. During the nine-day festival more than 500 hot-air balloons drift on variable air currents created by surrounding mountains.**

⬭ **PAINFUL BITE.**
The most venomous lizard native to the United States is the strikingly patterned Gila monster, which lives in desert areas of the Southwest.

ROADRUNNER
YUCCA

SPICY HOT!

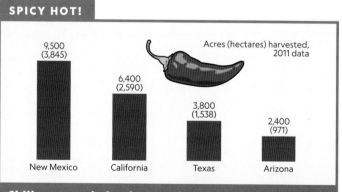

Acres (hectares) harvested, 2011 data

9,500 (3,845)	6,400 (2,590)	3,800 (1,538)	2,400 (971)
New Mexico	California	Texas	Arizona

Chili peppers help give southwestern food its distinctive taste. New Mexico leads the country in acres planted with this fiery flavor enhancer.

◖ **NUCLEAR MYSTERIES. Scientists at Los Alamos National Laboratory, a leading scientific and engineering research institution, use 3D simulations to study nuclear explosions.**

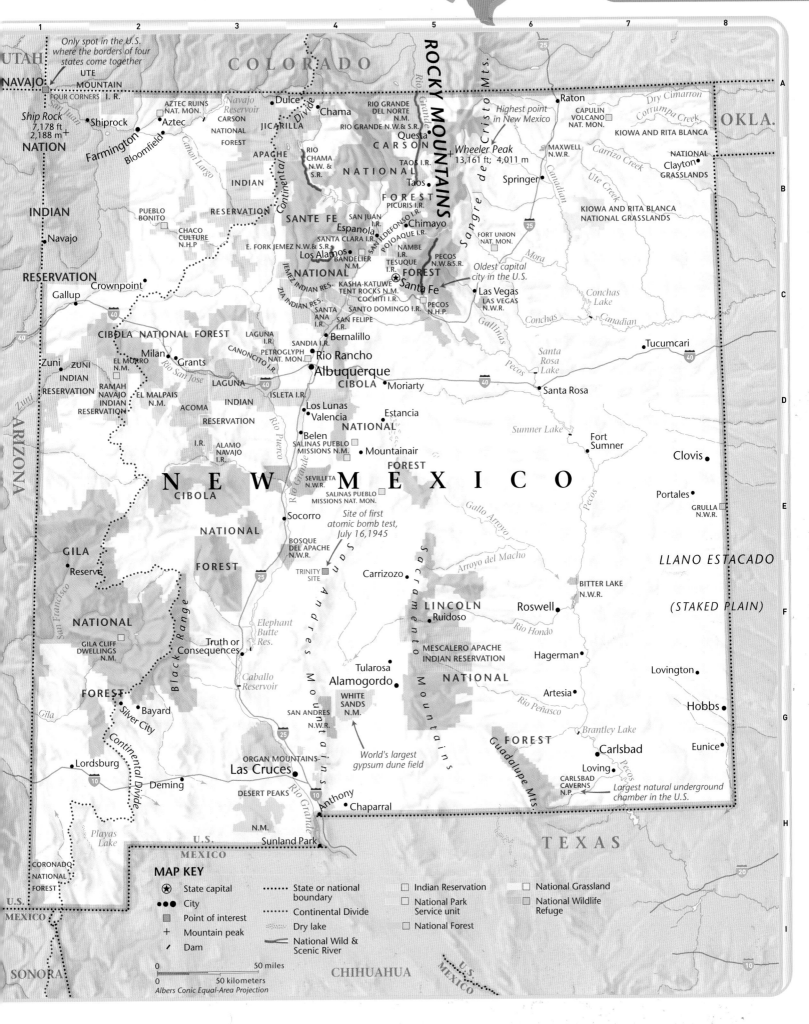

Only spot in the U.S. where the borders of four states come together

UTAH

COLORADO

OKLA.

NAVAJO

FOUR CORNERS I. R.

UTE MOUNTAIN I. R.

Ship Rock 7,178 ft 2,188 m

Shiprock

Farmington

Bloomfield

Aztec

AZTEC RUINS NAT. MON.

CARSON NATIONAL FOREST

Dulce

JICARILLA APACHE INDIAN RESERVATION

Chama

RIO GRANDE DEL NORTE

RIO GRANDE N.W. & S.R.

ROCKY MOUNTAINS

Raton

CAPULIN VOLCANO NAT. MON.

Dry Cimarron

Corrumpa Creek

Carrizo Creek

KIOWA AND RITA BLANCA

NATION

NATIONAL

Questa

Wheeler Peak 13,161 ft; 4,011 m

Highest point in New Mexico

MAXWELL N.W.R.

Clayton

Ute Creek

Canadian

NATIONAL GRASSLANDS

Sangre de Cristo Mts.

RIO CHAMA N.W. & S.R.

TAOS I.R.

Taos

Springer

PICURIS I.R.

FORT UNION NAT. MON.

KIOWA AND RITA BLANCA NATIONAL GRASSLANDS

Mora

INDIAN

PUEBLO BONITO

SANTE FE

Espanola

SAN JUAN I.R.

Chimayo

SANTA CLARA I.R.

SAN ILDEFONSO I.R.

NAMBE I.R.

PECOS N.W. & S.R.

Conchas Lake

RESERVATION

CHACO CULTURE N.H.P.

E. FORK JEMEZ N.W. & S.R.

Los Alamos

POJOAQUE I.R.

TESUQUE I.R.

Oldest capital city in the U.S.

Navajo

JEMEZ INDIAN RES.

BANDELIER N.M.

KASHA-KATUWE TENT ROCKS N.M.

Santa Fe

Las Vegas

LAS VEGAS N.W.R.

Conchas

Canadian

Crownpoint

ZIA INDIAN RES.

COCHITI I.R.

PECOS N.H.P.

Gallinas

Gallup

SANTA ANA I.R.

SANTO DOMINGO I.R.

Santa Rosa Lake

Tucumcari

CIBOLA NATIONAL FOREST

LAGUNA I.R.

SANDIA I.R.

SAN FELIPE I.R.

Milan

Grants

PETROGLYPH NAT. MON.

Rio Rancho

Bernalillo

CANONCITO I.R.

Pecos

Zuni

ZUNI

EL MORRO N.M.

Rio San Jose

Albuquerque

CIBOLA

Moriarty

Santa Rosa

INDIAN

RAMAH NAVAJO INDIAN RESERVATION

EL MALPAIS N.M.

ACOMA

LAGUNA

ISLETA I.R.

Sumner Lake

Fort Sumner

RESERVATION

INDIAN RESERVATION

Los Lunas

Valencia

Estancia

Clovis

ARIZONA

I.R.

ALAMO NAVAJO I.R.

Belen

SALINAS PUEBLO MISSIONS N.M.

Mountainair

NATIONAL

Portales

GRULLA N.W.R.

CIBOLA

SEVILLETA N.W.R.

SALINAS PUEBLO MISSIONS NAT. MON.

FOREST

N E W   M E X I C O

Socorro

Site of first atomic bomb test, July 16, 1945

BOSQUE DEL APACHE N.W.R.

Gallo Arroyo

LLANO ESTACADO

GILA

Reserve

NATIONAL

TRINITY SITE

Carrizozo

San Andres

Arroyo del Macho

BITTER LAKE N.W.R.

(STAKED PLAIN)

FOREST

LINCOLN

Roswell

San Francisco

Elephant Butte Res.

Black Range

Truth or Consequences

NATIONAL

Ruidoso

Rio Hondo

NATIONAL

Sacramento

MESCALERO APACHE INDIAN RESERVATION

Hagerman

Lovington

GILA CLIFF DWELLINGS N.M.

Caballo Reservoir

Tularosa

Alamogordo

NATIONAL

Artesia

Hobbs

FOREST

Bayard

Silver City

Gila

WHITE SANDS N.M.

SAN ANDRES N.W.R.

World's largest gypsum dune field

Mountains

Rio Peñasco

Brantley Lake

Continental Divide

Lordsburg

Deming

ORGAN MOUNTAINS-DESERT PEAKS N.M.

Las Cruces

FOREST

Guadalupe Mts.

Carlsbad

Eunice

Loving

CARLSBAD CAVERNS N.P.

Largest natural underground chamber in the U.S.

Anthony

Chaparral

Pecos

Playas Lake

U.S.

MEXICO

Sunland Park

TEXAS

CORONADO NATIONAL FOREST

U.S.

MEXICO

SONORA

CHIHUAHUA

MAP KEY

- ⭐ State capital
- ●●● City
- ▪ Point of interest
- + Mountain peak
- ⌐ Dam
- ⋯⋯ State or national boundary
- — — Continental Divide
- Dry lake
- National Wild & Scenic River
- ☐ Indian Reservation
- ☐ National Park Service unit
- ☐ National Forest
- ☐ National Grassland
- ☐ National Wildlife Refuge

0   50 miles

0   50 kilometers

Albers Conic Equal-Area Projection

OKLAHOMA

THE BASICS

Statehood
November 16, 1907; 46th state

Total area (land and water)
69,899 sq mi (181,037 sq km)

Land area
68,595 sq mi (177,660 sq km)

Population
3,943,079

Capital
Oklahoma City
Population 649,021

Largest city
Oklahoma City
Population 649,021

Racial/ethnic groups
74.3% white; 7.8% African American; 2.3% Asian; 9.2% Native American; 10.6% Hispanic (any race)

Foreign born
5.9%

Urban population
66.2%

Population density
57.5 per sq mi (22.2 per sq km)

GEO WHIZ

An area of Oklahoma City has earned the nickname Little Saigon. In the 1960s the city opened its doors to tens of thousands of refugees from Vietnam. Today, the area is a thriving business district that includes people of many Asian nationalities.

"Pocket dinosaur" is one of several nicknames for the armadillo. Native to South America, large populations of this armor-plated mammal are found throughout Oklahoma and in much of the southern United States.

Before it became a state in 1907, Oklahoma was known as Indian Territory. Today, 39 tribes have their headquarters in the state.

ROSE

SCISSOR-TAILED FLYCATCHER

Oklahoma

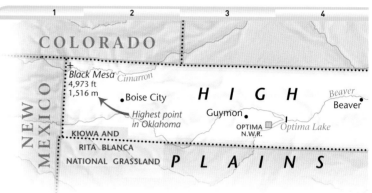

The U.S. government declared most of present-day Oklahoma as Indian Territory in 1834. To reach this new homeland, the Cherokee and other south-eastern tribes were forced to travel the Trail of Tears, named for its brutal conditions. By 1889 areas were opened for white homesteaders, who staked claims in frenzied land runs. White and Native American lands were combined to form the state of Oklahoma in 1907. During the 1930s many Oklahomans fled drought and dust storms that smothered everything in sight. Some traveled as far as California in search of work. Better farming methods and the return of rain helped agriculture recover, and today cattle and wheat are among the chief products. Oil and natural gas wells are found throughout the state. The Red River, colored by the region's iron-rich soils, marks the state's southern boundary. Along the eastern border, the Ozark Plateau and Ouachita Mountains form rugged bluffs and valleys. To the west, rolling plains rise toward the High Plains in the state's panhandle.

🌐 **NATURAL LANDSCAPE.** Bison graze in the Joseph H. Williams Tallgrass Prairie Preserve, near Pawhuska. Tallgrass prairie once covered 140 million acres (57 million ha), extending from Minnesota to Texas, but today less than 4 percent remains because of urban sprawl and cropland expansion. The preserve is the largest protected tallgrass prairie remaining on Earth.

THE SOONER STATE:
OKLAHOMA

KANSAS

MISSOURI

OKLAHOMA

TEXAS

ARKANSAS

MAP KEY

- ⭐ State capital
- ●●● City
- ✛ Mountain peak
- ⟍ Dam
- ····· State boundary
- ▥ Indian Reservation
- ☐ National Park Service unit
- ☐ National Forest
- ☐ National Grassland
- ▨ National Wildlife Refuge

0 ——— 50 miles
0 ——— 50 kilometers
Albers Conic Equal-Area Projection

🛩 HISTORY IN THE AIR. One of the Spirit of Tulsa Squadron's vintage PT-17 airplanes flies above the city. The squadron is part of the Commemorative Air Force, an organization committed to preserving aviation history.

FOOD SUPPLIER

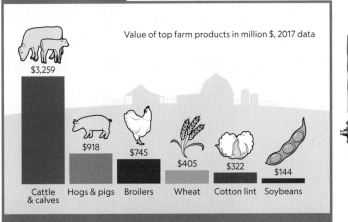

Value of top farm products in million $, 2017 data

Cattle & calves	Hogs & pigs	Broilers	Wheat	Cotton lint	Soybeans
$3,259	$918	$745	$405	$322	$144

With more than 78,000 farms, agriculture is important in Oklahoma, contributing more than $8 billion each year to the state's economy.

THE BASICS

Statehood
December 29, 1845; 28th state

Total area (land and water)
268,596 sq mi (695,662 sq km)

Land area
261,232 sq mi (676,587 sq km)

Population
28,701,845

Capital
Austin
Population 964,254

Largest city
Houston
Population 2,325,502

Racial/ethnic groups
79.2% white; 12.7% African American; 5.0% Asian; 1.0% Native American; 39.4% Hispanic (any race)

Foreign born
16.9%

Urban population
84.7%

Population density
109.9 per sq mi (42.4 per sq km)

GEO WHIZ

The Fossil Rim Wildlife Center in the Hill Country breeds endangered African animals. Offspring will be returned to the wild in Africa whenever possible.

Defeat at the 1836 Battle of the Alamo gave rise to the battle cry "Remember the Alamo" and inspired General Sam Houston's forces to win Texas independence from Mexico.

Texas

Various groups of Plains Native Americans were the early inhabitants of what would become Texas. In fact, the name Texas is derived from the word *Taysha*, which means "friend" in the Caddo language. Texas was an independent republic from 1836 until it became a state in 1845. Today, it is the second largest state in population (after California) and area (after Alaska), and a top producer of many agricultural products, including cattle, sheep, cotton, citrus fruits, vegetables, rice, and pecans. It also has huge oil and natural gas fields and is a manufacturing powerhouse. Pine forests cover East Texas while barrier islands protect the Gulf Coast, and grassy plains cover the northern panhandle. Wildflowers flourish in the Hill Country, and mountains and sandy plains sprawl across dry West Texas. The Rio Grande, sometimes barely a trickle, separates Texas and Mexico.

MOCKINGBIRD

BLUEBONNET

⬤ **BLACK GOLD.** Workers plug an oil well. Discovery of oil early in the 20th century transformed life in Texas. Today, the state leads the U.S. in oil and natural gas production.

WHIRLING DANGER

Average annual number of tornadoes, 1991–2015

147	92	65	55	55
Texas	Kansas	Florida	Oklahoma	Nebraska

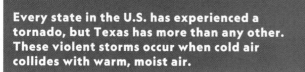

Every state in the U.S. has experienced a tornado, but Texas has more than any other. These violent storms occur when cold air collides with warm, moist air.

◗ **BORDER RELIC.** Los Ebanos Ferry, near Mission, Texas, takes its name from a nearby grove of ebony trees. It is the last remaining government-licensed, hand-pulled ferry on any U.S. border. It can carry three cars as it crosses the Rio Grande.

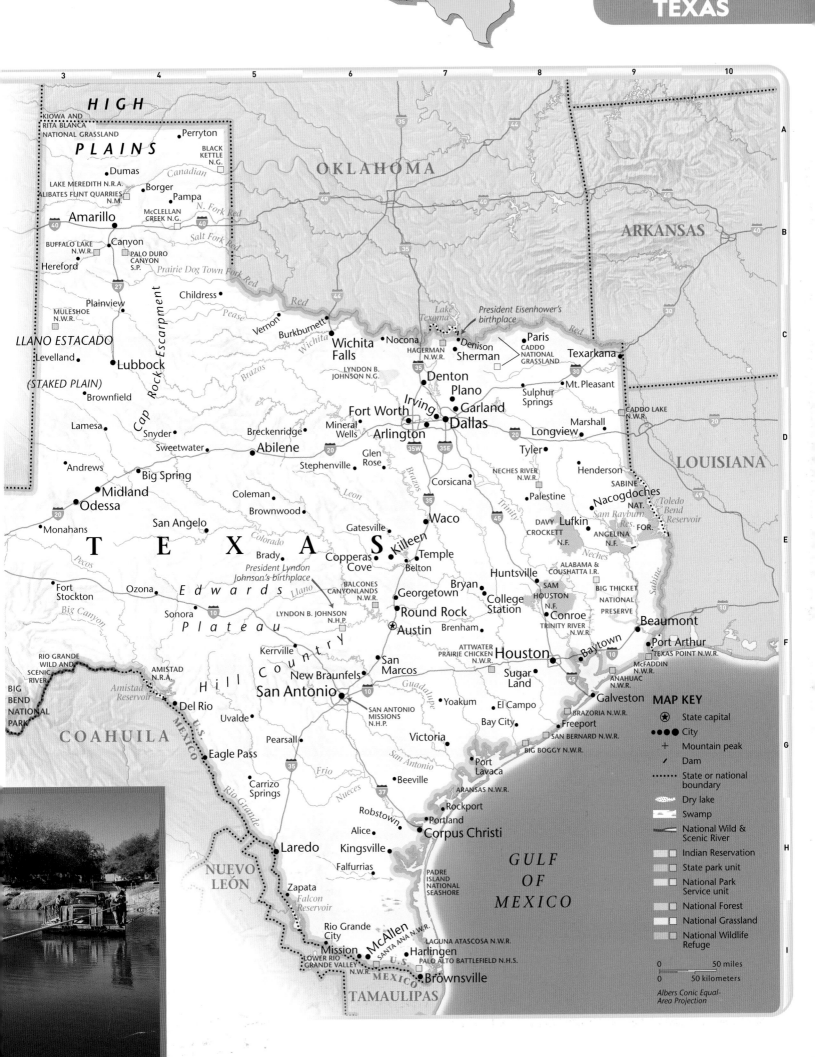

HIGH
PLAINS

KIOWA AND
RITA BLANCA
NATIONAL GRASSLAND

Perryton

BLACK
KETTLE
N.G.

Dumas   *Canadian*

LAKE MEREDITH N.R.A.   Borger
ALIBATES FLINT QUARRIES   Pampa
N.M.

McCLELLAN
CREEK N.G.

Amarillo

N. Fork Red

OKLAHOMA

ARKANSAS

BUFFALO LAKE   Canyon
N.W.R.

Hereford   PALO DURO
CANYON
S.P.

Salt Fork Red

MULESHOE
N.W.R.

Plainview

LLANO ESTACADO

Childress

Pease   *Prairie Dog Town Fork Red*   *Red*

Levelland

(STAKED PLAIN)

Vernon
Burkburnett

Nocona   President Eisenhower's
birthplace

Paris

Lubbock

Wichita   Wichita   HAGERMAN   Denison
Falls   N.W.R.   Sherman   CADDO
NATIONAL
GRASSLAND

Texarkana

Brownfield

Brazos   LYNDON B.
JOHNSON N.G.

Denton
Plano

Mt. Pleasant

Sulphur
Springs

CADDO LAKE
N.W.R.

Lamesa   Snyder   Breckenridge   Mineral   Irving   Garland   Marshall
Wells   Fort Worth   Dallas   Longview

Sweetwater   Abilene   Arlington   Tyler
Glen   35W 35E
Rose   20
Stephenville   NECHES RIVER   Henderson
N.W.R.   SABINE
Corsicana   Nacogdoches   *Toledo*
Palestine   NAT.   *Bend*
Coleman   *Leon*   DAVY   Lufkin   ANGELINA   *Reservoir*
Brownwood   CROCKETT   N.F.   N.F.   FOR.

Andrews   Big Spring

Midland
Odessa   San Angelo

Monahans   *Colorado*   Gatesville   Waco

T E X A S   Brady   Copperas   Killeen
Cove   Temple
Belton
President Lyndon
Johnson's birthplace   *Trinity*   Huntsville   ALABAMA &
COUSHATTA I.R.
Neches

Fort
Stockton   Ozona   *Edwards* *Llano*   Bryan   SAM   BIG THICKET
BALCONES   Georgetown   HOUSTON
CANYONLANDS   College   N.F.   NATIONAL
Big Canyon   N.W.R.   Round Rock   Station   PRESERVE
Sonora   LYNDON B. JOHNSON   Conroe   *Sabine*
Pecos   Plateau   N.H.P.   Austin   Brenham   TRINITY RIVER   Beaumont
N.W.R.

Kerrville   ATTWATER
PRAIRIE CHICKEN   Houston   Baytown   Port Arthur
RIO GRANDE   Country   N.W.R.   TEXAS POINT N.W.R.
WILD AND   New Braunfels   Sugar
SCENIC   AMISTAD   San   Land   McFADDIN
RIVER   N.R.A.   Hill   Marcos   *Guadalupe*   N.W.R.
BIG   *Amistad   San Antonio   ANAHUAC
BEND   Reservoir*   Country   N.W.R.
NATIONAL   Del Rio   Yoakum   El Campo   Galveston
PARK   Uvalde   SAN ANTONIO   *San*
MISSIONS   *Antonio*   Bay City   BRAZORIA N.W.R.
N.H.P.   Freeport
Pearsall   Victoria   SAN BERNARD N.W.R.
Eagle Pass   *Frio*   BIG BOGGY N.W.R.
Port
Carrizo   Lavaca
Springs   *Nueces*   37   Beeville

COAHUILA   Robstown   ARANSAS N.W.R.
Rockport
Alice   Portland
Laredo   Kingsville   Corpus Christi
Falfurrias
NUEVO
LEÓN   Zapata   GULF
*Falcon
Reservoir*   PADRE   OF
ISLAND   MEXICO
NATIONAL
SEASHORE
Rio Grande
City   McAllen   SANTA ANA N.W.R.
Mission   Harlingen   PALO ALTO BATTLEFIELD N.H.S.
LOWER RIO
GRANDE VALLEY   LAGUNA ATASCOSA N.W.R.
N.W.R.   MEXICO   Brownsville
TAMAULIPAS

Rio Grande

Cap Rock Escarpment

LOUISIANA

MAP KEY

⊛ State capital

●●●● City

+ Mountain peak

╱ Dam

••••• State or national
boundary

Dry lake

Swamp

National Wild &
Scenic River

Indian Reservation

State park unit

National Park
Service unit

National Forest

National Grassland

National Wildlife
Refuge

0   50 miles
0   50 kilometers

Albers Conic Equal-
Area Projection

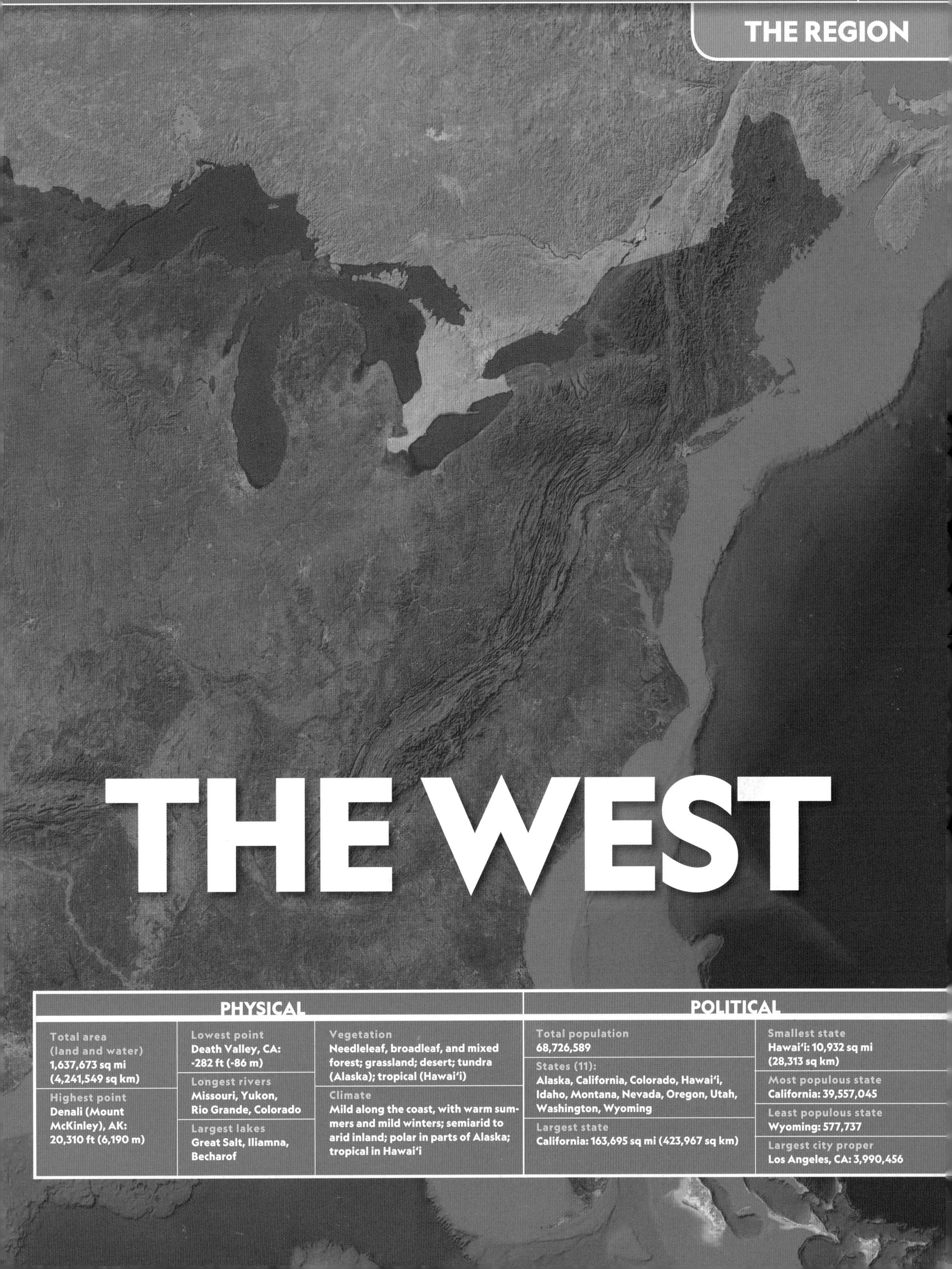

THE REGION

THE WEST

PHYSICAL

**Total area
(land and water)**
1,637,673 sq mi
(4,241,549 sq km)

Highest point
Denali (Mount
McKinley), AK:
20,310 ft (6,190 m)

Lowest point
Death Valley, CA:
-282 ft (-86 m)

Longest rivers
Missouri, Yukon,
Rio Grande, Colorado

Largest lakes
Great Salt, Iliamna,
Becharof

Vegetation
Needleleaf, broadleaf, and mixed
forest; grassland; desert; tundra
(Alaska); tropical (Hawai'i)

Climate
Mild along the coast, with warm summers and mild winters; semiarid to
arid inland; polar in parts of Alaska;
tropical in Hawai'i

POLITICAL

Total population
68,726,589

States (11):
Alaska, California, Colorado, Hawai'i,
Idaho, Montana, Nevada, Oregon, Utah,
Washington, Wyoming

Largest state
California: 163,695 sq mi (423,967 sq km)

Smallest state
Hawai'i: 10,932 sq mi
(28,313 sq km)

Most populous state
California: 39,557,045

Least populous state
Wyoming: 577,737

Largest city proper
Los Angeles, CA: 3,990,456

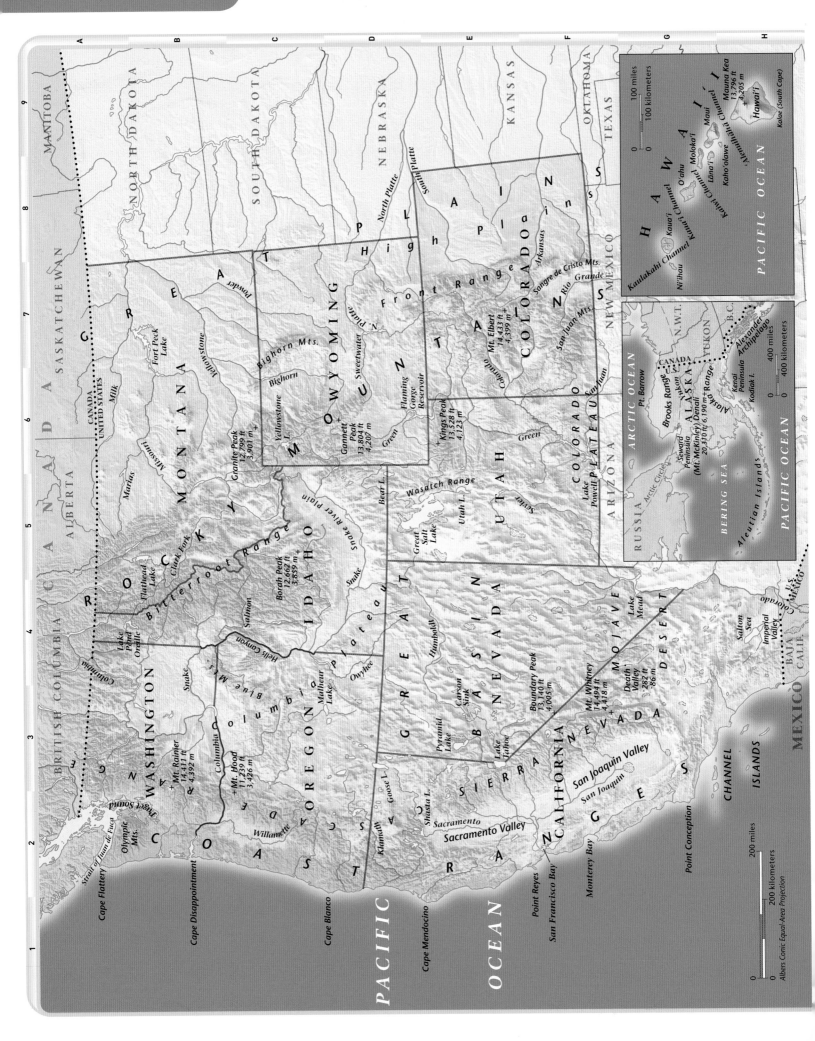

MANITOBA

SASKATCHEWAN

ALBERTA

BRITISH COLUMBIA

CANADA
UNITED STATES

NORTH DAKOTA

SOUTH DAKOTA

NEBRASKA

KANSAS

OKLAHOMA

TEXAS

NEW MEXICO

COLORADO

ARIZONA

UTAH

NEVADA

CALIFORNIA

OREGON

WASHINGTON

IDAHO

MONTANA

WYOMING

G R E A T   P L A I N S

High Plains

R O C K Y

M O U N T A I N S

Front Range

Sangre de Cristo Mts.

San Juan Mts.

Rio Grande

Mt. Elbert
14,433 ft
4,399 m

Kings Peak
13,528 ft
4,123 m

San Juan

COLORADO PLATEAU

Lake
Powell

Gannett
Peak
13,804 ft
4,207 m

Granite Peak
12,799 ft
3,901 m

Yellowstone
L.

Bighorn Mts.

Bighorn

Fort Peck
Lake

Yellowstone

Powder

Milk

Marias

Missouri

Sweetwater

N. Platte

North Platte

South Platte

Arkansas

Flaming
Gorge
Reservoir

Green

Colorado

Green

Bear L.

Wasatch Range

Utah L.

Great
Salt
Lake

Sevier

Borah Peak
12,662 ft
3,859 m

Snake River Plain

Snake

Salmon

Hells Canyon

Clark Fork

Flathead
Lake

Lake
Pend
Oreille

Bitterroot Range

Columbia

Mt. Rainier
14,411 ft
4,392 m

Puget Sound

Olympic
Mts.

Strait of Juan de Fuca

Cape Flattery

Cape Disappointment

Mt. Hood
11,239 ft
3,426 m

Columbia

Blue Mts.

Malheur
Lake

Owyhee

Klamath

Goose L.

Shasta L.

Sacramento

Sacramento Valley

Willamette

Cape Blanco

Cape Mendocino

Point Reyes

San Francisco Bay

Monterey Bay

Point Conception

CHANNEL
ISLANDS

San Joaquin Valley

San Joaquin

S I E R R A

N E V A D A

C O A S T   R A N G E S

Mt. Whitney
14,494 ft
4,418 m

MOJAVE
DESERT

Death
Valley
−282 ft
−86 m

Lake
Mead

Salton
Sea

Imperial
Valley

Colorado

BAJA CALIF.

MEXICO
U.S.

Boundary Peak
13,140 ft
4,005 m

Lake
Tahoe

Pyramid
Lake

Carson
Sink

Humboldt

G R E A T   B A S I N

PACIFIC

OCEAN

HAWAI'I

PACIFIC OCEAN

Kaua'i Channel

Kau'i Channel

Kaulakahi Channel

Ni'ihau

Kaua'i

O'ahu

Moloka'i

Lāna'i

Maui

Kaho'olawe

'Alenuihāhā Channel

Kalohi Channel

Kaiwi Channel

Mauna Kea
13,796 ft
4,205 m

Hawai'i

Kalae (South Cape)

0   100 miles

0   100 kilometers

ALASKA

ARCTIC OCEAN

Arctic Circle

Pt. Barrow

Brooks Range

Seward
Peninsula
(Mt. McKinley) Denali
20,310 ft / 6,190 m

Alaska Range

Kenai
Peninsula

Kodiak I.

Aleutian Islands

BERING SEA

RUSSIA

CANADA

N.W.T.

YUKON

B.C.

Alexander
Archipelago

PACIFIC OCEAN

0   400 miles

0   400 kilometers

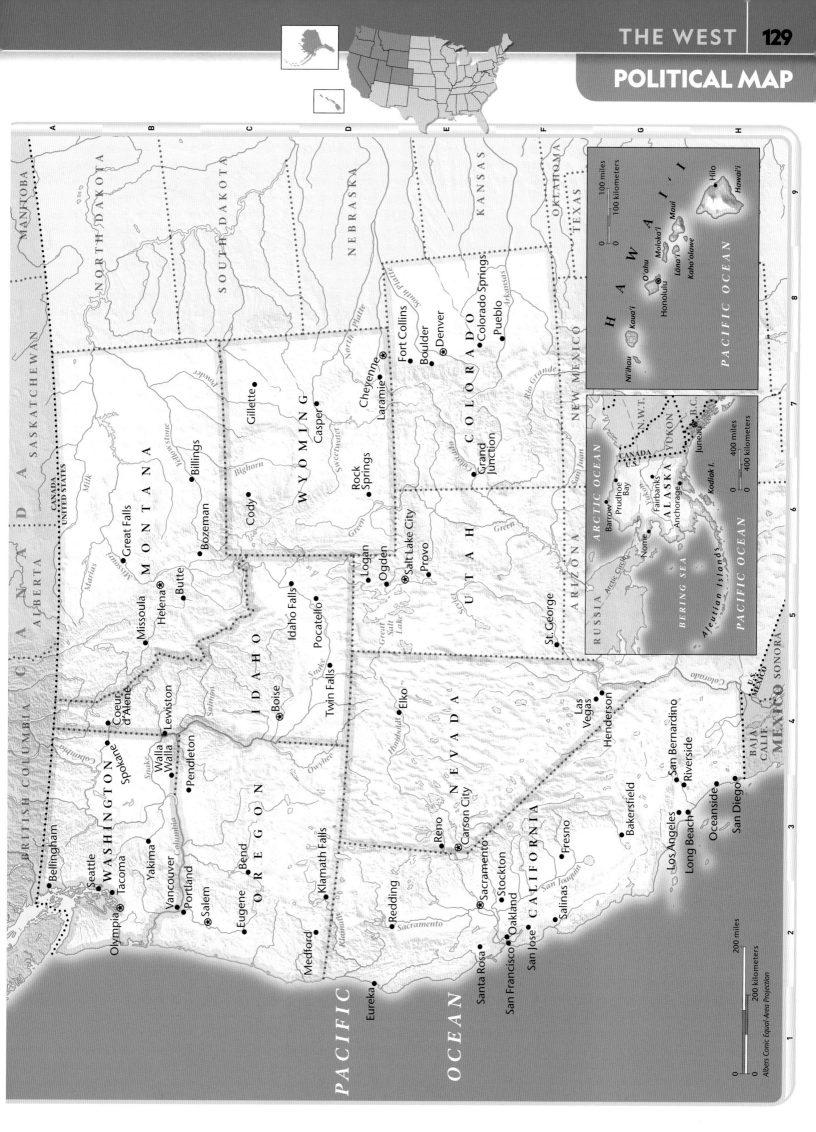

PACIFIC OCEAN

THE WEST
POLITICAL MAP

MANITOBA

NORTH DAKOTA

SOUTH DAKOTA

NEBRASKA

KANSAS

OKLAHOMA

TEXAS

NEW MEXICO

SASKATCHEWAN

CANADA
UNITED STATES

ALBERTA

CANADA

BRITISH COLUMBIA

MONTANA

Great Falls
Missoula
Helena
Butte
Billings
Bozeman

WYOMING

Gillette
Cody
Casper
Cheyenne
Laramie
Rock Springs

COLORADO

Fort Collins
Boulder
Denver
Colorado Springs
Pueblo
Grand Junction

IDAHO

Coeur d'Alene
Lewiston
Idaho Falls
Pocatello
Boise
Twin Falls

UTAH

Logan
Ogden
Salt Lake City
Provo
St. George

NEVADA

Elko
Reno
Carson City
Las Vegas
Henderson

WASHINGTON

Bellingham
Seattle
Tacoma
Olympia
Yakima
Vancouver
Spokane
Walla Walla

OREGON

Portland
Salem
Eugene
Bend
Medford
Klamath Falls
Pendleton

CALIFORNIA

Redding
Santa Rosa
San Francisco
Oakland
San Jose
Sacramento
Stockton
Salinas
Fresno
Bakersfield
Los Angeles
Long Beach
San Bernardino
Riverside
Oceanside
San Diego

ARIZONA

SONORA
MEXICO
BAJA CALIF.

U.S.
MEXICO

Eureka

PACIFIC OCEAN

Milk
Missouri
Marias
Yellowstone
Powder
Bighorn
Sweetwater
Green
North Platte
South Platte
Arkansas
Rio Grande
San Juan
Colorado
Great Salt Lake
Sevier
Snake
Salmon
Owyhee
Humboldt
Columbia
Klamath
Sacramento
San Joaquin

Albers Conic Equal-Area Projection

200 miles
200 kilometers

HAWAI'I

Ni'ihau
Kaua'i
O'ahu
Honolulu
Moloka'i
Lāna'i
Maui
Kaho'olawe
Hawai'i
Hilo

PACIFIC OCEAN

100 miles
100 kilometers

ALASKA

Barrow
Prudhoe Bay
Nome
Fairbanks
Anchorage
Juneau
Kodiak I.
Aleutian Islands

ARCTIC OCEAN
BERING SEA
PACIFIC OCEAN

RUSSIA
CANADA
U.S.
N.W.T.
YUKON
B.C.

Arctic Circle
Yukon

400 miles
400 kilometers

The West

THE HIGH FRONTIER

The western states, which make up almost half of the country's land area, have diverse landscapes and climates, ranging from the frozen heights of Denali, in Alaska, to the desolation of Death Valley, in California, and the lush, tropical islands of Hawai'i. More than half the region's population lives in California, and the Los Angeles metropolitan area is second in population only to that of New York City. Yet many parts of the region are sparsely populated, and much of the land is set aside as parkland and military bases. The region also faces many natural hazards—earthquakes, landslides, wildfires, and even volcanic eruptions.

◗ **OLD AND NEW.**
A cable car carries passengers in San Francisco. In the background, modern buildings rise above older neighborhoods in this earthquake-prone city.

◗ **NORTHERN GIANT.**
Denali, a name meaning "High One" in the Athabascan language, rises more than 20,000 feet (6,100 m) in the Alaska Range. Also known as Mount McKinley, it is North America's highest peak. The same tectonic forces that trigger earthquakes in Alaska are slowly pushing this huge block of granite ever higher.

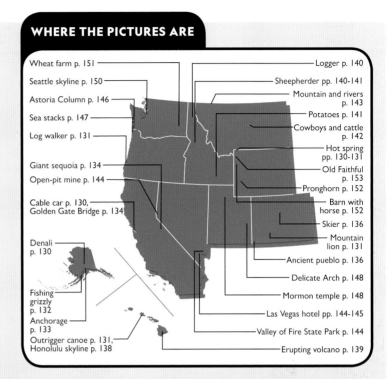

WHERE THE PICTURES ARE

Wheat farm p. 151
Seattle skyline p. 150
Astoria Column p. 146
Sea stacks p. 147
Log walker p. 131
Giant sequoia p. 134
Open-pit mine p. 144
Cable car p. 130,
Golden Gate Bridge p. 134
Denali p. 130
Fishing grizzly p. 132
Anchorage p. 133
Outrigger canoe p. 131,
Honolulu skyline p. 138

Logger p. 140
Sheepherder pp. 140-141
Mountain and rivers p. 143
Potatoes p. 141
Cowboys and cattle p. 142
Hot spring pp. 130-131
Old Faithful p. 153
Pronghorn p. 152
Barn with horse p. 152
Skier p. 136
Mountain lion p. 131
Ancient pueblo p. 136
Delicate Arch p. 148
Mormon temple p. 148
Las Vegas hotel pp. 144-145
Valley of Fire State Park p. 144
Erupting volcano p. 139

ELUSIVE PREDATOR. Known by many names, including cougar and mountain lion, these big cats are found mainly in remote mountainous areas of the West, where they hunt deer and smaller animals.

STEAMY BATH. Mineral-rich hot springs are a colorful feature of Yellowstone National Park. Runoff from rain and snowmelt seeps into cracks in the ground, sinking to a depth of 10,000 feet (3,050 m), where it is heated by molten rock before rising back to the surface.

BALANCING ACT. For many years rivers have been used to move logs from forest to market, taking advantage of the buoyancy of logs and the power of moving water. A logger stands on a floating log raft in Coos Bay, Oregon.

TRADITIONAL SAILING CRAFT. A Hawaiian outrigger canoe on Waikiki Beach promises fun in the surf for visitors to the 50th state. An important part of Polynesian culture, the canoes were once used to travel from island to island.

Alaska

THE BASICS

Statehood
January 3, 1959; 49th state

Total area
(land and water)
665,384 sq mi
(1,723,337 sq km)

Land area
570,641 sq mi
(1,477,953 sq km)

Population
737,438

Capital
Juneau
Population 32,113

Largest city
Anchorage
Population 291,538

Racial/ethnic groups
65.8% white; 3.7% African
American; 6.5% Asian; 15.3%
Native American; 7.1% Hispanic
(any race)

Foreign born
7.6%

Urban population
66.0%

Population density
1.3 per sq mi (0.5 per sq km)

GEO WHIZ

**During summer, migrating
humpback whales work
together in Alaskan waters to
catch fish. While swimming in
circles, the whales blow bub-
bles that form a net around
schools of herring. Each whale
can eat hundreds of fish in
one gulp.**

**Climate change and population
growth are changing the route
of the famous Iditarod sled-
dog race. Since 2002, lack of
snow in Wasilla has forced the
starting point for the competition first to Willow and then as
far north as Fairbanks.**

**The Tongass National Forest
in southeastern Alaska is the
largest U.S. national forest.**

Alaska—from *Alyeska*, an Aleut word meaning "great land"—was purchased by the U.S. from Russia in 1867 for just two cents an acre. Many people thought it was a bad investment, but it soon paid off when gold was discovered, and again when major petroleum deposits were discovered in 1968. Today, an 800-mile (1,287-km)-long pipeline links North Slope oil fields to the ice-free port at Valdez, but critics worry about the long-term environmental impact. Everything is big in Alaska. It is the largest state, with one-sixth of the country's land area; it has the highest peak in the United States as well as in North America, Denali (Mount McKinley); and the largest earthquake ever recorded in the United States—a 9.2 magnitude—occurred there in 1964. It is first in forestland, a leading source of seafood, and a major oil producer. Alaska's population has a higher percentage of native people than that of any other state.

🐾 **TIME FOR LUNCH.**
**A grizzly bear fishes
for salmon at Brooks
Falls in Katmai
National Park
and Preserve.**

FORGET-ME-NOT

WILLOW PTARMIGAN

◗ **NORTHERN METROPOLIS.** Anchorage,
established in 1915 as a construction port
for the Alaska Railroad, sits in the shadow
of the snow-covered Chugach Mountains.

THE LAST FRONTIER STATE:
ALASKA

ARCTIC OCEAN

BEAUFORT SEA

NUNAVUT

Utqiaġvik (Barrow) • Point Barrow — Northernmost point in the U.S.

Prudhoe Bay

NORTHWEST TERRITORIES

Point Hope

ALASKA MARITIME N.W.R.

North Slope

Meade

Utukok

Colville

B R O O K S   R A N G E

NOATAK N.W.&S.R.

NOATAK NAT. PRESERVE

CAPE KRUSENSTERN NATIONAL MONUMENT

SALMON N.W.&S.R.

KOBUK VALLEY N.P.

GATES OF THE ARCTIC NAT. PARK & PRESERVE

JOHN N.W.&S.R.

TINAYGUK N.W.&S.R.

ALATNA N.W.&S.R.

KOBUK N.W.&S.R.

KOYUKUK, NORTH FORK N.W.&S.R.

IVISHAK N.W.&S.R.

ARCTIC NATIONAL WILDLIFE REFUGE

WIND N.W.&S.R.

SHEENJEK N.W.&S.R.

Sagavanirktok

Porcupine

YUKON

CANADA / U.S.

Kotzebue

BERING LAND BRIDGE NATIONAL PRESERVE

SELAWIK N.W.R.

SELAWIK N.W.&S.R.

KOYUKUK N.W.R.

Koyukuk

Lowest recorded temperature in the U.S. -80°F (-62°C)

ARCTIC CIRCLE

YUKON FLATS

Fort Yukon

NAT. WILDLIFE REF.

KANUTI N.W.R.

BEAVER CREEK N.W.&S.R.

BIRCH CREEK N.W.&S.R.

YUKON-CHARLEY RIVERS NAT. PRES.

CHARLEY N.W.&S.R.

TRANS-ALASKA PIPELINE

Seward Peninsula

Norton Sound

UNALAKLEET N.W.&S.R.

Unalakleet

INNOKO NAT. WILDLIFE REFUGE

Galena

NOWITNA N.W.R.

Melozitna

Yukon

Tanana

College
Fairbanks • North Pole

FORTYMILE N.W.&S.R.

Tok

TETLIN N.W.R.

A L A S K A

NOWITNA N.W.&S.R.

DENALI NATIONAL PARK & PRES.

Denali (Mt. McKinley) 20,310 ft; 6,190 m
Highest point in North America

IDITAROD NATIONAL HISTORIC TRAIL

DELTA N.W.&S.R.

GULKANA N.W.&S.R.

WRANGELL-ST. ELIAS NATIONAL PARK & PRESERVE
Largest national park in the U.S.
Mt. St. Elias 18,008 ft; 5,489 m

A L A S K A   R A N G E

Susitna

Mountain Village

ANDREAFSKY N.W.&S.R.

Yukon

Kuskokwim

Aniak

Stony

N. Fk.

S. Fk.

Willow
Wasilla • Palmer

Anchorage

Matanuska

Cook Inlet

CHUGACH S.P.

Chugach Mts.

Valdez

Copper

CHUGACH NAT. FOREST

ALASKA HIGHWAY

St. Elias Mountains

KLONDIKE GOLD RUSH N.H.P.

Skagway • Haines

GLACIER BAY NAT. PARK & PRESERVE

Juneau

COAST MOUNTAINS

BRITISH COLUMBIA

Bethel

MULCHATNA N.W.R.

CHILIKADROTNA N.W.&S.R.

TLIKAKILA N.W.&S.R.

LAKE CLARK NAT. PK. & PRESERVE

Iliamna Lake

WOOD-TIKCHIK STATE PARK

TOGIAK N.W.R.

ALAGNAK N.W.&S.R.

Dillingham
Naknek

KATMAI NAT. PARK & PRESERVE

Becharof L.

BECHAROF N.W.R.

ANIAKCHAK NAT. MON. & PRESERVE

Kenai
KENAI N.W.R.
Seward
Kenai Peninsula
KENAI FJORDS NATIONAL PARK
Homer

Prince William Sound
Cordova

MALASPINA GLACIER
Largest piedmont glacier in the world

Largest national forest in the U.S.

TONGASS N.F.
TONGASS NATIONAL FOREST

ADMIRALTY ISLAND N.M.

Chichagof I.
ALEXANDER
Sitka
SITKA N.H.P.
Capital of Russian America until 1867
Baranof I.

ARCHIPELAGO
Prince of Wales I.

Petersburg
Wrangell

MISTY FIORDS NAT. MON.

FOREST
Ketchikan
ANNETTE ISLAND I.R.

U.S. / CANADA

GULF OF ALASKA

KODIAK N.W.R.
Afognak Island
Kodiak
KODIAK N.W.R.
Kodiak Island
Trinity Islands

Bristol Bay

Alaska Peninsula
ANIAKCHAK N.W.&S.R.

Shumagin Islands
REFUGE

PACIFIC OCEAN

Dixon Entrance

A L E U T I A N   I S L A N D S
ALASKA MARITIME NATIONAL WILDLIFE REFUGE

Attu I.
NEAR IS.
Agattu I.
RAT ISLANDS
Kiska I.
Amchitka I.
Semisopochnoi Island
Tanaga I.
Gareloi I.
Adak I.
ADAK NAVAL STATION
ANDREANOF ISLANDS
Atka I. Amlia I.
Seguam I.
Yunaska I.

Continuation of the Aleutian Islands at same scale as main map

LARGEST STATE

Alaska

From the western Aleutians to its southern panhandle, Alaska would extend from coast to coast in the lower 48 states.

200 miles
200 kilometers

Azimuthal Equidistant Projection

MAP KEY

★ State capital
●●● City
■ Point of interest
+ Mountain peak
③ State highway shield
---- Arctic Circle

•—•—• Pipeline
---- Trail
•••••• State or national boundary
Glacier
National Wild & Scenic River

Indian Reservation
State Park unit
National Park Service unit
National Forest
National Wildlife Refuge

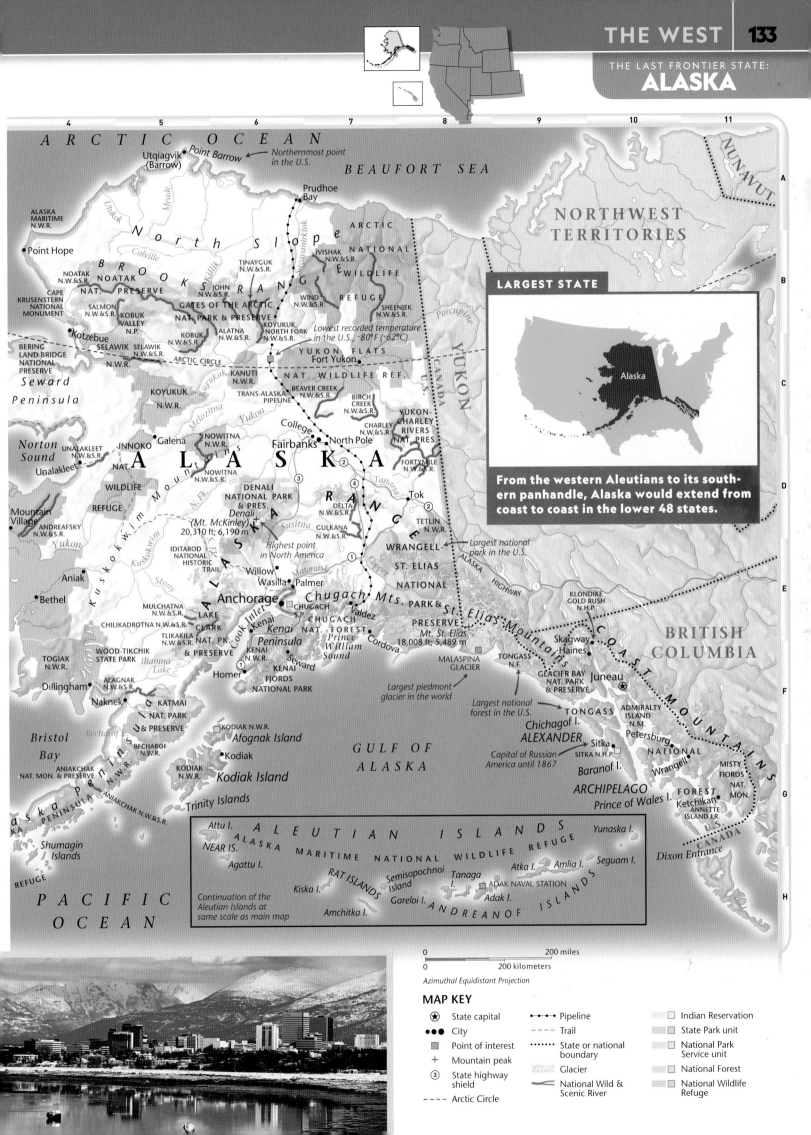

CALIFORNIA REPUBLIC

THE BASICS

Statehood
September 9, 1850; 31st state

Total area (land and water)
163,695 sq mi (423,967 sq km)

Land area
155,779 sq mi (403,466 sq km)

Population
39,557,045

Capital
Sacramento
Population 508,529

Largest city
Los Angeles
Population 3,990,456

Racial/ethnic groups
72.4% white; 6.5% African American; 15.2% Asian; 1.6% Native American; 39.1% Hispanic (any race)

Foreign born
27.0%

Urban population
95.0%

Population density
253.9 per sq mi (98.0 per sq km)

GEO WHIZ

The Monterey Bay Aquarium has worked to save endangered sea otters for more than 20 years.

Castroville, south of San Jose, is known as the Artichoke Capital of the World.

California

The coast of what is now California was visited by Spanish and English explorers in the mid-1500s, but colonization did not begin until 1769 when the first of 21 Spanish missions was established in San Diego. The missions, built mainly to convert (often forcibly) Native Americans to Christianity, eventually extended up the coast as far as Sonoma along a road known as El Camino Real. The United States gained control of California in 1847, following a war with Mexico. The next year gold was discovered near Sutter's Mill, triggering a gold rush and migration from the eastern United States and around the world. Today, California is the most populous state, and its economy ranks above that of most of the world's countries. It is a major source of fruits, nuts, and vegetables and a leader in the entertainment industry and in the production of high-tech equipment.

⬯ **ENGINEERING WONDER.** Stretching more than a mile (1.6 km) across the entrance to San Francisco Bay, the Golden Gate Bridge opened to traffic in 1937. The bridge is painted vermilion orange, a color chosen in part because it is visible in fog.

CALIFORNIA QUAIL
GOLDEN POPPY

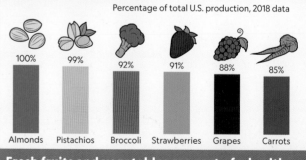

BOUNTIFUL HARVEST

Percentage of total U.S. production, 2018 data

Almonds	Pistachios	Broccoli	Strawberries	Grapes	Carrots
100%	99%	92%	91%	88%	85%

Fresh fruits and vegetables are part of a healthy diet. California leads the country in the overall production of these beneficial crops.

◖ **FOREST GIANT.** Sequoias in Yosemite National Park's Mariposa Grove exceed 200 feet (61 m), making them the world's tallest trees. The trees, some of which are 3,000 years old, grow in isolated groves on the western slopes of the Sierra Nevada.

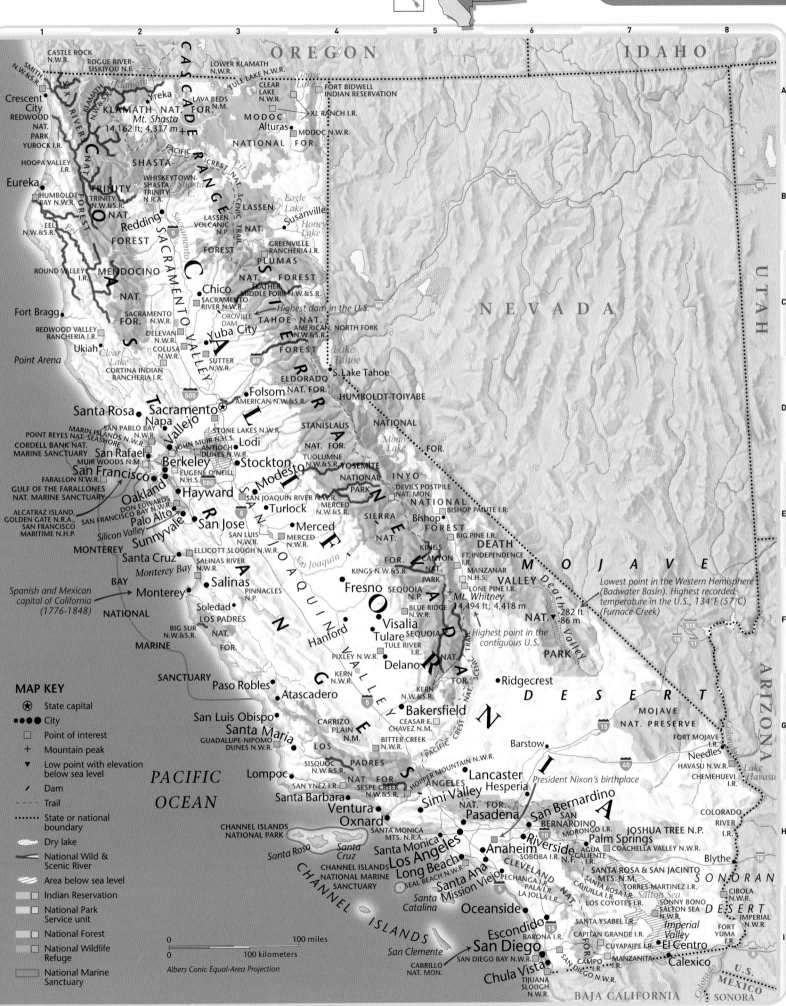

OREGON

IDAHO

NEVADA

UTAH

ARIZONA

MAP KEY

- ⊛ State capital
- ●●●● City
- □ Point of interest
- + Mountain peak
- ▼ Low point with elevation below sea level
- ⟋ Dam
- --- Trail
- ······ State or national boundary
- Dry lake
- National Wild & Scenic River
- Area below sea level
- Indian Reservation
- National Park Service unit
- National Forest
- National Wildlife Refuge
- National Marine Sanctuary

PACIFIC OCEAN

0   100 miles
0   100 kilometers
Albers Conic Equal-Area Projection

Mt. Shasta 14,162 ft; 4,317 m

Highest dam in the U.S.

Lowest point in the Western Hemisphere (Badwater Basin). Highest recorded temperature in the U.S., 134°F (57°C) (Furnace Creek)

-282 ft -86 m

Mt. Whitney 14,494 ft; 4,418 m

Highest point in the contiguous U.S.

Spanish and Mexican capital of California (1776-1848)

President Nixon's birthplace

MOJAVE DESERT

SONORAN DESERT

BAJA CALIFORNIA | SONORA
U.S. | MEXICO

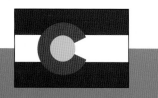

THE BASICS

Statehood
August 1, 1876; 38th state

Total area (land and water)
104,094 sq mi (269,601 sq km)

Land area
103,642 sq mi (268,431 sq km)

Population
5,695,564

Capital
Denver
Population 716,492

Largest city
Denver
Population 716,492

Racial/ethnic groups
87.3% white; 4.5% African American; 3.4% Asian; 1.6% Native American; 21.5% Hispanic (any race)

Foreign born
9.8%

Urban population
86.2%

Population density
55.0 per sq mi (21.2 per sq km)

GEO WHIZ

The Black Canyon of the Gunnison is one of the newest national parks in the Rockies. As it flows through the canyon, the Gunnison River drops an average of 95 feet (29 m) per mile—one of the steepest descents in North America. The craggy rock walls are a mecca for rock climbers.

Colorado's lynx population is making a comeback, thanks to a program that, between 1999 and 2006, released 214 wild cats captured in Canada and Alaska into Colorado's southern Rockies. Based on data from tracking and camera traps, the program has been declared a success.

Colorado

Ancestors of today's Native Americans were the earliest inhabitants of present-day Colorado. Some were cliff dwellers; others were plains dwellers. Spanish explorers arrived in Colorado in 1541. In 1803 eastern Colorado became a U.S. territory as part of the Louisiana Purchase. Gold was discovered in 1858, and thousands were attracted by the prospect of quick wealth. The sudden jump in population led to conflict with the Cheyenne and Arapaho tribes over control of the land, but the settlers prevailed. Completion of the transcontinental railroad in 1869 helped link Colorado to the eastern states and opened its doors for growth. Cattle ranching and farming developed on the High Plains of eastern Colorado, while mining was the focus in the mountainous western part of the state. Mining is still important in Colorado, but the focus has shifted to energy resources—oil, natural gas, coal, and wind. Agriculture is also a major source of income, with cattle accounting for half of farm income. And Colorado's majestic mountains attract thousands of tourists each year.

⬒ THRILLING SPORT. Colorado's snow-covered mountains attract winter sports enthusiasts from near and far. In the past, skis were used by gold prospectors. Today, skiing and snowboarding are big moneymakers in the state's recreation and tourism industry.

COLUMBINE

LARK BUNTING

◖ ANCIENT CULTURE. Ancestors of today's pueblo-dwelling people lived from about A.D. 600 to 1300 in the canyons that today are part of Mesa Verde National Park. More than 600 stone structures were built on protected cliffs of the canyon walls; others were located on mesas. These dwellings hold many clues to a past way of life.

Only spot in the U.S. where the borders of 4 states come together

THE CENTENNIAL STATE:
COLORADO

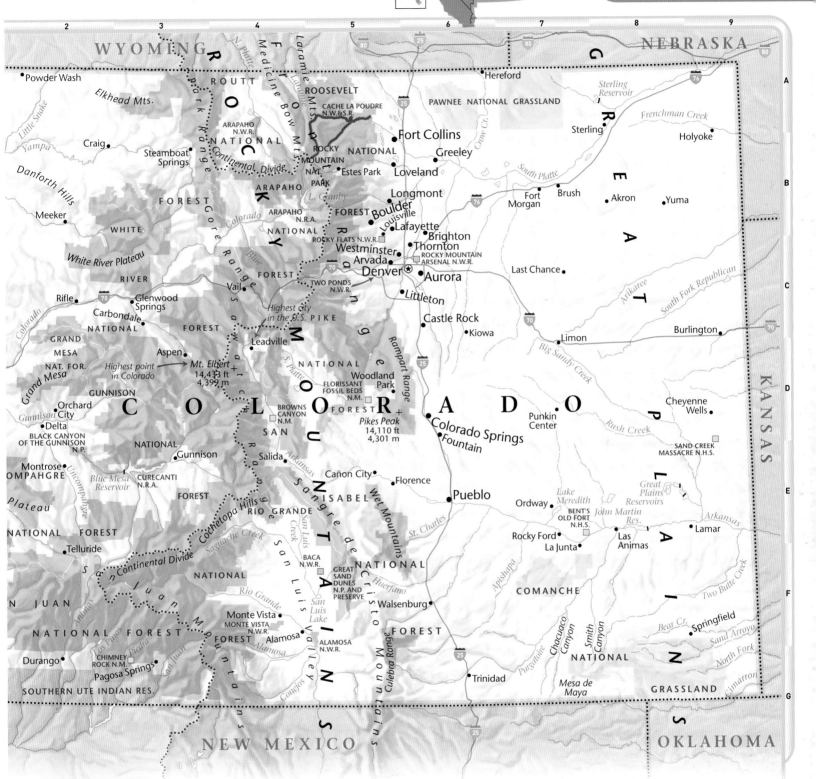

NEBRASKA

WYOMING

• Powder Wash

Elkhead Mts.

Little Snake

Yampa

Danforth Hills

• Craig

Steamboat
Springs

• Meeker

ROUTT

Park Range

ARAPAHO
N.W.R.

NATIONAL

Continental Divide

FOREST

WHITE

White River Plateau

RIVER

GORE

N. Platte

Medicine Bow Mts.

Laramie Mts.

Laramie

Fort
Collins

ROOSEVELT

CACHE LA POUDRE
N.W.&S.R.

ROCKY
MOUNTAIN
NAT.
PARK

Estes Park

L. Granby

Colorado

ARAPAHO
N.R.A.

ARAPAHO

NATIONAL

FOREST

Blue

Gore Range

Vail

NATIONAL

FOREST

TWO PONDS
N.W.R.

ROCKY FLATS N.W.R.

NATIONAL

Boulder
Louisville
Lafayette
Brighton
Thornton

Westminster
Arvada
Denver
Aurora

Littleton

Longmont

Greeley

Loveland

PAWNEE NATIONAL GRASSLAND

Sterling
Reservoir

Sterling

Fort
Morgan

Brush

Last Chance

ROCKY MOUNTAIN
ARSENAL N.W.R.

Akron

Frenchman Creek

Holyoke

Yuma

Crow Cr.

South Platte

GREAT

NEBRASKA

• Rifle

Glenwood
Springs

Carbondale

NATIONAL

GRAND
MESA

NAT. FOR.

Grand Mesa

• Orchard
City

Gunnison
• Delta

BLACK CANYON
OF THE GUNNISON
N.P.

• Montrose

UMPAHGRE

Plateau

NATIONAL FOREST

• Telluride

Continental Divide

SAN JUAN

NATIONAL FOREST

• Durango

Colorado

Leadville

Highest city
in the U.S. PIKE

Highest point
in Colorado
Mt. Elbert
14,433 ft
4,399 m

• Aspen

COLORADO

Sawatch Range

GUNNISON

NATIONAL

FOREST

BROWNS
CANYON
N.M.

• Gunnison

Blue Mesa
Reservoir

CURECANTI
N.R.A.

Gunnison

FOREST

Uncompahgre

San Juan

Rio Grande

Animas

Los Pinos

CHIMNEY
ROCK N.M.

Pagosa Springs

SOUTHERN UTE INDIAN RES.

San Juan Mountains

Piedra

Continental Divide

Cochetopa Hills

Saguache Creek

RIO GRANDE

NATIONAL

FOREST

Salida

SAN

Arkansas

Cañon City

Florence

S. Platte

NATIONAL

Woodland
Park

FLORISSANT
FOSSIL BEDS
N.M.

Pikes Peak
14,110 ft
4,301 m

Range

MOUNTAINS

Sangre de Cristo Mountains

San Luis

Creek

San Luis
Lake

BACA
N.W.R.

GREAT
SAND
DUNES
N.P. AND
PRESERVE

MONTE VISTA
N.W.R.

Monte Vista

Alamosa
ALAMOSA
N.W.R.

Rio Grande

Alamosa

Conejos

Valley

Castle Rock

Kiowa

Colorado Springs
Fountain

Pueblo

Ordway

Rampart Range

ISABEL

Wet Mountains

St. Charles

NATIONAL

Huerfano

Walsenburg

FOREST

Culebra Range

Trinidad

Punkin
Center

BENT'S
OLD FORT
N.H.S.

Rocky Ford

La Junta

COMANCHE

Purgatoire

Limon

Big Sandy Creek

Rush Creek

Lake
Meredith

John Martin
Res.

Las
Animas

Apishapa

Chacuaco
Canyon

Smith
Canyon

Mesa de
Maya

NATIONAL

GRASSLAND

Cheyenne
Wells

Arikaree

Burlington

SAND CREEK
MASSACRE N.H.S.

Great
Plains
Reservoirs

Lamar

Bear Cr.

Springfield

Sand Arroyo

North Fork

Cimarron

Two Butte Creek

Arkansas

South Fork Republican

GREAT

PLAINS

KANSAS

OKLAHOMA

NEW MEXICO

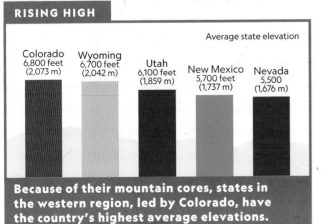

RISING HIGH

Average state elevation

Colorado	Wyoming	Utah	New Mexico	Nevada
6,800 feet (2,073 m)	6,700 feet (2,042 m)	6,100 feet (1,859 m)	5,700 feet (1,737 m)	5,500 feet (1,676 m)

Because of their mountain cores, states in the western region, led by Colorado, have the country's highest average elevations.

MAP KEY

⊛ State capital

●●● City

◻ Point of interest

+ Mountain peak

/ Dam

Indian Reservation

···· State boundary

······ Continental Divide

National Wild &
Scenic River

National Park
Service unit

National Forest

National Grassland

National Wildlife
Refuge

0   50 miles

0   50 kilometers

THE BASICS

Statehood
August 21, 1959; 50th state

Total area (land and water)
10,932 sq mi (28,313 sq km)

Land area
6,423 sq mi (16,635 sq km)

Population
1,420,491

Capital
Honolulu/Honolulu County
Population 980,080

Largest city
Honolulu/Honolulu County
Population 980,080

Racial/ethnic groups
25.7% white; 2.2% African American; 37.8% Asian; 10.2% Pacific Islander; 10.5% Hispanic (any race)

Foreign born
18.1%

Urban population
91.9%

Population density
129.9 per sq mi (50.2 per sq km)

GEO WHIZ

Hawai'i is the world's most isolated population center — 2,300 miles (3,700 km) from California; and 3,850 miles (6,196 km) from Japan.

You can ski two ways in Hawai'i: on the water at the beach and on snow at Mauna Kea on the Big Island.

HIBISCUS

HAWAIIAN GOOSE
(NENE)

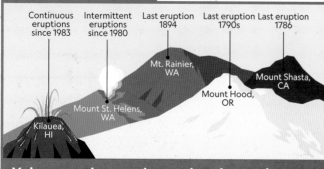

DANGER FROM BELOW

Volcanoes release molten rock and gases from beneath Earth's crust, often with explosive force that can put people and property at great risk.

Hawai'i

Some 1,500 years ago Polynesians traveling in large canoes arrived from the south to settle the volcanic islands that make up Hawai'i. In 1778 Captain James Cook claimed the islands for Britain, and soon Hawai'i became a center of the whaling industry and a major producer of sugarcane. The spread of sugarcane plantations led to the importation of workers from Asia. Hawai'i became a U.S. territory in 1900. Naval installations, established as fueling depots and to protect U.S. interests in the Pacific, were attacked by the Japanese in 1941, an act that officially brought the United States into World War II. In 1959 Hawai'i became the 50th state. Tourism, agriculture, and the military, with bases centered on O'ahu's Pearl Harbor, are the cornerstone of Hawai'i's economy today. Jet airline service makes the state accessible to tourists from both the mainland United States and Asia as well as from Australia and New Zealand. Hawai'i is still a major producer of sugarcane and other plant products.

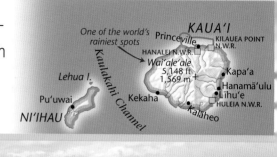

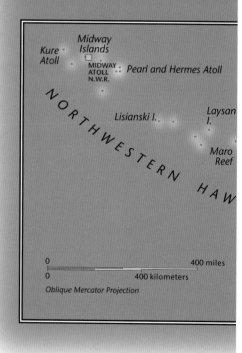

⬤ **ISLAND PARADISE.**
Waikiki, where sandy beaches attract thousands of visitors, is the center of Honolulu's tourist industry.

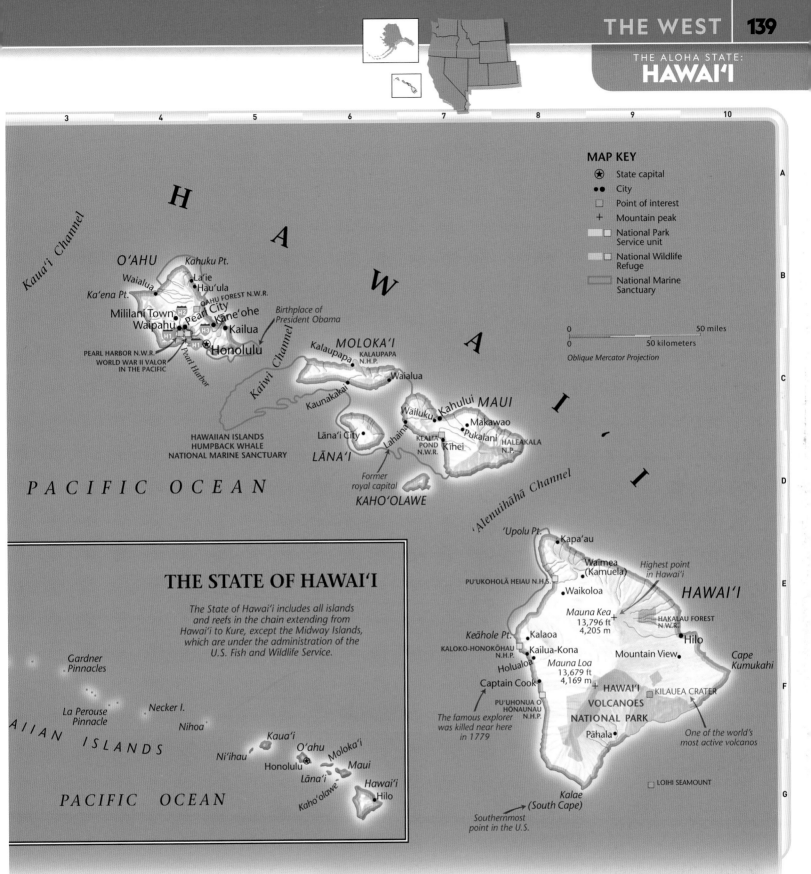

MAP KEY

★ State capital
•• City
□ Point of interest
+ Mountain peak
National Park Service unit
National Wildlife Refuge
National Marine Sanctuary

0   50 miles
0   50 kilometers
Oblique Mercator Projection

3   4   5   6   7   8   9   10

A B C D E F G

PACIFIC OCEAN

H A W A I I

Kaua'i Channel

O'AHU
Kahuku Pt.
Waialua
La'ie
Hau'ula
Ka'ena Pt.
Mililani Town
Pearl City
Kāne'ohe
Waipahu
Kailua
Birthplace of President Obama
PEARL HARBOR N.W.R.
WORLD WAR II VALOR IN THE PACIFIC
★ Honolulu
OAHU FOREST N.W.R.
Pearl Harbor

Kaiwi Channel

MOLOKA'I
Kalaupapa
KALAUPAPA N.H.P.
Waialua
Kaunakakai

LĀNA'I
Lāna'i City
Lahaina
Former royal capital

KAHO'OLAWE

Wailuku
Kahului
MAUI
Makawao
Pukalani
KEALIA POND N.W.R.
Kīhei
HALEAKALA N.P.

HAWAIIAN ISLANDS HUMPBACK WHALE NATIONAL MARINE SANCTUARY

'Alenuihāhā Channel

'Upolu Pt.
Kapa'au
Waimea (Kamuela)
Highest point in Hawai'i
PU'UKOHOLĀ HEIAU N.H.S.
Waikoloa
HAWAI'I
Keāhole Pt.
Kalaoa
Mauna Kea
13,796 ft
4,205 m
HAKALAU FOREST N.W.R.
Hilo
KALOKO-HONOKŌHAU N.H.P.
Kailua-Kona
Mountain View
Holualoa
Mauna Loa
13,679 ft
4,169 m
Cape Kumukahi
Captain Cook
HAWAI'I VOLCANOES NATIONAL PARK
KILAUEA CRATER
PU'UHONUA O HŌNAUNAU N.H.P.
The famous explorer was killed near here in 1779
Pāhala
One of the world's most active volcanos
□ LOIHI SEAMOUNT
Kalae (South Cape)
Southernmost point in the U.S.

THE STATE OF HAWAI'I

The State of Hawai'i includes all islands and reefs in the chain extending from Hawai'i to Kure, except the Midway Islands, which are under the administration of the U.S. Fish and Wildlife Service.

Gardner Pinnacles
La Perouse Pinnacle
Necker I.
Nihoa
HAWAIIAN ISLANDS
Kaua'i
Ni'ihau
O'ahu
Moloka'i
Honolulu ★
Lāna'i
Maui
Kaho'olawe
Hawai'i
Hilo
PACIFIC OCEAN

◗ **FIERY CREATION.** Hawai'i is the fastest-growing U.S. state—not in people, but in land. Active volcanoes are constantly creating new land as lava continues to flow. Recent eruptions on Kilauea, Hawai'i's most active volcano, have added more than 700 acres (283 ha) of new land to the state.

THE BASICS

Statehood
July 3, 1890; 43rd state

Total area (land and water)
83,569 sq mi (216,443 sq km)

Land area
82,643 sq mi (214,045 sq km)

Population
1,754,208

Capital
Boise
Population 228,790

Largest city
Boise
Population 228,790

Racial/ethnic groups
93.2% white; 0.9% African American; 1.5% Asian; 1.7% Native American; 12.5% Hispanic (any race)

Foreign born
5.9%

Urban population
70.6%

Population density
21.2 per sq mi (8.2 per sq km)

GEO WHIZ

Before the last ice age, huge mammals roamed what is now Idaho. Fossils of these creatures are displayed at the Museum of Idaho, in Idaho Falls.

Apollo astronauts trained for their moon mission in the harsh environment of Craters of the Moon National Monument and Preserve.

SYRINGA
(MOCK ORANGE)

MOUNTAIN BLUEBIRD

Idaho

Some of the earliest Native American sites in what is now Idaho date back more than 10,000 years. In the 18th century, contact between native people and Europeans not only brought trade and cultural change, but also diseases that wiped out many native groups. Present-day Idaho was part of the 1803 Louisiana Purchase and was explored during the Lewis and Clark expedition. In 1843 wagons crossed into Idaho on the Oregon Trail. The arrival of white settlers caused conflict with Native Americans, which continued until 1890 when Idaho became a state. Today, almost half the land is planted with crops, especially wheat, sugar beets, barley, and potatoes. The state encourages the use of alternative energy, such as wind, geothermal, and biomass, including ethanol. Manufacturing and high-tech industries have diversified the economy, and the state's natural beauty attracts tourists.

⬡ **WOOLLY RUSH HOUR.** Sheep fill a roadway in Idaho's Salmon River Valley. The herds move twice a year. In the spring they migrate north to mountain pastures. In the fall they return to the Snake River Plain in the south.

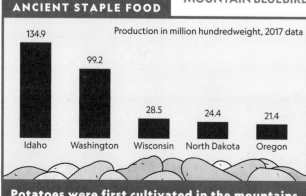

ANCIENT STAPLE FOOD

Production in million hundredweight, 2017 data

State	Production
Idaho	134.9
Washington	99.2
Wisconsin	28.5
North Dakota	24.4
Oregon	21.4

Potatoes were first cultivated in the mountains of South America by native peoples. Today, Idaho leads in U.S. potato production.

⬡ **TIMBER!** More than 60 percent of Idaho's land area is tree-covered, much of it in national forests. Lumber and paper products, most of which are sold to other states, are important to the state economy.

⬡ **ROLLING SPUDS.** Growing more than 30 varieties of potatoes, Idaho leads the country in production of this staple food crop. More than 60 percent of all potatoes grown in the state end up as french fries. Much of the rest goes to fresh-food markets and for making chips.

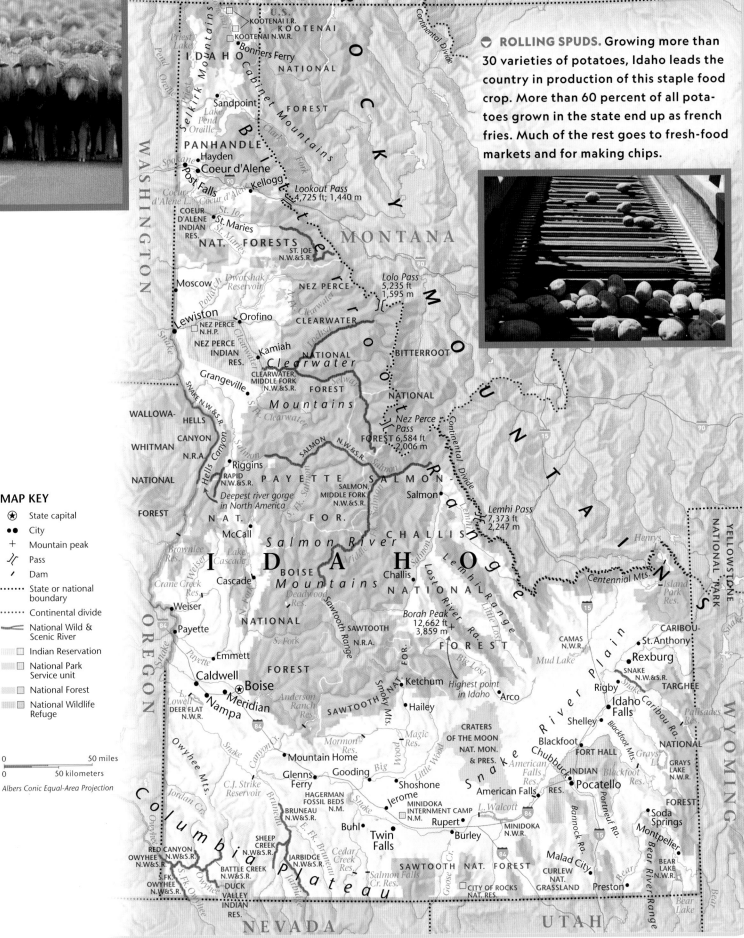

MAP KEY

- ⭐ State capital
- ●● City
- ✛ Mountain peak
-)(Pass
- ⸌ Dam
- ⋯⋯ State or national boundary
- ∙∙∙∙ Continental divide
- National Wild & Scenic River
- Indian Reservation
- National Park Service unit
- National Forest
- National Wildlife Refuge

0 ___ 50 miles
0 ___ 50 kilometers

Albers Conic Equal-Area Projection

BRITISH COLUMBIA
CANADA
U.S.
ALBERTA

KOOTENAI I.R.
KOOTENAI N.W.R.
Bonners Ferry
IDAHO
KOOTENAI
NATIONAL
FOREST

Priest Lake
Selkirk Mountains
Cabinet Mountains
Clark Fork
Pend Oreille
Lake Pend Oreille
Sandpoint

ROCKY

PANHANDLE
Hayden
Coeur d'Alene
Post Falls
Coeur d'Alene Lake
Spokane
Kellogg
Lookout Pass
4,725 ft; 1,440 m

MONTANA

COEUR D'ALENE INDIAN RES.
St. Joe
St. Maries
NAT. FORESTS
ST. JOE N.W.&S.R.

Moscow
Dworshak Reservoir
NEZ PERCE
Lolo Pass
5,235 ft
1,595 m

Lewiston
Orofino
NEZ PERCE N.H.P.
Kamiah
NEZ PERCE INDIAN RES.
CLEARWATER
NATIONAL
BITTERROOT

Clearwater
CLEARWATER, MIDDLE FORK N.W.&S.R.
Grangeville
FOREST
Mountains
NATIONAL
Selway

WALLOWA-
WHITMAN
HELLS CANYON N.R.A.
SNAKE N.W.&S.R.
Snake
S.F. Clearwater
Nez Perce Pass
6,584 ft
2,006 m
FOREST

NATIONAL
Salmon
Riggins
RAPID N.W.&S.R.
PAYETTE
SALMON N.W.&S.R.
SALMON, MIDDLE FORK N.W.&S.R.
Salmon
Salmon

FOREST
Deepest river gorge in North America
Hells Canyon
S. FK. Salmon
CHALLIS
Lemhi Pass
7,373 ft
2,247 m

McCall
Brownlee Res.
Lake Cascade
Salmon River
Mountains
Challis
NATIONAL
Lost River Ra.
Lemhi Range

IDAHO

Weiser Res.
Crane Creek Res.
Cascade
BOISE
Deadwood Res.
FOR.
Borah Peak
12,662 ft
3,859 m
Highest point in Idaho
FOREST
Centennial Mts.
Henrys L.
Island Park Res.

Weiser
NATIONAL
Sawtooth Range
SAWTOOTH
N.R.A.
Big Lost
Little Lost
CAMAS N.W.R.
Mud Lake

Payette
Emmett
FOREST
S. Fork
Anderson Ranch Res.
Ketchum
Arco
SNAKE N.W.&S.R.
Snake River Plain
CARIBOU
St. Anthony
Rexburg

Caldwell
Nampa
Meridian
Boise
Hailey
CRATERS OF THE MOON NAT. MON. & PRES.
Rigby
Idaho Falls
TARGHEE

OREGON

DEER FLAT N.W.R.
L. Lowell
Smoky Mts.
SAWTOOTH
Magic Res.
Shelley
Blackfoot Mts.
Palisades Res.
NATIONAL

Mountain Home
Glenns Ferry
Gooding
Shoshone
Jerome
Blackfoot
FORT HALL
Chubbuck
Grays L.
GRAYS LAKE N.W.R.

C.J. Strike Reservoir
Mormon Res.
Big Wood
Little Wood
MINIDOKA INTERNMENT CAMP N.M.
American Falls
FORT HALL INDIAN RES.
Pocatello
FOREST
WYOMING

Owyhee Mts.
Canyon Cr.
HAGERMAN FOSSIL BEDS N.M.
L. Walcott
Rupert
L. Walcott
American Falls Res.
Bannock Ra.
Soda Springs
Montpelier

Jordan Cr.
Bruneau
Buhl
Twin Falls
MINIDOKA N.W.R.
Burley
Portneuf Ra.
BEAR LAKE N.W.R.
Bear

RED CANYON OWYHEE N.W.&S.R.
SHEEP CREEK N.W.&S.R.
BRUNEAU N.W.&S.R.
E. FK. Bruneau
JARBIDGE N.W.&S.R.
Cedar Creek Res.
Salmon Falls Cr. Res.
SAWTOOTH NAT. FOREST
Malad City
CURLEW NAT. GRASSLAND
Bear Lake

Columbia Plateau
BATTLE CREEK N.W.&S.R.
DUCK VALLEY INDIAN RES.
S. FK. OWYHEE N.W.&S.R.
Owyhee
Bruneau
CITY OF ROCKS NAT. RES.
Preston
Bear River Range

NEVADA
UTAH

ROCKY
Bitterroot
Continental Divide
MOUNTAINS
Continental Divide

YELLOWSTONE NATIONAL PARK

WASHINGTON

Snake
Goose Cr.

THE BASICS

Statehood
November 8, 1889; 41st state

Total area (land and water)
147,040 sq mi (380,831 sq km)

Land area
145,546 sq mi (376,962 sq km)

Population
1,062,305

Capital
Helena
Population 32,315

Largest city
Billings
Population 109,550

Racial/ethnic groups
89.1% white; 0.6% African
American; 0.8% Asian; 6.7%
Native American; 3.8%
Hispanic (any race)

Foreign born
2.1%

Urban population
55.9%

Population density
7.3 per sq mi (2.8 per sq km)

GEO WHIZ

The fossil of a turkey-size
dinosaur is being called the
missing link between Asian
and North American horned
dinosaurs. Paleontologist
Paul Horner discovered the
fossil while sitting on it
during a lunch break at a
dig near Choteau.

Montana is the only state
with river systems that
empty southeast into the
Gulf of Mexico, north into
Canada's Hudson Bay, and
west into the Pacific Ocean.

WESTERN
MEADOWLARK

BITTERROOT

⬤ **STEP BACK IN TIME.** Just like in the past,
Montana ranchers move their cattle herds from
low winter pastures to higher elevations for summer grazing. Some ranches allow adventurous
tourists to participate in the drives.

Montana

Long before the arrival of
Europeans, numerous native groups
lived and hunted in the plains and
mountains of present-day Montana.
Although contact between European
explorers and these Native Americans
was often peaceful, Montana was the
site of the historic 1876 Battle of the
Little Bighorn, in which Lakota (Sioux)
and Cheyenne warriors defeated George
Armstrong Custer's troops. In the mid-19th
century, the discovery of gold and silver
attracted many prospectors, and later cattle
ranching became big business, adding to tensions
with the native people. Montana became the 41st
state in 1889. Today, Native Americans make up almost
7 percent of the state's population—only four other
states have a larger percentage. Agriculture is important to the economy, producing wheat, hay, and barley
as well as beef cattle. Mining and timber industries have
seen a decline, but service industries and tourism are
growing. Montana's natural environment, including Glacier and
Yellowstone National Parks, remains one of its greatest resources.

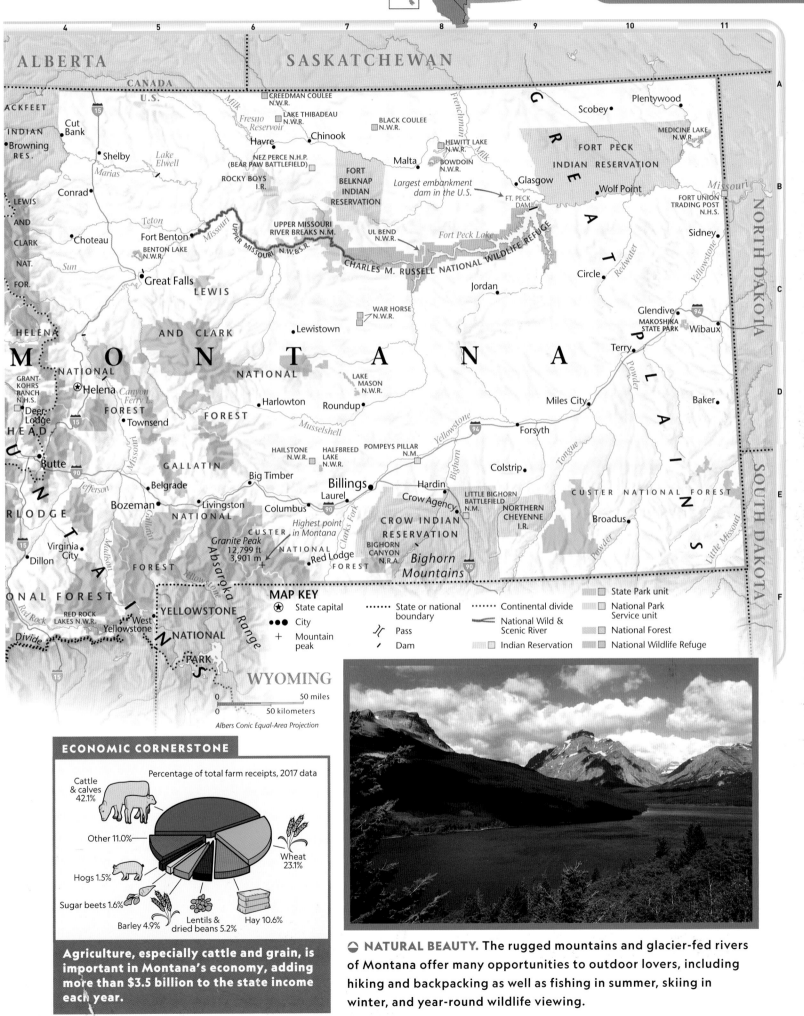

ALBERTA

SASKATCHEWAN

CANADA
U.S.

ACKFEET

INDIAN

RES.

- Browning

LEWIS

AND

CLARK

NAT.

FOR.

HELENA

Cut Bank

Shelby

Conrad

Choteau

Fort Benton

BENTON LAKE
N.W.R.

Great Falls

Lake
Elwell

Marias

Teton

Missouri

Sun

LEWIS

AND CLARK

NATIONAL

CREEDMAN COULEE
N.W.R.

Fresno
Reservoir

Havre

Chinook

NEZ PERCE N.H.P.
(BEAR PAW BATTLEFIELD)

ROCKY BOYS
I.R.

LAKE THIBADEAU
N.W.R.

BLACK COULEE
N.W.R.

Malta

FORT
BELKNAP
INDIAN
RESERVATION

UPPER MISSOURI
RIVER BREAKS N.M.

UPPER MISSOURI   N.W.&.R.

UL BEND
N.W.R.

HEWITT LAKE
N.W.R.

BOWDOIN
N.W.R.

Frenchman

Milk

Largest embankment
dam in the U.S.

Glasgow

FT. PECK
DAM.

CHARLES M. RUSSELL NATIONAL WILDLIFE REFUGE

Fort Peck Lake

Scobey

Plentywood

FORT PECK
INDIAN RESERVATION

Wolf Point

G
R
E
A
T

MEDICINE LAKE
N.W.R.

FORT UNION
TRADING POST
N.H.S.

Missouri

Sidney

M O N T A N A

NATIONAL

FOREST

HELENA

NATIONAL

GRANT-
KOHRS
RANCH
N.H.S.

Deer
Lodge

Butte

Helena

Canyon
Ferry L.

Townsend

FOREST

Missouri

Jefferson

90

15

Harlowton

Roundup

Musselshell

Lewistown

WAR HORSE
N.W.R.

LAKE
MASON
N.W.R.

Jordan

Circle

Redwater

Glendive

MAKOSHIKA
STATE PARK

Terry

Miles City

Forsyth

94

Powder

Yellowstone

T

Wibaux

Baker

P

L

A

I

N

S

N O R T H   D A K O T A

S O U T H   D A K O T A

GALLATIN

Belgrade

Bozeman

Gallatin

HEAD

RLODGE

Virginia
City

Dillon

Livingston

Big Timber

NATIONAL

Columbus

Madison

HAILSTONE
N.W.R.

HALFBREED
LAKE
N.W.R.

Laurel

Billings

Clarks Fork

Highest point
in Montana

CUSTER

Granite Peak
12,799 ft
3,901 m

NATIONAL

Red Lodge

FOREST

POMPEYS PILLAR
N.M.

Yellowstone

94

Hardin

Crow Agency

CROW INDIAN
RESERVATION

BIGHORN
CANYON
N.R.A.

Bighorn
Mountains

LITTLE BIGHORN
BATTLEFIELD
N.M.

NORTHERN
CHEYENNE
I.R.

Colstrip

Bighorn

Tongue

CUSTER NATIONAL FOREST

Broadus

Powder

Little Missouri

90

RED ROCK
LAKES N.W.R.

Red Rock

YELLOWSTONE

NATIONAL

PARK

West
Yellowstone

Absaroka Range

Yellowstone

Divide

15

WYOMING

MAP KEY

★ State capital

●●● City

+ Mountain peak

⋯⋯ State or national
boundary

)(Pass

⌐ Dam

⋯⋯ Continental divide

〰 National Wild &
Scenic River

▱ Indian Reservation

▢ State Park unit

▢ National Park
Service unit

▨ National Forest

▨ National Wildlife Refuge

0 ___ 50 miles
0 ___ 50 kilometers
Albers Conic Equal-Area Projection

ECONOMIC CORNERSTONE

Percentage of total farm receipts, 2017 data

Cattle
& calves
42.1%

Other 11.0%

Hogs 1.5%

Sugar beets 1.6%

Barley 4.9%

Lentils &
dried beans 5.2%

Hay 10.6%

Wheat
23.1%

Agriculture, especially cattle and grain, is important in Montana's economy, adding more than $3.5 billion to the state income each year.

NATURAL BEAUTY. The rugged mountains and glacier-fed rivers of Montana offer many opportunities to outdoor lovers, including hiking and backpacking as well as fishing in summer, skiing in winter, and year-round wildlife viewing.

THE BASICS

Statehood
October 31, 1864; 36th state

Total area (land and water)
110,572 sq mi (286,380 sq km)

Land area
109,781 sq mi (284,332 sq km)

Population
3,034,392

Capital
Carson City
Population 55,414

Largest city
Las Vegas
Population 644,644

Racial/ethnic groups
74.6% white; 9.8% African
American; 8.8% Asian; 1.7%
Native American; 28.8%
Hispanic (any race)

Foreign born
19.5%

Urban population
94.2%

Population density
27.6 per sq mi (10.7 per sq km)

GEO WHIZ

The Applegate Trail, named
for two brothers, offered a
shorter alternative to the
Oregon Trail.

Highway 375 is named
Extraterrestrial Highway
because of all the reported
extraterrestrial sightings.

MOUNTAIN BLUEBIRD
SAGEBRUSH

Nevada

Nevada's earliest inhabitants were ancestors of today's Native Americans. Around 2,000 years ago, they began establishing permanent dwellings of clay and stone perched atop rocky ledges in what today is the state of Nevada. This was what Spanish explorers saw when they arrived in 1776. In years that followed, many expeditions passing through the area faced challenges of a difficult environment and Native Americans protecting their land. In the mid-1800s gold and silver were discovered. In 1861 the Nevada Territory was created, and three years later statehood was granted. Today, the Nevada landscape is dotted with ghost towns—places once prosperous but now abandoned except for curious tourists. Mining is now overshadowed by other economic activities. Casinos, modern hotels, and lavish entertainment attract thousands of visitors each year. Hoover Dam, on the Colorado River, supplies power to much of Nevada, as well as Arizona and California. But limited water promises to be a challenge to Nevada's future growth.

⬭ **TURNING BACK TIME.** The Luxor, re-creating a scene from ancient Egypt, is one of the many hotel-casinos that attract thousands of tourists to the four-mile (6-km) section of Las Vegas known as the Strip.

⬭ **DESERT BEAUTY.** A beavertail cactus thrives in the dry environment of Valley of Fire State Park. The park, Nevada's oldest, gets its name from red sandstone formations visible in the distance.

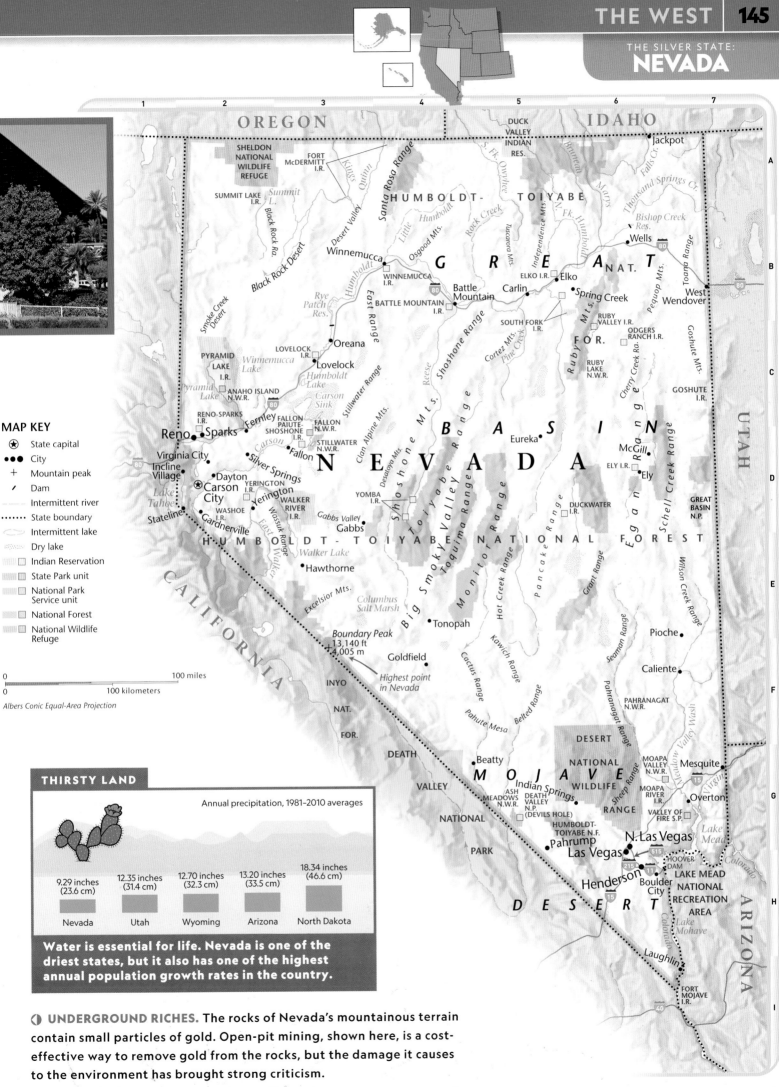

MAP KEY

⊛ State capital
●●● City
+ Mountain peak
⟋ Dam
— Intermittent river
····· State boundary
····· Intermittent lake
Dry lake
☐ Indian Reservation
☐ State Park unit
☐ National Park Service unit
☐ National Forest
☐ National Wildlife Refuge

0 ——— 100 miles
0 ——— 100 kilometers
Albers Conic Equal-Area Projection

Boundary Peak
13,140 ft
4,005 m
Highest point in Nevada

THIRSTY LAND

Annual precipitation, 1981–2010 averages

9.29 inches (23.6 cm)	12.35 inches (31.4 cm)	12.70 inches (32.3 cm)	13.20 inches (33.5 cm)	18.34 inches (46.6 cm)
Nevada	Utah	Wyoming	Arizona	North Dakota

Water is essential for life. Nevada is one of the driest states, but it also has one of the highest annual population growth rates in the country.

◖ **UNDERGROUND RICHES.** The rocks of Nevada's mountainous terrain contain small particles of gold. Open-pit mining, shown here, is a cost-effective way to remove gold from the rocks, but the damage it causes to the environment has brought strong criticism.

THE BEAVER STATE:
OREGON

THE BASICS

Statehood
February 14, 1859; 33rd state

Total area (land and water)
98,379 sq mi (254,799 sq km)

Land area
95,988 sq mi (248,608 sq km)

Population
4,190,713

Capital
Salem
Population 173,442

Largest city
Portland
Population 653,115

Racial/ethnic groups
87.1% white; 2.2% African American; 4.7% Asian; 1.8% Native American; 13.1% Hispanic (any race)

Foreign born
9.9%

Urban population
81.0%

Population density
43.7 per sq mi (16.9 per sq km)

GEO WHIZ

To recover wetlands and save two endangered fish species, 100 tons (90 t) of explosives were used to blast through levees so that water from the Williamson River could again flow into Upper Klamath Lake.

Crater Lake (1,932 ft/589 m) is the deepest in the United States. It fills a depression created when an eruption caused the top of a mountain to collapse. Wizard Island, at the center of the lake, is the top of the volcano.

Mount Hood, a dormant volcano near Portland, is Oregon's highest peak, rising 11,239 feet (3,426 m). Its last major eruption was in the 1790s, a few years before the Lewis and Clark expedition reached the region.

Oregon

Long before the Oregon Trail brought settlers from the eastern United States, Native Americans fished and hunted in Oregon's coastal waters and forested valleys. Spanish explorers sailed along Oregon's coast in 1543, and in the 18th century fur traders from Europe set up forts in the region. In the mid-1800s settlers began farming the rich soil of the Willamette Valley. Oregon achieved statehood in 1859, and by 1883 railroads linked Oregon to the East, and Portland had become an important shipping center. Today, forestry, fishing, and agriculture make up a significant part of the state economy, but Oregon is diversifying into manufacturing and high-tech industries. Dams on the Columbia River generate inexpensive electricity to support energy-hungry industries, such as aluminum production. Computers, electronics, and research-based industries are expanding. Snowcapped volcanoes, old-growth forests, and a rocky coastline help make tourism an important growth industry.

TOWER OF HISTORY. The 125-foot (38-m) Astoria Column, built in 1926 near the mouth of the Columbia River, is decorated with historic scenes of exploration and settlement along the Pacific Northwest coast.

OREGON GRAPE
WESTERN MEADOWLARK

HOLIDAY EVERGREENS

Christmas trees harvested, 2016 data

State	Trees harvested
Oregon	5.2 million
North Carolina	3.5 million
Michigan	3.0 million
Pennsylvania	2.3 million
Washington	1.5 million

Oregon's marine west coast climate provides an ideal environment for growing firs and spruce for the lucrative Christmas tree market.

MAP KEY

★ State capital
●●● City
+ Mountain peak
∕ Dam
- - - Trail
⋯⋯ State boundary

▨ Dry lake
〰 National Wild & Scenic River
☐ Indian Reservation
☐ National Park Service unit

☐ National Forest
☐ National Grassland
☐ National Wildlife Refuge

0   50 miles
0   50 kilometers
Albers Conic Equal-Area Projection

WASHINGTON

Columbia

LEWIS & CLARK N.W.R.
Nehalem
Rainier
St. Helens
Scappoose
Hillsboro
Forest Grove
Beaverton
Tigard
Portland
Lake Oswego
Gresham
McLOUGHLIN HOUSE N.H.S.
Oregon City
Newburg
BASKETT SLOUGH N.W.R.
McMinnville
Woodburn
Sheridan
GRAND RONDE I.R.
Dallas
Monmouth
Salem
Stayton
ANKENY N.W.R.
Albany
Corvallis
Lebanon
WILLIAM L. FINLEY N.W.R.
Sweet Home
Junction City
Eugene
Springfield
Cottage Grove
Sutherlin
N. Umpqua
UMPQUA
NORTH UMPQUA N.W.&S.R.
Roseburg
Winston
COW CREEK I.R.
S. Umpqua
NATIONAL
UPPER ROGUE N.W.&S.R.
Rogue
FOREST
RIVER-SISKIYOU
Grants Pass
White City
Central Point
Medford
OREGON CAVES N.M.
Ashland
N.F.
KLAMATH NATIONAL FOREST

Columbia
BONNEVILLE DAM
COLUMBIA RIVER GORGE NATIONAL SCENIC AREA
Hood River
The Dalles
Mt. Hood 11,239 ft 3,426 m   Highest point in Oregon
MOUNT HOOD NAT. FOR.
SANDY N.W.&S.R.
SALMON N.W.&S.R.
ROARING R.
CLACKAMAS
ELKHORN CREEK N.W.&S.R.
QUARTZVILLE CR. N.W.&S.R.
McKenzie
McKENZIE N.W.&S.R.
SQUAW CREEK N.W.&S.R.
WARM SPRINGS INDIAN RES.
Madras
METOLIUS N.W.&S.R.
CROOKED RIVER NATIONAL GRASSLAND
Redmond
Bend
DESCHUTES
WILLAMETTE N.W.&S.R.
NEWBERRY NAT. VOLCANIC MON.
CRESCENT CREEK N.W.&S.R.
LITTLE DESCHUTES N.W.&S.R.
BIG MARSH CREEK N.W.&S.R.
High Desert
Christmas Lake Valley
Crater Lake   Deepest lake in the U.S., 1,932 ft (589 m)
CRATER LAKE N.P.
KLAMATH MARSH N.W.R.
FREMONT-
Sycan
UPPER KLAMATH N.W.R.
Upper Klamath Lake
WINEMA
NORTH FORK SPRAGUE N.W.&S.R.
SYCAN N.W.&S.R.
KLAMATH I.R.
Sprague
Klamath Falls
Altamont
CASCADE SISKIYOU N.M.
BEAR VALLEY N.W.R.
KLAMATH N.W.&S.R.
N.F.

White River
Deschutes
JOHN DAY N.W.&S.R.
Heppner
John Day
JOHN DAY FOSSIL BEDS NAT. MON.
OCHOCO
Ochoco Mts.
Prineville
NATIONAL
CROOKED N.W.&S.R.
Crooked
FOREST
Newberry
Christmas Lake Valley
Harney Basin
Summer Lake
Lake Abert
HART MT. NATIONAL ANTELOPE REFUGE
Warner Valley
Goose Lake
Lakeview

UMATILLA N.W.R.
COLD SPRINGS N.W.R.
Milton-Freewater
Hermiston
Pendleton
McKAY CREEK N.W.R.
UMATILLA INDIAN RES.
La Grande
JOHN DAY, NORTH FORK N.W.&S.R.
MALHEUR
John Day, SOUTH FORK N.W.&S.R.
CROOKED, NORTH FORK N.W.&S.R.
NATIONAL
Burns
BURNS PAIUTE I.R.
FOREST
MALHEUR N.W.&S.R.
MALHEUR, NORTH FORK N.W.&S.R.
N. Fk. Malheur
Malheur
Harney Lake
Malheur Lake
MALHEUR NATIONAL WILDLIFE REFUGE
GREAT
DONNER UND BLITZEN N.W.&S.R.
Steens Mountain
BASIN
NEVADA

WENAHA N.W.&S.R.
UMATILLA
GRANDE RONDE N.W.&S.R.
JOSEPH CREEK N.W.&S.R.
Grande Ronde
SNAKE N.W.&S.R.
WALLOWA-
HELLS CANYON N.R.A.
WALLOWA N.W.&S.R.
WHITMAN
Enterprise
NAT.
MINAM N.W.&S.R.
LOSTINE N.W.&S.R.
Wallowa
IMNAHA N.W.&S.R.
Hells Canyon   Deepest river gorge in North America
NATIONAL
EAGLE CREEK N.W.&S.R.
N. Powder
N. POWDER N.W.&S.R.
Powder
Baker City
Brownlee Res.
IDAHO
DEER FLAT N.W.R.
Ontario
Snake
Malheur
Owyhee
Lake Owyhee
OWYHEE NATIONAL WILD & SCENIC RIVER
WEST LITTLE OWYHEE N.W.&S.R.
OWYHEE, NORTH FORK N.W.&S.R.
Owyhee
FORT McDERMITT I.R.

Columbia Plateau
Blue Mountains

O R E G O N

CALIFORNIA   B A S I N

◑ **CHANGING LANDSCAPE.**
Oregon's Pacific coast is a lesson on erosion and deposition. Rocky outcrops called sea stacks are leftovers of a former coastline that has been eroded by waves. The sandy beach is a result of eroded material being deposited along the shore.

THE BASICS

Statehood
January 4, 1896; 45th state

Total area (land and water)
84,897 sq mi (219,882 sq km)

Land area
82,170 sq mi (212,818 sq km)

Population
3,161,105

Capital
Salt Lake City
Population 200,591

Largest city
Salt Lake City
Population 200,591

Racial/ethnic groups
90.9% white; 1.4% African American; 2.6% Asian; 1.5% Native American; 14.0% Hispanic (any race)

Foreign born
8.2%

Urban population
90.6%

Population density
38.5 per sq mi (14.9 per sq km)

GEO WHIZ

A giant duck-billed dinosaur is among the many kinds of dinosaur fossils that have been found in the Grand Staircase–Escalante National Monument. Scientists think the plant-eater had 300 teeth and was at least 30 feet (9 m) long.

Great Salt Lake is the largest natural lake west of the Mississippi River. As a result of high levels of evaporation, the lake contains about 4.5 billion tons (4 billion t) of salt.

Utah

For thousands of years, present-day Utah was populated by Native Americans living in small hunter-gatherer groups, including the Ute for whom the state is named. Spanish explorers passed through Utah in 1776, and in the early 19th century trappers came from the East searching for beavers. In 1847 the arrival of Mormons marked the beginning of widespread settlement of the territory. They established farms and introduced irrigation. Discovery of precious metals in the 1860s brought miners to the territory. Today, 63 percent of Utah's land is managed by the federal government for military and defense industries and as national parks. As a result, the government is a leading employer in the state. Another important force in Utah is the Church of Jesus Christ of Latter-day Saints (Mormons), which has influenced culture and politics in the state for more than a century. Salt Lake City is the world headquarters of the church.

⬡ **MONUMENT TO FAITH.** Completed in 1893, the Salt Lake Temple is where Mormons gather to participate in religious ceremonies. Members regard their temples as Earth's most sacred places.

SEGO LILY

CALIFORNIA GULL

SPREADING THE FAITH

Mormon Church membership, 2018 data

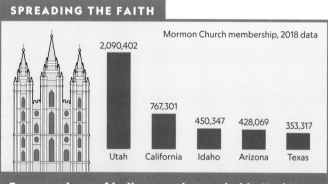

Utah	California	Idaho	Arizona	Texas
2,090,402	767,301	450,347	428,069	353,317

From a colony of believers who settled in Utah's Salt Lake basin in the 1840s, followers of the Mormon faith have expanded into nearby states.

◑ **NATURE'S HANDIWORK.** Arches National Park includes more than 2,000 arches carved by forces of water and ice, extreme temperatures, and the shifting of underground salt beds over a period of 100 million years. Delicate Arch stands on the edge of a canyon, with the snowcapped La Sal Mountains in the distance.

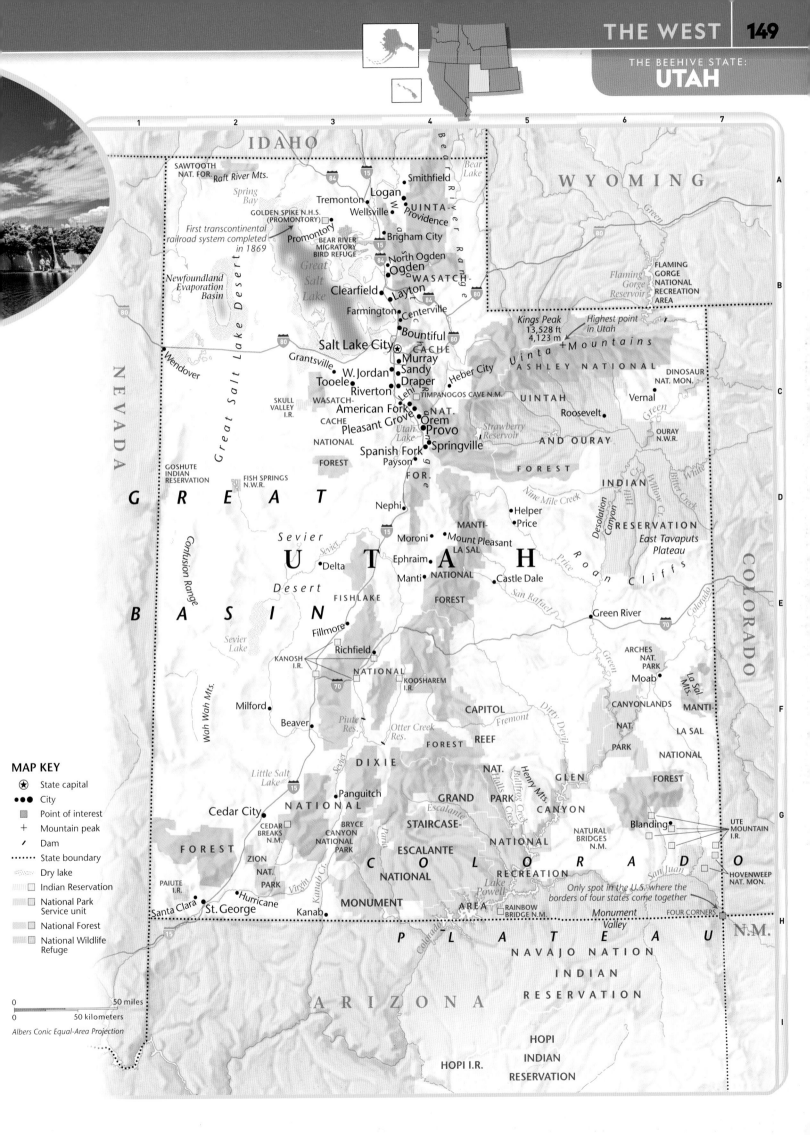

THE BASICS

Statehood
November 11, 1889; 42nd state

Total area (land and water)
71,298 sq mi (184,661 sq km)

Land area
66,456 sq mi (172,119 sq km)

Population
7,535,591

Capital
Olympia
Population 52,555

Largest city
Seattle
Population 744,955

Racial/ethnic groups
79.5% white; 4.2% African
American; 8.9% Asian; 1.9%
Native American; 12.7%
Hispanic (any race)

Foreign born
13.8%

Urban population
84.1%

Population density
113.4 per sq mi (43.8 per sq km)

GEO WHIZ

**The Olympic Peninsula is
among the world's rainiest
places, and its Hoh Rainforest
is one of the world's few
temperate rainforests.**

**Mount St. Helens, the most
active volcano in the lower 48
states, is close to Seattle and
to Portland, in Oregon. The
eruption in May 1980 reduced
its elevation by 1,314 feet
(401 m) and caused the largest
landslide in recorded history.**

**Orcas, also known as killer
whales, are the world's largest
dolphins. The fewer than 80
living in the waters of Puget
Sound have been placed on
the government's Endangered
Species List.**

AMERICAN GOLDFINCH
COAST RHODODENDRON

Washington

Long before Europeans explored along the coast of the Pacific Northwest, Native Americans inhabited the area, living mainly off abundant seafood found in coastal waters and rivers. In the late 18th century Spanish sailors and then British explorers, including Captain James Cook, visited the region. Under treaties with Spain (1819) and Britain (1846), the United States gained control of the land, and in 1853 the Washington Territory was formally separated from the Oregon Territory. Settlers soon based their livelihood on fishing, farming, and lumbering. Washington became the 42nd state in 1889. The 20th century was a time of growth and development for the state. Seattle became a major Pacific seaport. The Grand Coulee Dam, completed in 1941, provided the region with inexpensive electricity. Today, industry, led by Boeing and Microsoft, is a mainstay of the economy. Washington leads the country in production of apples and sweet cherries, and the state is the headquarters of the Starbucks chain of coffee shops.

◗ **PACIFIC GATEWAY.** Seattle, easily recognized by its distinctive Space Needle tower, is a major West Coast port and home to the North Pacific fishing fleet.

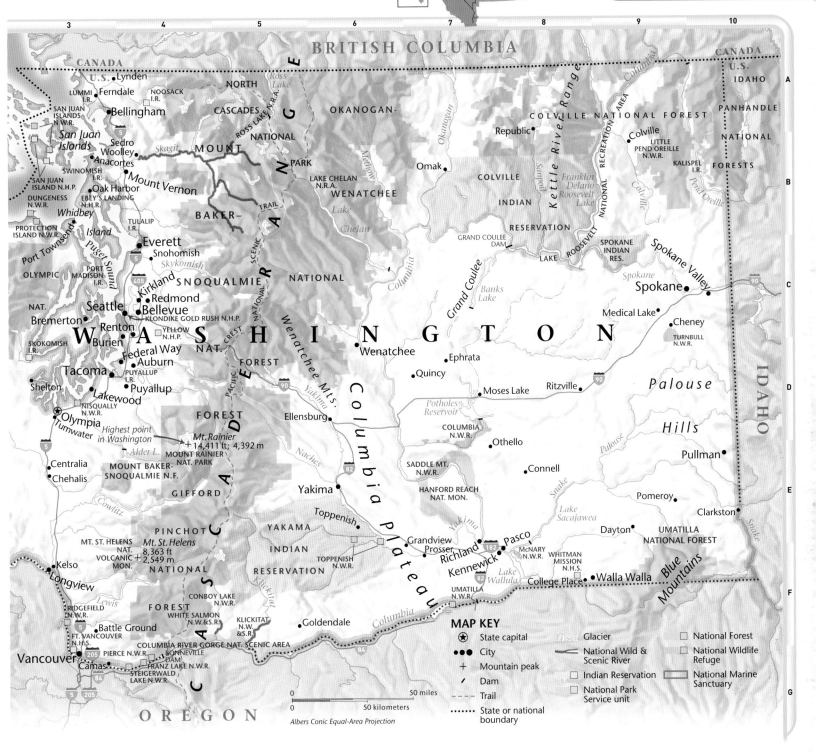

Map

BRITISH COLUMBIA

CANADA
U.S.

Lynden
LUMMI I.R. Ferndale
NOOSACK I.R.
Bellingham
SAN JUAN ISLANDS N.W.R.
San Juan Islands
Sedro Woolley
Anacortes
Mount Vernon
Oak Harbor
Whidbey Island
Port Townsend
OLYMPIC
NAT.
Bremerton
Seattle
Renton
Burin
WASHINGTON
Tacoma
Shelton
Lakewood
Puyallup
Federal Way
Auburn
Olympia
Tumwater
Highest point in Washington
Centralia
Chehalis
MOUNT BAKER-SNOQUALMIE N.F.
Mt. Rainier
+14,411 ft; 4,392 m
MOUNT RAINIER NAT. PARK
GIFFORD
PINCHOT
Mt. St. Helens
8,363 ft
2,549 m
MT. ST. HELENS NAT. VOLCANIC MON.
Kelso
NATIONAL
Longview
FOREST
Ridgefield N.W.R.
Battle Ground
Vancouver
Camas
FT. VANCOUVER N.H.S.

NORTH CASCADES NATIONAL PARK
Ross Lake
MOUNT BAKER-SNOQUALMIE
Skagit
CASCADE RANGE
SNOQUALMIE NATIONAL FOREST
WENATCHEE
Lake Chelan
LAKE CHELAN N.R.A.
Wenatchee Mts.
Columbia Plateau
Ellensburg
Naches
Yakima
Toppenish
YAKAMA INDIAN RESERVATION
TOPPENISH N.W.R.
Klickitat
Goldendale
Columbia River Gorge Nat. Scenic Area
CONBOY LAKE N.W.R.
WHITE SALMON N.W.&S.R.
KLICKITAT N.W. &S.R.
BONNEVILLE DAM

OKANOGAN-
Omak
Republic
Lake Chelan
Wenatchee
Ephrata
Quincy
GRAND COULEE DAM
Grand Coulee
Banks Lake
Moses Lake
Ritzville
Othello
COLUMBIA N.W.R.
SADDLE MT. N.W.R.
HANFORD REACH NAT. MON.
Grandview
Prosser
Richland
Kennewick
Pasco
McNARY N.W.R.
WHITMAN MISSION N.H.S.
College Place
Walla Walla
UMATILLA N.W.R.
Columbia
Lake Wallula
WASHINGTON

COLVILLE NATIONAL FOREST
Colville
LITTLE PEND OREILLE N.W.R.
KALISPEL I.R.
COLVILLE INDIAN RESERVATION
Franklin Delano Roosevelt Lake
LAKE ROOSEVELT
SPOKANE INDIAN RES.
Kettle River Range
Spokane Valley
Spokane
Medical Lake
Cheney
TURNBULL N.W.R.
Palouse Hills
Pullman
Connell
Pomeroy
Clarkston
Dayton
UMATILLA NATIONAL FOREST
Blue Mountains
Snake
Lake Sacajawea

CANADA
U.S.
IDAHO
PANHANDLE
NATIONAL
FORESTS
IDAHO

OREGON

Map Key

MAP KEY

- ★ State capital
- ●●● City
- + Mountain peak
- / Dam
- --- Trail
- ···· State or national boundary

- Glacier
- ～ National Wild & Scenic River
- ☐ Indian Reservation
- ☐ National Park Service unit

- ☐ National Forest
- ☐ National Wildlife Refuge
- National Marine Sanctuary

50 miles
50 kilometers
Albers Conic Equal-Area Projection

⬡ **HARVEST TIME.** Once a semiarid grassland, the Palouse Hills north of the Snake River in eastern Washington is now a major wheat-producing area.

WATER POWER

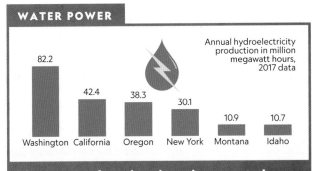

Annual hydroelectricity production in million megawatt hours, 2017 data

Washington	82.2
California	42.4
Oregon	38.3
New York	30.1
Montana	10.9
Idaho	10.7

The energy of roaring rivers is converted into inexpensive electricity to light homes and power industries in Washington and other states.

Wyoming

When Europeans arrived in the 18th century in what would become Wyoming, various groups of Native Americans were already there, following herds of deer and bison across the plains. In the early 19th century fur traders moved into the area, and settlers followed later along the Oregon Trail. Laramie and many other towns developed around army forts built to protect wagon trains traveling through the territory. Today, fewer than 600,000 people live in all of Wyoming. The state's economy is based on agriculture—mainly grain and livestock production—and mining, especially energy resources. Wyoming has some of the world's largest surface coal mines as well as large deposits of petroleum and natural gas. The environment is also a major resource. Yellowstone, established in 1872, was the world's first national park.

THE BASICS

Statehood
July 10, 1890; 44th state

Total area
(land and water)
97,813 sq mi
(253,335 sq km)

Land area
97,093 sq mi (251,470 sq km)

Population
577,737

Capital
Cheyenne
Population 63,957

Largest city
Cheyenne
Population 63,957

Racial/ethnic groups
92.8% white; 1.3% African American; 1.0% Asian; 2.7% Native American; 10% Hispanic (any race)

Foreign born
3.6%

Urban population
64.8%

Population density
6.0 per sq mi (2.3 per sq km)

GEO WHIZ

The successful reintroduction of wolves into Yellowstone National Park has become a model for saving other species of endangered carnivores.

Devils Tower in northeast Wyoming was the first U.S. national monument.

⬤ **WANT TO RACE?** Unique to the High Plains of the West, the pronghorn can sprint up to 60 miles an hour (97 km/h).

WESTERN MEADOWLARK

INDIAN PAINTBRUSH

⬤ **DRAMATIC LANDSCAPE.** Rising more than 13,000 feet (3,900 m), the Tetons, one of the youngest western mountain ranges, tower over a barn on the valley floor.

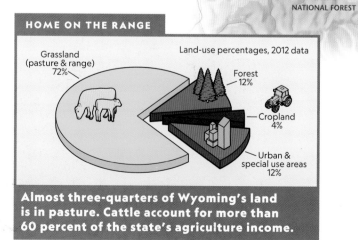

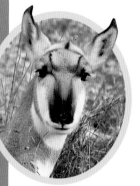

HOME ON THE RANGE

Land-use percentages, 2012 data

Grassland (pasture & range) 72%

Forest 12%

Cropland 4%

Urban & special use areas 12%

Almost three-quarters of Wyoming's land is in pasture. Cattle account for more than 60 percent of the state's agriculture income.

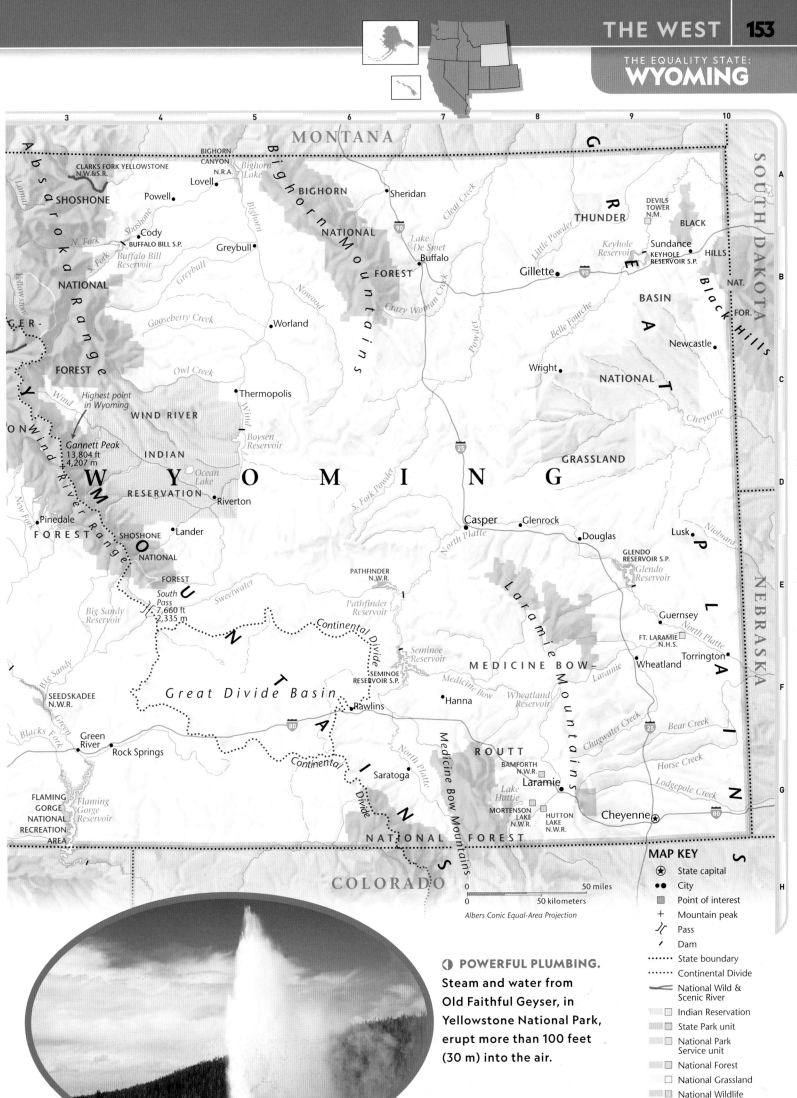

MONTANA

SOUTH DAKOTA

NEBRASKA

COLORADO

Absaroka Range

CLARKS FORK YELLOWSTONE
N.W.&S.R.

SHOSHONE

Lamar

Yellowstone

TIGER-

NATIONAL

FOREST

Wind River Range

Wind

Highest point
in Wyoming

Gannett Peak
13,804 ft
4,207 m

New Fork

Pinedale

FOREST

SHOSHONE

NATIONAL

FOREST

South
Pass
7,660 ft
2,335 m

Big Sandy
Reservoir

Big Sandy

SEEDSKADEE
N.W.R.

Blacks Fork

Green

Green
River

Rock Springs

FLAMING
GORGE
NATIONAL
RECREATION
AREA

Flaming
Gorge
Reservoir

Powell

Lovell

Cody

N. Fork

BUFFALO BILL S.P.

S. Fork

Buffalo Bill
Reservoir

Greybull

Greybull

Gooseberry Creek

Owl Creek

Thermopolis

WIND RIVER

INDIAN

RESERVATION

Ocean
Lake

W   Y   O   M   I

Riverton

Lander

BIGHORN
CANYON
N.R.A.

Bighorn
Lake

Bighorn

Bighorn Mountains

BIGHORN

NATIONAL

FOREST

Nowood

Worland

Wind

Boysen
Reservoir

M   O   U   N

Sweetwater

Continental Divide

Great Divide Basin

Continental

Divide

Sheridan

Clear Creek

Lake
De Smet

Buffalo

Crazy Woman Creek

90

Little Powder

Powder

S. Fork Powder

N   G

Casper

25

North Platte

PATHFINDER
N.W.R.

Pathfinder
Reservoir

SEMINOE
RESERVOIR S.P.

Seminoe
Reservoir

Rawlins

80

T   A   I   N   S

Saratoga

North Platte

Medicine Bow Mountains

NATIONAL FOREST

THUNDER

GREAT

DEVILS
TOWER
N.M.

BLACK

HILLS

Keyhole
Reservoir

Sundance

KEYHOLE
RESERVOIR S.P.

Gillette

BASIN

Newcastle

Wright

NATIONAL

GRASSLAND

Glenrock

Douglas

MEDICINE BOW-

Medicine Bow

Hanna

Wheatland
Reservoir

ROUTT

BAMFORTH
N.W.R.

Lake
Hattie

MORTENSON
LAKE
N.W.R.

HUTTON
LAKE
N.W.R.

Laramie

Belle Fourche

Cheyenne

Black Hills

NAT.

FOR.

Cheyenne

Lusk

Niobrara

GLENDO
RESERVOIR S.P.

Glendo
Reservoir

Guernsey

North Platte

FT. LARAMIE
N.H.S.

Laramie

Laramie Mountains

Chugwater Creek

Bear Creek

Horse Creek

Lodgepole Creek

Torrington

Wheatland

P   L   A   I   N   S

Cheyenne

25

80

MAP KEY

⊛ State capital

●● City

◼ Point of interest

+ Mountain peak

)(Pass

⌐ Dam

········· State boundary

········· Continental Divide

National Wild &
Scenic River

Indian Reservation

State Park unit

National Park
Service unit

National Forest

National Grassland

National Wildlife
Refuge

0 ___ 50 miles
0 ___ 50 kilometers

Albers Conic Equal-Area Projection

◑ **POWERFUL PLUMBING.**

Steam and water from
Old Faithful Geyser, in
Yellowstone National Park,
erupt more than 100 feet
(30 m) into the air.

POLITICAL MAP

U.S. Territories
ACROSS TWO SEAS

Listed below are the five largest* of the fourteen U.S. territories, along with their flags and key information. Two of these territories are in the Caribbean Sea, and three are in the Pacific Ocean.

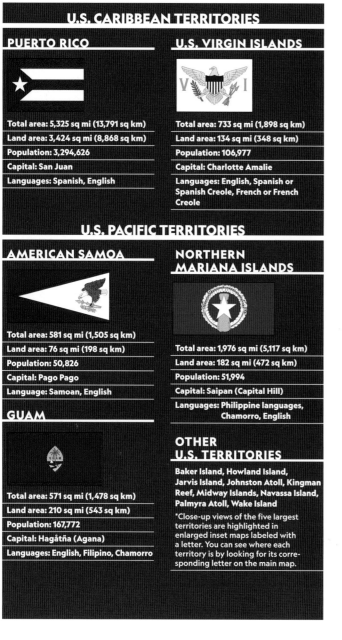

U.S. CARIBBEAN TERRITORIES

PUERTO RICO

Total area:	5,325 sq mi (13,791 sq km)
Land area:	3,424 sq mi (8,868 sq km)
Population:	3,294,626
Capital:	San Juan
Languages:	Spanish, English

U.S. VIRGIN ISLANDS

Total area:	733 sq mi (1,898 sq km)
Land area:	134 sq mi (348 sq km)
Population:	106,977
Capital:	Charlotte Amalie
Languages:	English, Spanish or Spanish Creole, French or French Creole

U.S. PACIFIC TERRITORIES

AMERICAN SAMOA

Total area:	581 sq mi (1,505 sq km)
Land area:	76 sq mi (198 sq km)
Population:	50,826
Capital:	Pago Pago
Language:	Samoan, English

NORTHERN MARIANA ISLANDS

Total area:	1,976 sq mi (5,117 sq km)
Land area:	182 sq mi (472 sq km)
Population:	51,994
Capital:	Saipan (Capital Hill)
Languages:	Philippine languages, Chamorro, English

OTHER U.S. TERRITORIES

Baker Island, Howland Island, Jarvis Island, Johnston Atoll, Kingman Reef, Midway Islands, Navassa Island, Palmyra Atoll, Wake Island

*Close-up views of the five largest territories are highlighted in enlarged inset maps labeled with a letter. You can see where each territory is by looking for its corresponding letter on the main map.

GUAM

Total area:	571 sq mi (1,478 sq km)
Land area:	210 sq mi (543 sq km)
Population:	167,772
Capital:	Hagåtña (Agana)
Languages:	English, Filipino, Chamorro

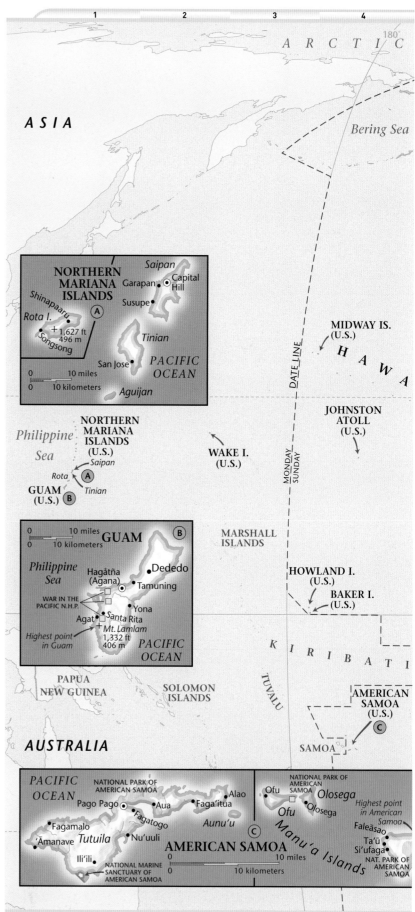

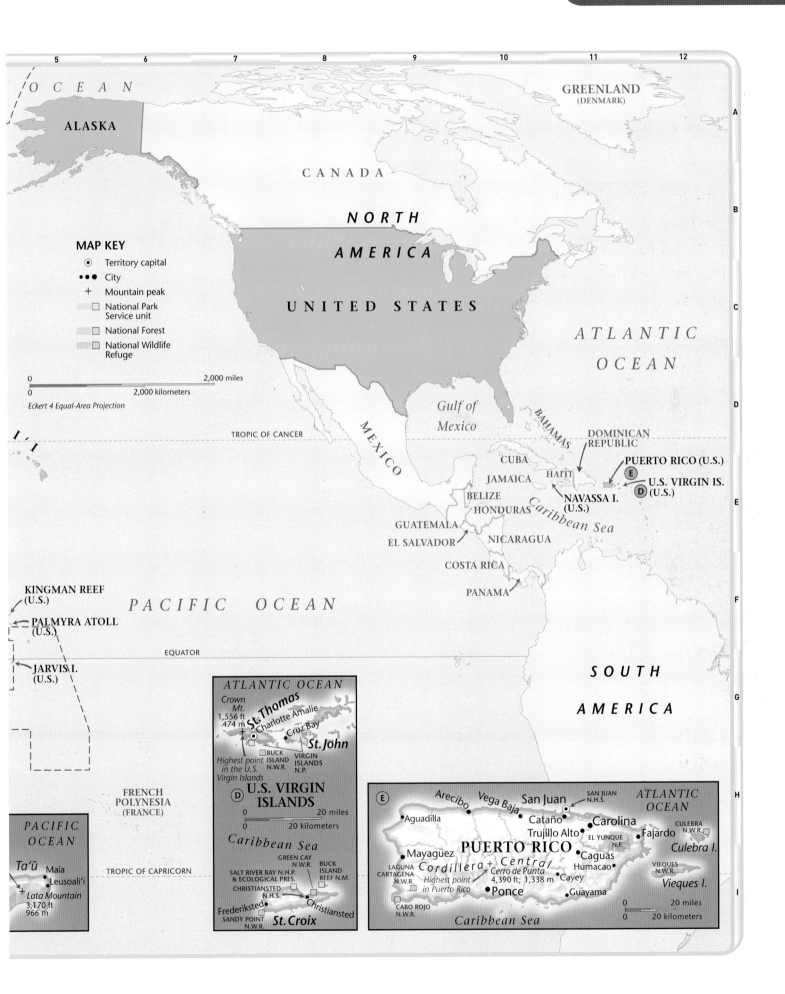

OCEAN

ALASKA

GREENLAND
(DENMARK)

CANADA

NORTH

AMERICA

UNITED STATES

MAP KEY

⊙ Territory capital
••• City
+ Mountain peak
▢ National Park Service unit
▢ National Forest
▢ National Wildlife Refuge

0 — 2,000 miles
0 — 2,000 kilometers
Eckert 4 Equal-Area Projection

ATLANTIC

OCEAN

Gulf of
Mexico

BAHAMAS

DOMINICAN
REPUBLIC

TROPIC OF CANCER

MEXICO

CUBA

JAMAICA   HAITI

PUERTO RICO (U.S.)
Ⓔ
U.S. VIRGIN IS.
Ⓓ (U.S.)

BELIZE
HONDURAS

NAVASSA I.
(U.S.)

GUATEMALA
EL SALVADOR

Caribbean Sea

NICARAGUA

COSTA RICA

KINGMAN REEF
(U.S.)

PACIFIC   OCEAN

PANAMA

PALMYRA ATOLL
(U.S.)

EQUATOR

JARVIS I.
(U.S.)

SOUTH

AMERICA

ATLANTIC OCEAN

Crown
Mt.
1,556 ft
474 m +
⊙ Charlotte Amalie
St. Thomas
Cruz Bay
St. John

FRENCH
POLYNESIA
(FRANCE)

Highest point
in the U.S.
Virgin Islands

▢ BUCK
ISLAND
N.W.R.

VIRGIN
ISLANDS
N.P.

Ⓓ U.S. VIRGIN
ISLANDS

0 — 20 miles
0 — 20 kilometers

Caribbean Sea

PACIFIC
OCEAN

Ta'ū   Maia
• Leusoali'i

TROPIC OF CAPRICORN

+ Lata Mountain
3,170 ft
966 m

GREEN CAY
N.W.R.
SALT RIVER BAY N.H.P.
& ECOLOGICAL PRES.
CHRISTIANSTED
N.H.S.

BUCK
ISLAND
REEF N.M.

Frederiksted•
SANDY POINT
N.W.R.

•Christiansted

St. Croix

Ⓔ Arecibo Vega Baja San Juan SAN JUAN
N.H.S.
ATLANTIC
OCEAN

•Aguadilla
Cataño Carolina
Trujillo Alto EL YUNQUE
N.F. Fajardo

CULEBRA
N.W.R.

PUERTO RICO

•Mayagüez Cordillera + Central
LAGUNA
CARTAGENA
N.W.R. Highest point
in Puerto Rico

Cerro de Punta
4,390 ft; 1,338 m
Cayey

Caguas
Humacao

Culebra I.

VIEQUES
N.W.R.

CABO ROJO
N.W.R.

•Ponce

Guayama

Vieques I.

0 — 20 miles
0 — 20 kilometers

Caribbean Sea

U.S. Territories

ISLANDS IN THE FAMILY

PRESERVING TRADITION. Dancers from American Samoa, dressed in traditional costumes, prepare to perform in the Pacific Arts Festival.

Fourteen territories and commonwealths scattered across the Pacific and Caribbean came under U.S. influence after wars or various international agreements. Although they are neither states nor independent countries, the U.S. government provides economic and military aid. Puerto Rico's 3.3 million residents give it a population greater than that of 21 U.S. states. Many tourists seeking sunny beaches visit the U.S. Virgin Islands, purchased from Denmark for $25 million in 1917. American Samoa, Guam, and the Northern Mariana Islands in the Pacific have sizable populations, but several tiny atolls have no civilian residents and are administered by U.S. military or government departments.

RELIC OF THE PAST. Sugar mill ruins on St. John, in the U.S. Virgin Islands, recall a way of life that dominated the Caribbean in the 18th and 19th centuries, when plantations used slave labor to grow sugarcane.

WHERE THE PICTURES ARE

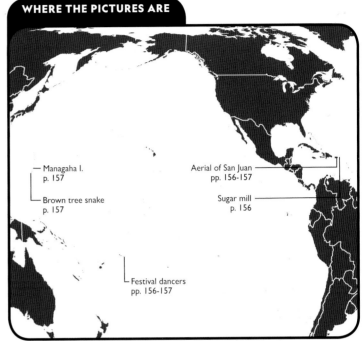

Managaha I.
p. 157

Brown tree snake
p. 157

Aerial of San Juan
pp. 156-157

Sugar mill
p. 156

Festival dancers
pp. 156-157

◖ PACIFIC JEWEL. Managaha Island sits in the blue-green waters of a lagoon along Saipan's western coast. Portions of the reef around it are dying due to overfishing, warming ocean water, and pollution. The lagoon holds wrecks from battles fought in Northern Mariana waters during World War II.

◗ ATLANTIC PLAYGROUND. Modern hotels, catering to more than four million tourists annually, rise above surf and sandy beaches in San Juan, Puerto Rico. The city was founded by the Spanish in 1521.

⬢ STOWAWAY. The brown tree snake probably arrived in Guam in the 1950s. Since then, it has reduced the island's bird populations and causes power outages when it climbs electric poles.

U.S. FACTS & FIGURES

THE BASICS

Founding
1776

Total area (land and water)
3,796,742 sq mi (9,833,517 sq km)

Land area
3,531,905 sq mi (9,147,593 sq km)

Population
327,167,434

Capital
Washington, D.C.
Population 702,455

Largest city
New York
Population 8,398,748

Racial/ethnic groups
76.6% white; 13.4% African
American; 5.8% Asian; 1.3%
Native American; 18.1% Hispanic
origin (any race)

Foreign born
13.4%

Urban population
80.7%

Population density
92.6 per sq mi (35.8 per sq km)

Language
No official national language;
language spoken at home:
English 78.2%; Spanish 13.4%

Economy
Agriculture: 0.9%; Industry:
19.1 %; Services: 80.0%

BALD EAGLE,
NATIONAL SYMBOL

TOP STATES

Listed below are major producers of selected
agriculture products, fish and seafood, and
minerals.

AGRICULTURE PRODUCTS

**Top 10 Agriculture Producing States
(based on cash receipts, 2017)**

1. California
2. Iowa
3. Texas
4. Nebraska
5. Minnesota
6. Illinois
7. Kansas
8. North Carolina
9. Wisconsin
10. Indiana

**Leading Agriculture Products and Top
Producers (based on cash receipts, 2017)**

Cattle and calves: Nebraska, Texas, Kansas,
Iowa, Colorado

Corn: Iowa, Illinois, Nebraska, Minnesota,
Indiana

Soybeans: Illinois, Iowa, Minnesota, Indiana,
Nebraska

Milk/dairy products: California, Wisconsin,
New York, Idaho, Texas

Broilers: Georgia, Arkansas, North Carolina,
Alabama, Mississippi

Hogs: Iowa, Minnesota, North Carolina,
Illinois, Indiana

Wheat: North Dakota, Kansas, Montana,
Washington, Minnesota

Chicken eggs: Iowa, Georgia, Indiana,
Arkansas, Ohio

Cotton lint: Texas, Georgia, California,
Mississippi, Arkansas

Grapes: California, Washington, Oregon,
New York, Texas

FISH AND SEAFOOD

Volume of wild catch (2017): 9.9 billion lb
(4.5 billion kg)
Volume of farmed catch (2016): 633.5 million lb
(287.4 million kg)

**Top 5 States in Fish and Seafood
(based on value of commercial landings,
2017)**

1. Alaska
2. Massachusetts
3. Maine
4. Louisiana
5. Washington

MINERALS

Leading Fossil Fuels and Top Producers

Petroleum: Texas, North Dakota, Alaska,
California, New Mexico (2017)

Natural gas: Texas, Pennsylvania, Alaska,
Oklahoma, Louisiana (2018)

Coal: Wyoming, West Virginia, Pennsylvania,
Illinois, Kentucky (2017)

**Top 10 Nonfuel Mineral Producing States
(based on production value, 2017)**

1. Nevada
2. Arizona
3. Texas
4. Alaska
5. California
6. Minnesota
7. Florida
8. Utah
9. Missouri
10. Michigan

**Leading Nonfuel Minerals (based on
production value, 2017)**

1. Crushed stone
2. Gold
3. Cement
4. Copper
5. Sand/gravel
6. Iron ore
7. Lime
8. Zinc
9. Phosphate rock
10. Salt
11. Soda ash
12. Clay

EXTREMES

Strongest Surface Wind in U.S.
231 miles an hour (372 km/h), Mount
Washington, New Hampshire, April 12, 1934

World's Tallest Living Tree
Hyperion; a coast redwood in Redwood
National Park, California, 380.2 ft
(115.9 m) high

World's Largest Gorge
Grand Canyon, Arizona: 277 mi (446 km)
long, along the river, 600 ft to 18 mi (183 m
to 29 km) wide, 1 mile (1.6 km) deep

**Highest Recorded Air Temperature
in the World**
134°F (56.7°C), Death Valley, California,
July 10, 1913

Lowest Recorded Air Temperature in U.S.
Minus 80°F (-62°C), at Prospect Creek,
Alaska, January 23, 1971

Highest Point in U.S.
Denali (Mount McKinley), Alaska: 20,310 ft
(6,190 m)

Lowest Point in U.S.
Death Valley, California: 282 feet (86 m)
below sea level

Longest River System in U.S.
Mississippi-Missouri: 3,710 mi (5,971 km)

Rainiest Spot in U.S.
Waiʻaleʻale (mountain), Hawaiʻi: average
annual rainfall 460 in (1,168 cm)

METROPOLITAN AREAS*
(with more than 5 million people)

1. New York, pop. 19,979,477
2. Los Angeles, pop. 13,291,486
3. Chicago, pop. 9,498,716
4. Dallas–Fort Worth, pop. 7,539,711
5. Houston, pop. 6,997,384
6. Washington, D.C., pop. 6,249,950
7. Miami, pop. 6,198,782
8. Philadelphia, pop. 6,096,372
9. Atlanta, pop. 5,949,951

* A metropolitan area is a city and its
surrounding suburban areas.

GLOSSARY

atoll a circular coral reef enclosing a tropical lagoon

arid climate type of dry climate in which annual precipitation is generally less than 10 inches (25 cm)

biomass total weight of all organisms found in a given area; organic matter used as fuel

bituminous coal a soft form of coal used in industries and power plants

bog a poorly drained area with wet, spongy ground

broadleaf forest trees with wide leaves that are shed during the winter season

canal an artificial waterway that is used by ships or to carry water for irrigation

center-pivot irrigation an irrigation system that rotates around a piped water source at its middle, often resulting in circular field patterns

city proper an incorporated urban place with boundaries and central government

continental climate temperature extremes with long cold winters and heavy snowfall

continental divide an elevated area that separates rivers flowing toward opposite sides of a continent

Creole a modified form of a language, such as French or Spanish, used for communication between two groups; spoken in some Caribbean islands

delta lowland formed by silt, sand, and gravel deposited by a river at its mouth

desert vegetation plants such as cactus and dry shrubs that have adapted to conditions of low, often irregular precipitation

estuary area near a river's mouth where freshwater and saltwater are mixed by ocean tides

fork place in a river where the stream divides

Fortune 500 company one of the top 500 U.S. companies ranked by revenue

fossil remains of or an impression left by the remains of plants or animals preserved in rock

geothermal energy a clean, renewable form of energy provided by heat from Earth's interior

grassland areas with medium to short grasses; found where precipitation is not sufficient to support tree growth

gross domestic product (GDP) the total value of goods and services produced in a country in a year

highland climate a type of climate found in association with high mountains where elevation affects temperature and precipitation

hundredweight in the U.S., a commercial unit of measure equal to 100 pounds

ice age a very long period of cold climate when glaciers often cover large areas of land

intermittent river/lake a stream or lake that contains water only part of the time, usually after heavy rainfall or snowmelt

Latin America cultural region made up of Mexico and the countries of Central America, the Caribbean, and South America

levee an embankment, usually made of earth or concrete, built to prevent a river from overflowing

lignite low-grade coal used mainly to produce heat in thermal-electric generators

marine west coast climate type of mild climate found on the mid-latitude west coast of continents poleward of the Mediterranean climate

Mediterranean climate type of mild climate found on the mid-latitude west coast of continents

mesa a high, extensive, flat-topped hill; an eroded remnant of a plateau

metropolitan area a city and its surrounding suburbs or communities

mild climate a type of climate that has moderate temperatures with distinct seasons and ample precipitation

pinnacle a tall pillar of rock standing alone or on a summit

plain a large area of relatively flat land that is often covered with grasses

population density the average number of people living on each square mile (sq km) of a specific land area

rangeland areas of grass prairie that are used for grazing livestock

reactor a device that uses controlled nuclear fission to divide an atomic nucleus to generate power

Richter scale ranking of the power of an earthquake; the higher the number, the stronger the quake

Rust Belt a region made up of northeastern and midwestern states that have experienced a decline in heavy industry and an out-migration of population

scale on a map, a means of explaining the relationship between distances on the map and actual distances on Earth's surface

stalactite column of limestone hanging from the ceiling of a cave that forms as underground water drips down and evaporates, leaving dissolved minerals behind

stalagmite column of limestone that forms on the floor of a cave when underground water drips down and evaporates, leaving dissolved minerals behind

staple main item in an economy; also, main food for domestic consumption

subtropical climate type of mild climate found in the southeastern areas of continents

Sunbelt a region made up of southern and western states that are experiencing major in-migration of population and rapid economic growth

tectonic plate one of several thick slabs of Earth's crust that, according to geologic theory, move slowly over the semi-molten rock below

temperate rainforest forests in the coastal Pacific Northwest region of the U.S. with heavy rainfall and mild temperatures

territory land that is under the jurisdiction of a country but that is not a state or a province of that country

tropical zone the area bounded by the Tropic of Cancer and the Tropic of Capricorn, where it is usually warm year-round

tundra vegetation plants, often stunted in size, that have adapted to a cold, short growing season; found in polar regions and at high elevations

urban area associated with a town or city in which most people are engaged in nonagricultural employment

volcanic pipe a vertical opening beneath a volcano through which molten rock has passed

wetland land that is either covered with or saturated by water; includes swamps, marshes, and bogs

POSTAL ABBREVIATIONS

AK- Alaska
AL- Alabama
AR- Arkansas
AS- American Samoa
AZ- Arizona
CA- California
CO- Colorado
CT- Connecticut
DC- District of Columbia

DE- Delaware
FL- Florida
GA- Georgia
GU- Guam
HI- Hawai'i
IA- Iowa
ID- Idaho
IL- Illinois
IN- Indiana
KS- Kansas

KY- Kentucky
LA- Louisiana
MA- Massachusetts
MD- Maryland
ME- Maine
MI- Michigan
MN- Minnesota
MO- Missouri
MP- Northern Mariana Islands

MS- Mississippi
MT- Montana
NC- North Carolina
ND- North Dakota
NE- Nebraska
NH- New Hampshire
NJ- New Jersey
NM- New Mexico
NV- Nevada
NY- New York

OH- Ohio
OK- Oklahoma
OR- Oregon
PA- Pennsylvania
PR- Puerto Rico
RI- Rhode Island
SC- South Carolina
SD- South Dakota
TN- Tennessee
TX- Texas

UT- Utah
VA- Virginia
VI- U.S. Virgin Islands
VT- Vermont
WA- Washington
WI- Wisconsin
WV- West Virginia
WY- Wyoming

MAP ABBREVIATIONS

°E .... degrees East	ME. .... Maine	OREG. .... Oregon
°N .... degrees North	mi .... miles	p., pp. .... page, pages
°S .... degrees South	MICH. .... Michigan	PA. .... Pennsylvania
°W .... degrees West	MINN. .... Minnesota	Pen. .... Peninsula
°C .... degrees Celsius	MISS. .... Mississippi	Pk. .... Peak
°F .... degrees Fahrenheit	MO. .... Missouri	Pres. .... Preserve
ALA. .... Alabama	MONT. .... Montana	Pt. .... Point
ARIZ. .... Arizona	Mt., Mts. .... Mount, Mountain, Mountains	R. .... River
ARK. .... Arkansas	N. .... North	Ra. .... Range
Br. .... Branch	Nat. .... National	Res. .... Reservoir
CALIF. .... California	NAT. MEM. .... National Memorial	RES. .... Reservation
COLO. .... Colorado	NAT. MON., N.M. .... National Monument	R.I. .... Rhode Island
CONN. .... Connecticut	NAT. RES. .... National Reserve	S. .... South
Cr. .... Creek	N.B. .... National Battlefield	S.C. .... South Carolina
D.C. .... District of Columbia	N.B.P. .... National Battlefield Park	S. DAK. .... South Dakota
DEL. .... Delaware	N.B.S. .... National Battlefield Site	S.H.P. .... State Historical Park
E. .... East	N.C. .... North Carolina	S.H.S. .... State Historical Site
Fk. .... Fork	N. DAK. .... North Dakota	S.P. .... State Park
FLA. .... Florida	NEBR. .... Nebraska	Sprs. .... Springs
ft .... feet	NEV. .... Nevada	sq km .... square kilometers
Ft. .... Fort	N.F. .... National Forest	sq mi .... square miles
GA. .... Georgia	N.G. .... National Grassland	St., Ste. .... Saint, Sainte
GDP .... Gross Domestic Product	N.H. .... New Hampshire	Str., Strs. .... Strait, Straits
I., Is. .... Island, Islands	N.H.A. .... National Historical Area	TENN. .... Tennessee
ILL. .... Illinois	N.H.P. .... National Historical Park	TVA .... Tennessee Valley Authority
IND. .... Indiana	N.H.S. .... National Historical Site	U.S. .... United States
INDIAN RES., I.R. .... Indian Reservation	N.J. .... New Jersey	VA. .... Virginia
KANS. .... Kansas	N. MEX. .... New Mexico	VT. .... Vermont
km .... kilometers	N.M.P. .... National Military Park	W. .... West
KY. .... Kentucky	N.P. .... National Park	WASH. .... Washington
L. .... Lake	N.R.A. .... National Recreation Area	WIS. .... Wisconsin
LA. .... Louisiana	N.W.R. .... National Wildlife Refuge	W. VA. .... West Virginia
m .... meters	N.W.&S.R. .... National Wild & Scenic River	WYO. .... Wyoming
MASS. .... Massachusetts	N.Y. .... New York	
MD. .... Maryland	OKLA. .... Oklahoma	

OUTSIDE WEBSITES

The following websites will provide additional valuable information about topics included in this atlas. Other sites can be found by putting topics of interest into your favorite search engine.*

Natural Environment:
Biomes: www.blueplanetbiomes.org
Climate: www.eoearth.org
Climate change: climate.gov/news-features/understanding-climate/global-climate-indicators

Climate:
www.noaa.gov/climate
www.world-climates.com
www.cpc.ncep.noaa.gov

Natural Hazards:
General: www.usgs.gov/mission-areas/natural-hazards
Droughts: droughtmonitor.unl.edu
Earthquakes: earthquake.usgs.gov
Hurricanes: www.nhc.noaa.gov
Tornadoes: www.tornadoproject.com
Tsunamis: www.tsunami.noaa.gov
Volcanoes: www.geo.mtu.edu/volcanoes
Wildfires: www.nifc.gov and www.fs.fed.us/managing-land/fire

Population:
Cities: www.city-data.com
Foreign-born: www.census.gov/topics/population/foreign-born.html
Population clock: www.census.gov/popclock
Population mobility: www.census.gov/data/tables/time-series/demo/geographic-mobility/historic.html
States: www.census.gov/quickfacts/fact/table/US/PST045218

Energy:
www.eia.gov/energyexplained/?page=us_energy_home
www.nrdc.org/issues/increase-renewable-energy

Native American Facts and Resources:
www.native-languages.org/kids.htm

Projections:
gisgeography.com/map-projections

U.S. Territories:
www.cia.gov/library/publications/resources/the-world-factbook/index.html

*Check with an adult before going on the internet.

PLACE-NAME INDEX

Abbeville — Benton, AR

Map references are in bold-face (**59**) type. Letters and numbers following in lightface (G6) locate the place-names using the map grid. (Refer to page 7 for more details.)

Benton, IL — Cape Cod Bay

Cape Cod Canal — Conroe

Continental Divide – Elkhorn Creek N.W.&S.R.

Gladstone — Hood River

La'ie – Marion, IL

Natchez N.H.P. — Paris, AR

BACK OF
THE BOOK

Red, Elm Fork (river) — Seneca, SC

Sylvania — Washburn, WI

Previously released by the National Geographic Society as
National Geographic United States Atlas for Young Explorers.
First edition copyright © 1999 National Geographic Society
Updated edition copyright © 2004 National Geographic Society
Third and Fourth editions copyright © 2008, 2012
National Geographic Society
Fifth edition released by National Geographic Partners, LLC, as
National Geographic Kids United States Atlas. Fifth edition copyright
© 2017 National Geographic Partners, LLC
Sixth edition copyright © 2020 National Geographic Partners, LLC

Since 1888, the National Geographic Society has funded more than
12,000 research, exploration, and preservation projects around
the world. The Society receives funds from National Geographic
Partners, LLC, funded in part by your purchase. A portion of the
proceeds from this book supports this vital work. To learn more,
visit natgeo.com/info.

NATIONAL GEOGRAPHIC and Yellow Border Design are trademarks of
the National Geographic Society, used under license.

For more information, visit nationalgeographic.com,
call 1-877-873-6846, or write to the following address:

National Geographic Partners
1145 17th Street N.W.
Washington, DC 20036-4688 U.S.A.

Visit us online at nationalgeographic.com/books

For librarians and teachers: nationalgeographic.com/books/
librarians-and-educators

More for kids from National Geographic: natgeokids.com

National Geographic Kids magazine inspires children to explore their
world with fun yet educational articles on animals, science,
nature, and more. Using fresh storytelling and amazing
photography, *Nat Geo Kids* shows kids ages 6 to 14 the
fascinating truth about the world—and why they should care.
kids.nationalgeographic.com/subscribe

For rights or permissions inquiries, please contact
National Geographic Books Subsidiary Rights:
bookrights@natgeo.com

Designed by Kathryn Robbins

National Geographic supports K–12 educators with
ELA Common Core Resources. Visit natgeoed.org/commoncore
for more information.

The publisher would like to thank everyone who worked to make
this book come together: Martha Sharma, geographer/writer/
researcher; Suzanne Fonda, project manager; Angela Modany,
associate editor; Rachel Kenny, designer; Hilary Andrews, associate
photo editor; Mike McNey, map production; Maureen J. Flynn, map
edit; Chris Philpotts, illustrator; Sally Abbey and Vivian Suchman,
managing editors; Joan Gossett, production editorial manager; and
Gus Tello and Anne LeongSon, design production assistants.

Trade paperback ISBN: 978-1-4263-3821-2
Trade Hardcover ISBN: 978-1-4263-3822-9
Reinforced library binding ISBN: 978-1-4263-3823-6

Printed in Hong Kong
20/PPHK/1

Photo Credits

Art for state flowers and state birds by Robert E. Hynes.

Abbreviations: GI: Getty Images; IS: iStockphoto; NGIC: National Geographic Image Collection;
SS: Shutterstock

Front cover: (Space Needle), Xuanlu Wang/SS; (Mt. Rushmore), NaughtyNut/SS; (eagle), Chris Hill/SS;
(oranges), Astrid Gast/SS; **Back cover:** (wolf), Geoffrey Kuchera/SS; (Liberty Bell), Kenneth Garrett/NGIC;
(geyser), photoDISC; (girl), hartcreations/GI

Front of the Book
1, 1xpert/Adobe Stock; 2 (LE), eblue/Adobe Stock; 2 (CTR LE), Tim Laman/NGIC; 2 (CTR RT), NASA;
2 (RT), photoDISC; 3 (LE), Joseph H. Bailey/NGIC; 3 (CTR LE), Glenn Taylor/IS; 3 (CTR RT), Gerry Ellis/
Minden Pictures; 3 (RT), Annie Griffiths/NGIC; 4 (LE), photoDISC; 4 (RT), Brian J. Skerry/NGIC; 4-5, Lenice
Harms/SS; 5 (UP LE), italianestro/SS; 5 (UP RT), James Davis/Alamy Stock Photo; 5 (LO RT), Digital Stock;
9 (A), Lane V. Erickson/SS; 9 (B), Elena Elisseeva/SS; 9 (C), SNEHIT/SS; 9 (D), Nicole Watson/SS; 9 (E),
FloridaStock/SS; 9 (F), Sai Chan/SS; 9 (G), TTphoto/SS; 10, Sean Rayford/GI; 12 (LE), George F. Mobley/
NGIC; 12 (CTR LE), Skip Brown/NGIC; 12 (CTR CTR), Jan Brons/SS; 12 (CTR RT), Michelle Pacitto/SS;
12 (RT), Tammy Bryngelson/IS; 13 (LE), Carsten Peter/NGIC; 13 (CTR LE), Mark Thiessen/NGIC; 13 (CTR
CTR), Michael Nichols/NGIC; 13 (CTR RT), Steven Collins/SS; 13 (RT), Robert Madden/NGIC; 16, Ira Block/
NGIC; 18 (UP), Penny De Los Santos; 18 (LO LE), Mark Miller Photos/GI; 18 (LO RT), Cameron Davidson/GI;
21, Douglas Peebles/Danita Delimont/GI; 22-23, photoDISC; 23, Orhan Cam/SS

The Northeast
28 (UP), Michael Melford/NGIC; 28 (LO LE), MyTravelCurator/SS; 28 (LO RT), Les Byerley/SS; 29 (UP),
Donald Swartz/IS; 29 (LO), Tim Laman/NGIC; 30 (UP), Jerry and Marcy Monkman/Alamy Stock Photo;
30 (LO), David Arnold/NGIC; 31, Michael Tureski/Icon Sportswire via GI; 32 (LO LE), Kevin Fleming/NGIC;
32 (LO RT), Barry Winiker/GI; 32-33, Stephen St. John/NGIC; 34 (UP), photoDISC; 34 (LO), David Cannings-
Bushell/IS; 35, Roy Toft/NGIC; 36 (UP), Jeremy Edwards/IS; 36 (LO), Justine Gecewicz/IS; 37, James L.
Stanfield/NGIC; 38 (UP), Sarah Leen/NGIC; 38 (LO), Tim Laman/NGIC; 39, Darlyne A. Murawski/NGIC; 40
(UP), Medford Taylor/NGIC; 40 (LO), Yellow Dog Productions/GI; 41, Richard Nowitz/NGIC; 42 (UP), Richard
Nowitz/NGIC; 42 (LO), David Zimmerman/GI; 42-43, doncon402/Adobe Stock; 43, Yellow Dog Productions/
GI; 44 (UP), Glenn Taylor/IS; 44 (LO), James P. Blair/NGIC; 45, Kenneth Garrett/NGIC; 46 (UP), Kenneth
Garrett/NGIC; 46-47, Jeremy Edwards/IS; 47, William Albert Allard/NGIC; 48 (UP), Todd Gipstein/NGIC;
48 (LO), Onne van der Wal/GI; 48-49, Ira Block/NGIC; 50 (UP), Michael S. Yamashita/NGIC; 50 (LO),
Jupiterimages/GI; 51, slocummedia/Adobe Stock

The Southeast
56 (UP), Klaus Nigge/NGIC; 56 (LO LE), Tyrone Turner; 56 (LO RT), Richard T. Nowitz/GI; 57 (UP), Skip
Brown/NGIC; 57 (CTR), Raymond Gehman/NGIC; 57 (LO), Robert Clark/NGIC; 58 (UP), Raymond Gehman/
NGIC; 58 (LO), NASA; 60 (UP), Harrison Shull/Aurora Photos/Alamy Stock Photo; 60 (LO), Joel Sartore/
NGIC; 61, Cary Wolinsky/NGIC; 62 (UP), David Burnett/NGIC; 62 (LO), Brian J. Skerry/NGIC; 63, NASA;
64 (UP LE), William S. Weems/NGIC; 64 (UP RT), photoDISC; 64 (LO), Micheal Melford/NGIC; 66, Melissa
Farlow/NGIC; 67, Randy Olson/NGIC; 68 (UP), Tyrone Turner/NGIC; 68 (LO), Kylie McLaughlin/GI; 70 (UP),
Jim West/Alamy Stock Photo; 70 (LO), Ira Block/NGIC; 71, Elena Vdovina/IS; 72 (LE), Jack Fletcher/NGIC;
72 (RT), David Madison/GI; 73, Raymond Gehman/NGIC; 74, Terry Healy/IS; 74-75, Planetpix/Alamy Stock
Photo; 75, Raymond Gehman/NGIC; 76, Melissa Farlow/NGIC; 77 (LE), Dennis R. Dimick/NGIC; 77 (RT),
Jodi Cobb/NGIC; 78 (UP), Robert Clark/NGIC; 78 (LO), Mira/Alamy Stock Photo; 79, Digital Vision/GI; 80
(UP), James L. Stanfield/NGIC; 80 (LO), Joel Sartore/NGIC; 81, Robert Pernell/SS

The Midwest
86 (UP), James L. Stanfield/NGIC; 86 (LO LE), Jim Richardson/NGIC; 86-87, James P. Blair/NGIC; 87
(UP LE), Nadia M. B. Hughes/NGIC; 87 (UP RT), Sean Martin/IS; 87 (LO), Marilyn Angel Wynn/GI; 88 (UP),
Charles Brutlag/SS; 88 (LO), Jenny Solomon/SS; 88-89, Lenice Harms/SS; 90 (UP), Jello5700/IS; 90 (LO),
Melissa Farlow/NGIC; 92 (UP), idiz/SS; 92 (LO), Madeleine Openshaw/SS; 93, Charlie Neibergall/AP/
SS; 94, Cotton Coulson/NGIC; 95, Phil Schermeister/NGIC; 96 (UP), Jeff Kowalsky/AFP/GI; 96 (LO), Vince
Ruffa/SS; 97, Geoffrey Kuchera/SS; 98 (UP), Kirkikis/GI; 98 (LO), Medford Taylor/NGIC; 99, Lawrence
Sawyer/IS; 100 (UP), Marc Romanelli/Blend Images/Adobe Stock; 100 (LO), photoDISC; 101, Sarah Leen/
NGIC; 102, Joel Sartore/NGIC; 103, Sarah Leen/NGIC; 104, Farrell Grehan/NGIC; 105 (LE), Annie Griffiths/
NGIC; 105 (RT), Beverley Vycital/IS; 106 (UP), photoDISC; 106 (LO), Robert J Daveant/SS; 107, Ronald T.
Bennett; 108, Carol M. Highsmith/Library of Congress; 109, Dan Westergren/NGIC; 110 (UP LE), Paul
Damien/NGIC; 110 (UP RT), Anne Rippy/Alamy Stock Photo; 110 (LO), photoDISC

The Southwest
116 (UP), Joseph H. Bailey/NGIC; 116 (LO), Penny De Los Santos; 117 (UP), photoDISC; 117 (LO LE), Anton
Foltin/IS; 117 (LO RT), Joel Sartore/NGIC; 118 (UP), Joel Sartore/NGIC; 118 (LO), George Burba/SS; 120
(UP), italianestro/SS; 120 (CTR), James P. Blair/NGIC; 120 (LO), Lynn Johnson/NGIC; 122, Joel Sartore/
NGIC; 123, Annie Griffiths/NGIC; 124 (UP), Sarah Leen/NGIC; 124 (LO), Diane Cook & Len Jenshel/NGIC

The West
130, photoDISC; 131 (UP), eblue/Adobe Stock; 131 (CTR), Digital Stock; 131 (LO LE), Joel Sartore/NGIC;
131 (LO RT), Digital Stock; 132, Joel Sartore/NGIC; 133, Blue Poppy/GI; 134 (UP), Vacclav/SS; 134 (LO),
Randy Olson/NGIC; 136, photoDISC; 138, Andrew Zarivny/SS; 139, Charles Wood/REX/SS; 140 (UP),
Michael Melford/NGIC; 140 (LO), Joel Sartore/NGIC; 141, J. Cameron Gull/SS; 142, William Albert Allard/
NGIC; 143, 6015714281/SS; 144 (UP), Andrew Zarivny/SS; 144 (LO LE), Diane Johnson/Danita Delimont/
Alamy Stock Photo; 144 (LO RT), Raymond Gehman/NGIC; 146, Jennifer Lynn Arnold/SS; 147, Peter
Kunasz/SS; 148 (UP), photoDISC; 148 (LO), EunikaSopotnicka/GI; 150, Digital Stock; 151, photoDISC;
152 (UP), Michael Rubin/SS; 152 (LO), Digital Stock; 153, photoDISC

U.S. Territories and Back of the Book
156 (UP), James Davis/Alamy Stock Photo; 156 (LO), Kendra Nielsam/SS; 157 (UP), raksyBH/Adobe Stock;
157 (LO LE), littleny/Adobe Stock; 157 (LO RT), Gerry Ellis/Minden Pictures; 158, Eric Isselée/Adobe Stock

Map Acknowledgments

2-3, 24-25, 52-53, 82-83, 112-113, 126-127, Blue Marble: Next Generation NASA Earth Observatory; 10, US-
GCRP, 2017: Climate Science Special Report: Fourth National Climate Assessment, Volume I [Wuebbles, D.J.,
D.W. Fahey, K.A. Hibbard, D.J. Dokken, B.C. Stewart, and T.K. Maycock (eds.)]. U.S. Global Change Research
Program, Washington, DC, USA, 470 pp.; 10-11, Peel, M. C., Finlayson, B. L., and McMahon, T. A.: Updated
world map of the Köppen-Geiger climate classification, Hydrol. Earth Syst. Sci.; 11, National Climate Report-
Annual 2017, NOAA's National Centers for Environmental Information; 12-13, Billion Dollar Weather Disasters
1980-2018, NOAA's National Centers for Environmental Information; 16-17, LandScan (2016)™ High Resolution
global Population Data Set copyrighted by UT-Battelle, LLC, operator of Oak Ridge National Laboratory under
Contract No. DE-AC05-000R22725 with the United States Department of Energy. The United States Government
has certain rights in this Data Set. Neither UT-Battelle, LLC nor the United States Department of Energy, nor
any of their employees, makes any warranty, express or implied, or assumes any legal liability or responsibil-
ity for the accuracy, completeness, or usefulness of the data set.; 18-19, US Census Bureau: www.census.gov;
20, Rubinstein, J. L., and A. B. Mahani (2015). Myths and Facts on Wastewater Injection, Hydraulic Fracturing,
Enhanced Oil Recovery, and Induced Seismicity. Seismol. Res. Lett. 86, no. 4, doi: 10.1785/0220150067.; 20-21,
EIA (U.S. Energy Administration)